Social Media and the Public Interest

Social Media and the Public Interest

∎ ∎ ∎

Media Regulation in the Disinformation Age

Philip M. Napoli

Columbia University Press

New York

Columbia University Press
Publishers Since 1893
New York   Chichester, West Sussex
cup.columbia.edu
Copyright © 2019 Columbia University Press

Library of Congress Cataloging-in-Publication Data
Names: Napoli, Philip M., author.
Title: Social media and the public interest : media regulation in the
disinformation age / Philip M. Napoli.
Description: New York : Columbia University Press, 2019. |
Includes bibliographical references and index.
Identifiers: LCCN 2019021836 (print) | LCCN 2019008051 (e-book) |
ISBN 9780231184540 (cloth : alk. paper) | ISBN 9780231545549 (e-book)
Subjects: LCSH: Social media and journalism. |
Web usage mining in journalism. | Social media.
Classification: LCC PN4766 .N36 2019 (e-book) |
LCC PN4766 (print) | DDC 302.23—dc23
LC record available at https://lccn.loc.gov/2019021836

Columbia University Press books are printed on permanent
and durable acid-free paper.
Printed in the United States of America

Cover design: Lisa Hamm

For Donovan

Contents

Acknowledgments

My previous books have been relatively solitary endeavors. This time, though, I find myself with quite a laundry list of individuals and organizations to thank. All of them have helped to make this a better book than it otherwise would have been.

First and foremost, I need to thank Philip Leventhal of Columbia University Press, for convincing me to revive a project that I had let go dormant. Without his encouragement and gentle prodding, I might have let this project continue to sit among my other half-baked book ideas. His editorial feedback along the way has been incredibly helpful. The topic ended up being even more of a moving target than I imagined when I started the project (which was before the 2016 election), so I am also appreciative of his patience as I reworked chapters and adjusted small details right up until the very end. This is a book that just never felt *done*. I also appreciated the feedback of the two anonymous reviewers who generously read and commented upon both the original proposal and the completed manuscript. Thanks also to Peggy Tropp for a really superb job of copyediting, and to Ben Kolstad, for overseeing the production.

Also vitally important has been the support I received in the form of an Andrew Carnegie Fellowship from the Carnegie Corporation of New York. While this publication was made possible by a grant from the Carnegie Corporation of New York, the statements made and views expressed are, of course, solely my responsibility.

I have been able to road test some of the ideas presented in this book at a number of different conferences, where I received a tremendous amount of valuable feedback (along with a fair bit of pushback). Thank you to the organizers of all of these events for including me. Portions of this book were presented at the 2017 Data & Society Workshop on Propaganda and Media Manipulation in New York (thank you, danah boyd, for the invitation and feedback); the 2016, 2017, and 2018 Telecommunications Policy Research Conferences (TPRC) in Arlington, Virgina; the 2018 meeting of the American Political Science Association in Boston; the 2018 European Media Management Association Conference in Warsaw; the 2018 Algorithms, Automation, and Journalism Conference in Munich; the 2018 Defending Democracy Conference at Princeton University; the 2018 Collective Behavior, Social Media, and Systemic Risk Conference, also at Princeton; and the 2017 Nordic Political Science Congress in Copenhagen. I am particularly grateful for the detailed comments and suggestions I received from Mark Nadel of the Federal Communications Commission at TPRC and Kari Karppinen of the University of Helsinki at the Nordic Political Science Congress.

I was also fortunate to be able to present ideas from this book in more informal settings. Thanks to Sharon Strover and her colleagues at the University of Texas for inviting me speak there, and for the useful feedback that they provided. Thanks also to Fritz Mayer at the Sanford School at Duke for inviting me to speak in his Democracy Lab, and to the Duke Political Union and the Durham League of Women Voters for giving me the opportunity to present ideas from this book to their members as well. Thank you to Sanford Dean, Judith Kelly, for giving me the opportunity to present a couple of the chapters from this book as part of Sanford's weekly faculty seminar series, as well as to the Sanford School's Board of Visitors. Thanks also to Amit Schejter for agreeing to a last-minute request to read the entire manuscript.

My colleagues and students at Duke University's Sanford School of Public Policy have provided an incredibly fertile environment for working on this book. Particular thanks are due to the students in my undergraduate seminar on Algorithms, Journalism, and the Public Interest. I used the syllabus for the 2017 version of the course to essentially lay out the outline for the book, and the students in the 2018 version were subject to a (very) rough draft as part of their assigned reading. The discussions in these classes often had me taking more notes than the students. Thank you also to hall mate Bill Adair, director of Sanford's DeWitt Wallace Center for Media & Democracy, for serving as a sounding board for various ideas over the past couple of years and for keeping me abreast of developments in the relationship between social media and fact-checking. I also benefited tremendously while working on this book from the administrative support provided by Shelley Stonecipher and Kim Krzywy of the DeWitt Wallace Center.

I also benefited from incredibly helpful research assistance from some of my Duke University undergraduate students, including Petra Ronald (now at Microsoft), Peter Andringa, and Jake Schulman. I am eternally grateful for their help with the drudgery of tracking down articles and formatting the references.

Portions of the introduction to this book appeared in volume 22, issue 5, of the journal *First Monday* as "Why Media Companies Insist They're Not Media Companies, Why They're Wrong, and Why It Matters" (2017) and in volume 44, issue 4, of *Intermedia* as "Platform or Publisher?" (also 2017). Both of these articles were coauthored with my doctoral student Robyn Caplan, who has been working on her dissertation on algorithmic accountability and content moderation while I have been working on this book. Our conversations and collaborations over the past couple of years have been incredibly valuable to this book. Portions of chapter 3 appeared in volume 70, issue 1, of the *Federal Communications Law Journal* as "What If More Speech Is No Longer the Solution? First Amendment Theory Meets Fake News and the Filter Bubble" (2018). Thank you to these publications for allowing the material from those articles to be used here.

A huge thanks, as always, to my wife Anne, for listening as I bounced random ideas and dozens of title permutations off her, and as I fretted that the whole project was going off the rails. I don't know what I'd do without her patience, tolerance, insight, and support. Thanks also to my parents, who encouraged my love of writing, reading, and learning every step of the way. And then there's my son Donovan, who really knows how to help me keep things in perspective. When I asked him recently what he wants to be when he grows up (he's nine), his smart-ass response was "something more interesting than what you do." This book is dedicated to him.

Finally, as I mentioned, this book really involved taking aim at a fast-moving target, so apologies for whatever aspects of it seem out of date by the time you read it. For instance, as this book was going to press, the live streaming of a mass shooting took place in New Zealand. Soon after, Facebook's Mark Zuckerberg published an op-ed calling for a more active role for government regulators in areas such as harmful content, election integrity, privacy, and data portability. This shift in perspective, it should be noted, echoes broadcasters' calls for government regulation back in the 1920s. In addition, social media platforms have recently become much more aggressive in removing "inauthentic accounts" and certain categories of disinformation. And policymakers, particularly in countries such as Australia, France, Britain, and India, are moving forward with more comprehensive regulatory models for social media platforms. All of these developments suggest the emergence of the type of more public-interest-oriented media governance framework that I explore in this book. Hopefully this book can prove useful in informing these and future efforts.

Social Media and the Public Interest

Introduction

I n April 2018, Facebook CEO Mark Zuckerberg delivered nearly ten hours of testimony before Congress. At the hearing, he was asked to respond to a range of concerns about how the platform he had created was being used and misused. One key theme that emerged from his testimony was the extent to which Facebook was being used in ways its creator had never imagined or intended. Zuckerberg frequently mentioned how much Facebook had grown and changed since its humble beginnings in his Harvard dorm room.[1] Facebook, it is important to remember, was created for the narrow purpose of helping college undergraduates to identify attractive classmates. Twitter had similarly modest origins. The very word *Twitter* was coined to reflect the platform's modest founding ambitions, to facilitate the transmission of "inconsequential" bits of information.[2]

However, in less than two decades, these and other platforms such as YouTube, Twitter, Instagram, Snapchat, and WhatsApp have evolved in ways that have seen them credited (and blamed) for everything from overturning dictatorships to cultivating political extremism and terrorist organizations to destroying journalism to subverting elections.[3] Many of these hypothesized and demonstrated effects relate specifically to the ways in which these platforms have evolved into a significant component of our news and information ecosystem. They have unexpectedly become key platforms for how journalism (and disinformation posing as journalism) is produced, disseminated, and consumed. It is this aspect of social media's evolution that is the focus of this book.

Media Evolution

This kind of massive disconnect between a media technology's original intended function and its ultimate use is hardly new. One of the defining characteristics in the history of media is that technologies are created for purposes that prove to be very different from how they are used. Thomas Edison (who developed an early competitor to Bell's telephone) expected the telephone to be a way for people to listen to concerts.[4] Radio was created to enable ship-to-shore communication.[5] Cable television was developed to improve over-the-air broadcast television signals.[6] The VCR would enable time-shifted recording and viewing of television programs. The Internet was initially developed to facilitate a decentralized form of communication and shared access to computing power among academic researchers and government agencies.[7]

In all of these cases, the functions that ultimately drove the widespread usage of these technologies proved to be something very different. The telephone took hold primarily as a means of interpersonal communication. Only years later, when phone lines evolved into the initial infrastructure for the Internet, did the telephone system take on some of the mass media characteristics initially envisioned by Edison. Radio ultimately took hold as a mass entertainment medium and, secondarily, as a source of news. Cable television's initial functioning as an "antenna service" for broadcast television signals became a way of bringing additional, nonbroadcast, channels into the home. Later, like the telephone system, these cable systems evolved into a primary mechanism for accessing the Internet. As far as the VCR goes, the unimpressive legacy of time-shifting is reflected in the widely held belief that most VCR owners never even learned how to program their VCRs to record television programs.[8] Instead, an entirely unintended and unexpected industry propelled the popularity of the VCR, in which individuals rented or owned tapes of Hollywood movies.[9] And finally, it goes without saying that the Internet has evolved from its fairly narrow origins into a myriad of unexpected directions.[10]

These transitions are seldom smooth. As technologies—and the entire industries built around them—shift gears to accommodate the unexpected functions that resonate with media users, there are bound to be bumps in the road. In the early days of the radio industry, stations were so ill equipped to serve as freestanding sources of journalism that they resorted to simply reading print newspapers over the air. "News piracy" (as it was called at the time) was ultimately declared illegal. Radio stations would have to function as news organizations in their own right if they wanted to operate not just as providers of music and entertainment, but as providers of news and information as well.[11] Similarly, the introduction of the VCR and its recording capabilities appeared so threatening to the motion picture and television studios that they went all the way to the Supreme Court in an unsuccessful (and ultimately misguided) effort to ban a technology that would soon account for roughly 50 percent of their annual revenues.[12] As the cable television industry evolved into the primary means by which households accessed television, concerns about the cable industry's potential ability to strangle the life out of "free TV" (i.e., broadcast television) and the local news it provided (that cable at the time did not) led to a host of regulations designed to protect the economic welfare of broadcasters.[13] The continuing and still uncertain ripple effects of the Internet's evolving functionalities have been wide reaching, decimating the traditional business models of the music and newspaper industries and generating a host of associated lawsuits.

Social Media and News

As with some of the earlier examples (e.g., radio, cable TV), a key dimension of how the Internet has evolved (and associated tensions) is the extent to which it intercuts with the dynamics of journalism and the

construction of an informed citizenry. Needless to say, social media platforms have experienced what can only be described as a meteoric rise,
in terms of their ascension to prominence in the news and information
ecosystem. According to the online audience traffic measurement firm
Parse.ly, Facebook went from accounting for 16 percent of referrals to
online news sites in 2013[14] to more than 40 percent in 2017.[15] According
to recent research by the Pew Research Center, more than 67 percent
of adults get news from social media.[16] According to the same study,
68 percent of Facebook users obtain news through the platform (up
from 47 percent in 2013); 74 percent of Twitter users use it as a source
of news (up from 52 percent in 2013);[17] and 32 percent of YouTube users
use it as a news source (up from 20 percent in 2013).[18] As Columbia University's Emily Bell argues, this powerful gatekeeping position of a select
few companies represents "a far greater concentration of power . . . than
there has ever been in the past."[19] This functionality is a far cry from
being the place where people go to post pictures of their children, or
locate long-lost classmates or exes.

Social media platforms essentially fell into their role as significant
news sources. This helps explain why they have proven to be particularly
vulnerable to manipulation and exploitation by purveyors of disinformation. "Fake news" is hardly a new phenomenon.[20] As long there has
been journalism, there have been efforts to disguise disinformation as
journalism. However, many of the dynamics surrounding how fake news
is produced, disseminated, and consumed on social media are new. Of
particular importance here is the way that social media platforms, given
their origins, have, until recently, operated as news distributors without adopting any of the established norms, values, or practices of news
organizations. Mark Zuckerberg put it bluntly in his testimony before
Congress: "We didn't take a broad enough view of our responsibility, and
that was a big mistake."[21]

So, we find ourselves in a situation in which social media platforms
that never intended to be news media are operating as such—and with
a degree of reach and gatekeeping power that many have argued are
unprecedented in the history of media.[22] It should hardly be surprising that these platforms have found themselves a bit adrift, under fire

from many quarters in terms of effectively performing this function, and now are scrambling to improve their performance. Nor should it be surprising that policy makers have found themselves unsure of how to respond, if at all, to these platforms' emergent function as primary news and information gatekeepers.

Given the consequences of this function for an informed citizenry and a well-functioning democracy, it is crucial to understand the technological, economic, and behavioral forces that led us to a news ecosystem in which social media have become such a prominent source for news. In turn, we must develop mechanisms to address the problems that have emerged from this evolutionary shift.

This book will place these contemporary developments, problems, and controversies within the context of the history of media and how they have been governed. One of the most troubling tendencies of the digital media age is the extent to which the notion of "media" (and the normative and regulatory baggage that generally comes with this term) has been divorced from the platforms by which news and information are increasingly produced, disseminated, and consumed. Unlike newspapers, radio, and television, which eventually assumed the responsibilities of providing news, one of the primary characteristics of social media platforms, search engines, and content aggregators has been their resistance to being characterized as media companies, insisting instead that they be thought of as primarily—or exclusively—technology companies.[23] Given that the approach I take in this book is to analyze social media through a media governance lens, it is important to make clear why we need to think about social media from a media-centric, rather than a technology-centric, perspective.

When Media Companies Insist They're Not Media Companies

In today's digital media age, we have media companies that would rather not be seen as media companies—and that have seemed particularly

averse to being thought of as *news* media.[24] A big part of this (mis)
perception arises from what MIT's William Urrichio has termed the
"algorithmic turn" in the media sector.[25] As is now well known, journalistic, editorial, and media consumption decisions are increasingly
being influenced—if not dictated—by complex, data-driven algorithms
developed by large teams of engineers and computer scientists.[26] Microsoft Research's Tarleton Gillespie has succinctly defined algorithms
as "encoded procedures for transforming input data into a desired output, based on specified calculations."[27] This ongoing transformation in
how our new information ecosystem functions represents the application, and prioritization, of a particular type of specialized, technical
knowledge—and resulting technical systems—to the governance of the
processes and institutions through which news is produced, disseminated, and consumed.

As a result, we have seen a foregrounding of the technological dimensions of these social media platforms at the expense of thinking about
them, and trying to understand them, as *media*—and, specifically, as
news media. To some extent, this tendency is a reflection of broader
trends taking place throughout society and the economy, in which
algorithmic decision-making tools or technological infrastructures are
supplementing or supplanting traditional actors or organizations.[28] In
today's technology-driven business environment, firms increasingly see
their identity in terms of the technological approaches they take to their
business, rather than the particular business in which they operate. One
of the most prominent—and controversial—examples involves Uber.
Uber has steadfastly maintained that it is a technology company rather
than a transportation company because, according to one Uber representative, "we don't transport goods or people—our partners do. We just
facilitate that."[29]

The ramifications of accepting or rejecting this argument are profound. If regulators perceive Uber as a transportation company, then
it is subject to the regulations under which the transportation industry
operates. If, on the other hand, regulators perceive Uber as a technology
company, then these transportation industry regulations do not apply,
which could represent an important source of competitive advantage

for Uber.[30] Uber is certainly not alone in maintaining such a position. A variety of automotive, finance, and telecommunications companies have similarly argued that they should be seen purely as technology companies.[31] Even the Ford Motor Company wants to be seen as a technology company rather than an automobile manufacturer.[32]

Similarly, a defining characteristic of social media platforms (and digital content curators more broadly) is the consistency with which they have resisted being characterized as media companies and instead have insisted that they be thought of purely as technology companies.[33] Even companies that are—or were—unequivocally in the business of producing media content, such as Gawker and Vox, have had their CEOs maintain (even if only temporarily) that they are technology companies rather than media companies.[34]

However, if we are to address the question of Facebook, Twitter, and YouTube and their relationship to news, we must recognize that the technology-company-not-media-company position is fundamentally flawed.

"WE DON'T CREATE CONTENT"

The most prominent argument among digital media companies is that they do not produce original content; rather, they merely facilitate the distribution of content created by their users. Google's Eric Schmidt (along with other Google executives) has deployed this argument frequently over the years, declaring, "We don't do our own content. We get you to someone else's content faster."[35] Facebook also has long been a proponent of this argument. Facebook's VP of Global Marketing Solutions has stated, " 'We actually define ourselves as a technology company. . . . 'Media companies are known for the content that they create.' "[36] Facebook CEO Mark Zuckerberg has maintained this position over the years,[37] and as recently as November 2016, in his response to accusations that the dissemination of fake news stories via Facebook may have influenced the U.S. presidential election.[38] While serving as CEO of Twitter, Dick Costolo stated, "I think of us as a technology company because I think the future of the company is in building on an extensible platform that allows third-party developers and companies to add value to Twitter in a way that is accretive to Twitter and is accretive to our users. . . . I don't need to be or want to be in the content business.'"[39] The late Steve Jobs of Apple similarly emphasized this point at the time of the launch of iTunes. Bristling at the suggestion from an *Esquire* interviewer that Apple was becoming a media company, he argued, "We're not a media company. We don't own media. We don't own music. We don't own films or television. We're not a media company. We're just Apple.'"[40] The issue was sufficiently sensitive to Jobs that he abruptly ended the interview at that point.

This argument obviously invites discussion of the types of activities that are central to our understanding of what media companies do. Traditionally, the industrial organization of media has been described in terms of three fundamental—but seldom mutually exclusive—activities: (1) production (exemplified by content creators such as news outlets and television studios); (2) distribution (the process of moving content from producers toward consumers; and (3) exhibition (the process of providing content directly to audiences).[41]

Digitization and media convergence have meant that these processes have, in some cases, merged, as content can now be distributed directly to the end user. The decline of traditional exhibitors such as book and music retailers in the face of content digitization and digital distribution represents a case in point. One would be hard pressed to argue that traditional exhibitors such as movie theaters, bookstores, or record stores should be thought of as media companies. However, the replacements for these entities, such as Amazon, iTunes, and Netflix, are fundamentally different, utilizing an electronic media infrastructure to distribute content to audiences in a "pure public good"[42] form in a manner that more closely parallels traditional content curators and distributors such as cable systems and broadcast networks. This is in many ways also the case with social media platforms such as Twitter, YouTube, and Facebook, which now serve as central means of distribution for many content creators (ranging from news outlets to individuals to the NFL), while also serving as the exhibition end point for users, who access the content through these platforms. With services like Facebook Live (which allows direct and immediate broadcasting over the Facebook platform) and Facebook Instant Articles (through which Facebook directly hosts the content produced by news organizations),[43] the processes of production, distribution, and exhibition are even more integrated.

These evolving processes illustrate that distribution, as much as content creation, is a defining characteristic of media.[44] Content creation/ownership has never served as a point of distinction in defining a media company from the perspective of those charged with regulating the media sector. Consider, for instance, that both the cable television and satellite industries were built entirely on a foundation of serving exclusively (at least initially) as distributors of media content. This fact never served as a mechanism for keeping these companies beyond the bounds of Federal Communications Commission (FCC) regulatory authority, given the competition and diversity concerns that arise from distribution bottlenecks. And while the mechanisms of content distribution in the digital realm certainly differ from those employed by traditional media, digital media executive Elizabeth Spiers asks, " 'Will someone explain to me how digital distribution of your content makes your company primarily a tech company?' "[45] The argument, then, that content creation/ownership meaningfully separates these "technology" companies from the media sector reflects either a naïve or ill-informed understanding of media, or a more intentional, strategically motivated effort to redefine the parameters of a media company within business and policy discourse.

A final irony is that some of the companies that have made this argument have subsequently vertically integrated into content creation. This step follows a fairly predictable pattern in media history, in which content distributors inevitably pursue the strategic and economic advantages of also being content creators.[46] For example, in 2016 YouTube began producing original series on its subscription service. Facebook recently initiated a foray into original video content creation.[47] Thus, even if we accept the argument that a content distributor is not a media company, the odds are that company is not going to remain purely a content distributor for long.

"WE'RE COMPUTER SCIENTISTS"

The second prominent line of argument put forth by social media platforms and digital content curators focuses on the nature of their personnel. Specifically, representatives of these companies frequently point to their own and their employees' professional training and background in support of the argument that they are technology companies rather than media companies. Google's Eric Schmidt emphasized that Google is a technology company "because it is run by three computer scientists."[48] Similarly, Ben Huh, then CEO of user-generated content aggregator Cheezburger, emphasized the proportion of the company's employees who were developers when asserting that the company was a technology company.[49]

Here too we see an argument lacking in logical or historical grounding. Consider, for instance, that at the time of its introduction there was no greater technological marvel than over-the-air broadcasting. It represented a huge technological leap forward in the means of communication. Consequently, broadcasting was the province of the technologists and engineers of the time, given its relative technical complexity compared to other means of communication at the time, such as print newspapers. Technological expertise was at the core of early radio broadcasting companies such as RCA and the Marconi Company.[50] Satellite technology represented another dramatic advancement when employed by the cable television industry, once again requiring professionals with a high level of technical expertise.

Technological advancements—and the associated technical expertise—have been fundamental to the media sector since at least the advent of the printing press. As media scholar Mark Deuze notes, it is important that we recognize "the pivotal role technologies play in media work."[51] To argue that the technical orientation of the personnel or leadership of a company represents a logical grounding for precluding it from being thought of as a media company is most likely another strategic effort to narrow the definition of media relative to its traditional parameters.

"NO HUMAN EDITORIAL INTERVENTION"

A less explicit argument that these digital media platforms put forth, but one that certainly ties into the previous argument, is the frequent contention that the content that "surfaces" is a product not of human judgment but of algorithms and data-driven technologies that filter, categorize and classify information and reflect what users want back to them. Platforms such as Google and Facebook have frequently emphasized the lack of human intervention in their content curation processes and have been hesitant to acknowledge such human intervention when it does take place.[52] Facebook, in the wake of the 2016 Trending News controversy, in which a report contended that human editors employed by Facebook were suppressing conservative news stories in the platform's Trending list, downplayed as much as possible the role of direct human editorial intervention in the platform's operation. In the aftermath of the controversy, the company eliminated the positions of the journalists and editors overseeing its Trending module.[53]

This asserted/perceived lack of direct human editorial involvement is, in many ways, fundamental to the logic of perceiving these platforms as technology companies rather than media companies. Indeed, as Microsoft Research's Tarleton Gillespie has illustrated, the term *platform* itself has been strategically deployed as a means of casting these services strictly as neutral, technology-driven *facilitators* of content creation and dissemination.[54] Facebook's Mark Zuckerberg has favored emphasizing that the platform simply *provides tools* to users, to help them engage in their own content creation and curation,[55] a position that seems to ignore—or at least mischaracterize—the role that the platform's algorithms play in prioritizing and filtering content for users. The asserted absence of direct human editorial involvement furthers this perception of distance from the content selection process—a model that is thus fundamentally different from the kind of direct (and human) editorial discretion that has been a defining characteristic of traditional media companies.

However, simply because the mechanisms for exercising editorial discretion—for *gatekeeping*—have changed does not mean that the fundamental institutional identity of the gatekeepers should be recast. Representatives of these platforms would likely argue that the nature of their interaction with users is fundamentally different from that of traditional media, in that social media users play a much more autonomous role in determining the content that they receive. That is, the users, in collaboration with their social networks, ultimately dictate the content that they consume, with the platform serving as neutral facilitator. Again, this position is simply no longer tenable.

For starters, media have always, to some extent, tried to give audiences what they want. In this regard, Facebook, Twitter, or YouTube is no different from any print, broadcast, or digital news outlet desperately seeking to figure out what audiences want and then provide them with exactly that.[56] The real difference is simply that digital media platforms represent more effective and efficient mechanisms for doing so, given the increased quantity, scope, and depth of user data that they are able to draw upon, a function of the greater interactivity associated with these newer platforms. The relationship between social media platforms and users thus represents the next step in the ongoing progression of "the rationalization of audience understanding."[57] The rationalization of audience understanding is essentially the process by which media organizations increasingly use data and quantitative predictive analytics to understand their audiences. Today, this process of rationalization continues to move forward, as big data and algorithms facilitate more systematic and intensive reliance on such analytics across ever more decision-making contexts—and even, in some contexts, the complete or near-complete delegation of decision-making to algorithmic systems.[58]

Yet the notion that algorithms operate in a completely neutral and objective manner, free of the kind of biases that characterize direct human editorial decision-making, has been effectively challenged. Algorithms, though automated, classify, filter, and prioritize content based on values internal to the system and the preferences and actions of users.[59] Moreover, engineers and other company actors must make countless decisions in the design and development of algorithms. Through those decisions and relationships, subjective decisions and biases get encoded into systems, giving rise to algorithmic biases.[60]

In addition, regardless of the algorithmic gatekeeping mechanisms employed, platforms such as Facebook, YouTube, and Twitter find themselves having to navigate a range of editorial policy issues that place them firmly in line with traditional media organizations.[61] Issues related to protecting users from offensive, inflammatory, or adult content are central to the operation of these platforms.[62] This tension was well illustrated by the controversy that arose around Facebook's decision to censor a post by a Norwegian journalist that featured the well-known Vietnam War photo of a nude Vietnamese girl fleeing a napalm attack.[63] Amid the outcry, Facebook quickly reversed its decision on the basis of the photograph's historical importance.[64] Nonetheless, the controversy highlighted the extent to which editorial policy decisions not unlike those associated with traditional news publishers are essentially part and parcel of what it means to be a social media platform, even when the editorial decision-making is initially being handled by algorithms, as was the case with the Vietnam photo.

As the controversy surrounding Facebook's Trending list illustrated, human editorial intervention often plays a more significant role in the process of content curation than is commonly assumed.[65] Indeed, in the wake of increased concerns about disinformation and hate speech, many of these platforms are dramatically increasing their human staffing devoted to evaluating content. The guidelines these teams use are not unlike editorial guidelines used by many content companies to promote accuracy and limit bias.

As should be clear, these scenarios reveal that these companies operate as *news organizations*, given the extent to which they are engaged in editorial and gatekeeping decisions related to the flow of information. Even Facebook, despite its string of public pronouncements that it is not a media company, has acknowledged its editorial authority in a court case. In defending the company in a lawsuit from a failed start-up that accused Facebook of driving competitors out of business, Facebook's lawyers argued that, as a publisher, Facebook has the right to make decisions as to what to publish and what not to publish.[66] Facebook's lawyers contended, "The publisher discretion is a free speech right irrespective of what technological means is used. A newspaper has a publisher function whether they are doing it on their website, in a printed copy or through the news alerts." Thus, despite many public pronouncements to the contrary, within the legal arena Facebook analogized itself to a newspaper.

THE CENTRALITY OF ADVERTISING

Finally, it is worth noting that all of the arguments put forth by these platforms collapse under the fact that the primary revenue stream for the bulk of these platforms is advertising. Being in the business of providing content to audiences while selling those audiences to advertisers is a defining characteristic of the media sector.[67] When advertisers explore how best to reach potential consumers, the strengths and weaknesses of digital media platforms such as Facebook, Twitter, and YouTube are being evaluated right alongside those of more traditional media options. Moreover, these digital media platforms are proving increasingly effective at siphoning off advertising revenues from these other media sectors.[68] From this perspective, it is hard to dispute that these firms are all operating in the same business sector.

Reasons for Misrepresenting Media

The efforts by these platforms to cast themselves as technology companies rather than media companies serve a number of purposes. As Tarleton Gillespie notes, many digital media companies use terms like "platform" strategically, "to position themselves both to pursue current and future profits, to strike a regulatory sweet spot between legislative protections that benefit them and obligations that do not."[69] The self-definition as technology companies and the strong resistance to any classification as media companies have been a key dimension of this framing.

Such tendencies are not new. In 1981, Ronald Reagan appointed a deregulation-minded communications lawyer named Mark Fowler to head the Federal Communications Commission (FCC), the primary regulatory agency assigned to oversee the communications sector in the United States. In an interview granted shortly after he assumed his position as FCC chair, Fowler famously declared television to be nothing more than a "toaster with pictures."[70] Fowler's point was that television possesses no greater social, political, or cultural significance than a toaster. It is a mere appliance, and therefore policy makers should afford it no greater attention than other household appliances. Certainly, concerns about diversity or the cultivation of an informed citizenry that had previously characterized television regulation had no place within such a perspective on this media technology.

There are other reasons that today's media companies do not want to be thought of as media companies. Chief among these is that the technology company label brings with it the potential for much higher valuations from the investment community.[71] The investment community generally sees greater income potential in the technology sector than the media sector[72] and seems to have maintained a hard-line distinction between these two sectors, viewing media companies as having less potential than tech firms. Painting oneself as a technology company rather than a media company is "what venture capitalists [want] to hear."[73] As digital media executive Elizabeth Spiers has noted, "institutional investors don't fund media services."[74]

This also leads to a devaluing of media-related knowledge and skill sets within these organizations. Witness, for instance, the role of editors and journalists at Facebook. Editors and journalists occupy the lower rungs of the Facebook corporate hierarchy. The company brought them in as low-wage, contract employees. In some instances, their primary function has been to help train the algorithms designed to eventually replace them.[75]

Within a "tech company" environment, this kind of marginalization of journalists and editors is perhaps inevitable, but the implications for our news and information ecosystem may be profound. The 2016 U.S. presidential election, and the associated concerns about fake news and filter bubbles that it brought to the public agenda, forced policy makers, scholars, social media platforms, news media, and citizens all to take a hard look at how social media platforms function, and whether they are operating in a way that is helping or hurting democracy.

Social Media and the Public Interest

What has been largely missing from the platforms' conception of themselves as distributors of news and information is the concept of the "public interest." The term has a very long, complex, and contested history in the world of media and journalism[76] and has served as a central component of the professional and organizational missions of journalists and news organizations. It also has served as a guiding concept for regulators and policy makers who oversee the media sector, in an effort to assure that community information needs are being met and that the news media are playing their proper role in informing and facilitating the democratic process.[77]

In this book, I consider how the notion of the public interest translates into the social media context, in which the new news and information gatekeepers evolved from organizational, professional, and regulatory environments largely devoid of the public interest frameworks that characterized regulation and professional norms in the "old" media sector. I will consider the barriers to, and possibilities for, transitioning to a more public interest–oriented governance framework for social media.

Once again, some historical context is useful. Returning to our 1980s example, the rise of new communications technologies such as cable television and the VCR created the impression (or helped to bolster the preconceived notion) that the public interest concept was no longer relevant, or at least not relevant in its traditional sense. Mark Fowler (in addition to articulating his vision of television as a toaster with pictures) also sought to convince us that "the public's interest . . . defines the public interest."[78] What he meant was that, in a media environment of so much choice, one could safely assume that the operation of market forces represented an adequate substitute for the broader notions of public service and social responsibility that had previously characterized interpretations of the public interest.

We hear echoes of this perspective in contemporary assessments of our media ecosystem, which often emphasize that today's digital media platforms provide tools that empower individual media users, giving them easy access to a wealth of news and information sources, as well as the means to create and disseminate news and information on their own. Some have embraced this *democratization* of the media (as it has been described by those who unequivocally celebrate these developments) as being essentially synonymous with effective serving of the public interest.[79] Some have gone so far as to suggest that the very notion of the public interest is an idea with little relevance or resonance in today's media environment.[80] I will argue that this perspective should be reversed, and will offer some proposals for how.

In developing this argument, I will not focus exclusively on the realm of regulation and policy, but rather will consider the broader sphere of media governance. The term *media governance* refers to the rules that organize the structure and behavior of media systems and the use of media technologies.[81] Media governance is a broader, more inclusive concept than media regulation or media policy. In particular, media governance is more inclusive in terms of the range of stakeholders participating in the process of designing the rules and norms. These participants include policy makers, industry stakeholders, nongovernmental organizations (NGOs), civil society organizations, and even media users.[82] Media governance refers, then, not only to the laws, regulations, and policies governing the media, but also to the self-imposed regulations and organizational norms and practices that characterize the operation of media organizations, as well as the ways in which users can collectively shape and affect those regulations and organizational norms and practices.[83]

This notion of media governance better reflects the dynamics of our contemporary media ecosystem than narrower terms such as media regulation (which focuses more narrowly on government actors/actions). As this book will illustrate, many of the central gatekeepers in our digital media ecosystem operate outside of traditional regulatory parameters, which accentuates the importance of their own internal regulatory parameters and normative principles and compels broader stakeholder involvement if the public interest is to be well served. In addition, given the complexity and rate of change in the digital media realm, it is important to recognize the limits on what policy makers can accomplish. The sometimes clueless questions that members of Congress asked Mark Zuckerberg during his testimony certainly illustrated this point. Ultimately, social media platforms reflect Lawrence Lessig's famous pronouncement that "code is law."[84] That is, the operation of their algorithmic systems represents a system of governance in and of itself. Indeed, in previous work I have argued that algorithms should be thought of as institutions, alongside more traditional institutions such as law, journalism, and government.[85] For these reasons, this book will employ the broader, more inclusive governance orientation, rather than focus exclusively on regulation and policy, when considering the tensions and challenges emerging in this current stage in the evolution of our media ecosystem.

Plan of the Book

In chapter 1, I focus on providing historical context. I consider the relatively short history of the Internet, with a particular focus on broad evolutionary patterns within the structure and evolution of the Web. I argue that the initial structure of the Web (Web 1.0) was, in some ways, incompatible with the economics of media and the dynamics of media usage. The Web of the 1990s through the mid-2000s represented a simply untenable level of fragmentation that was inefficient for both media organizations and media users. The processes of searching for content and of reaching, measuring, and monetizing audiences all became more difficult than perhaps at any previous point in media history. Thus, many of the characteristics we associate with the social media age (once widely referred to as Web 2.0) essentially represent efforts to tame the Web, to reaggregate audiences that had become too fragmented, to reassert a "push" over a "pull" model of media consumption, and to reestablish the "walled gardens" that characterized the early days of dial-up Internet access. I highlight the largely neglected ways in which the evolution of the Web has been regressive—involving the adoption of characteristics more often associated with "old," traditional media—as a counterpoint to the more prominent narrative of progress and advancement toward unprecedented choice and interactivity. I will also illustrate how these processes simultaneously compelled and were facilitated by the increased reliance on algorithmic decision-making systems.

In chapter 2, I provide an overview and critical evaluation of the rise of these algorithmic decision-making systems that supplement and, in some cases, replace, human decision-making at virtually all stages of the production, distribution, and consumption of news. This analysis is grounded in established theoretical perspectives related to the production, dissemination, and consumption of news, including gatekeeping and the two-step flow. I argue that these perspectives need to be revised and expanded to reflect the contemporary dynamics of social media and offer some approaches to doing so. I position the rise of socially mediated news within the broader processes of technocratization and rationalization at work in the media sector and explore the concept of *algorithmic creep* in the journalistic sphere.

With the historical and technological contexts effectively established in chapters 1 and 2, in chapter 3, I begin the process of evaluating socially mediated news through the lens of specific media governance principles. I examine the role and interpretation of the First Amendment and the notion of counterspeech—the foundational idea that the best solution to bad/false speech is more speech. More specifically, I consider whether fundamental characteristics of social media undermine this core assumption of the First Amendment. The presence of false news and information on social media is an issue that has justifiably raised significant concerns, and, as this chapter illustrates, the technological infrastructure through which news and information are produced, disseminated, and consumed, has a number of innate characteristics that systematically favor false news over legitimate news. Thus, we may not be able to rely on counterspeech within the context of social media in the same way that we could with older media.

In chapter 4, I delve into the marketplace-of-ideas principle that is tightly associated with the First Amendment and the notion of counterspeech. In this chapter, the focus is on delineating criteria for evaluating how effectively a marketplace of ideas is functioning and then applying these criteria to the algorithmic marketplace of ideas constructed by social media. I begin by considering how economists analyze the functioning of traditional product markets and then adapt this approach to the more political (rather than economic) context of the marketplace of ideas. In particular, I consider the criteria and consequences related to the phenomenon of market failure and contend that recent political developments may represent compelling evidence of market failure in the algorithmic marketplace of ideas. I conclude by considering the media governance implications of such a market failure.

In light of the dangers reflected in chapters 3 and 4, in chapter 5, I explore the public interest concept, its position in media governance, and how historically it has functioned as a guiding principle for professional practice as well as for media regulation and policy. A key point is that the public interest concept is not the vague and amorphous term that critics have often claimed. Rather, an historical perspective demonstrates that the public interest concept is infused with specific criteria and principles directly related to the concerns raised by socially mediated news. Unfortunately, as this chapter also illustrates, manifestations of the public interest in the social media space have been quite rare and have reflected a very limited interpretation of the concept. Further, the rationales for media regulation that operate in the United States have facilitated an ongoing disconnect between social media (and digital media more broadly) and the public interest.

Building on the issues raised in chapter 5, in chapter 6, I put forth some proposals for a more robust public interest governance framework for social media. It is important to emphasize that the focus here is less on making highly specific behavioral or policy recommendations and more on constructing a revised media governance framework that would encourage and allow specific actions that might be deemed necessary.

The range of concerns that have arisen around social media has sparked a wide range of suggestions for courses of action, but far fewer evaluations and proposals related to the underlying legal, self-regulatory, and regulatory frameworks on which these specific suggestions must be built and justified. This chapter represents an effort to correct this imbalance, to develop a broader institutional framework that reflects the elements of continuity between our old and new media. Toward this end, I offer some institutional-level suggestions for how social media platforms can better regulate themselves and better integrate public interest values into the algorithmic curation of news. I also consider some ways in which the legal and regulatory frameworks that govern media can be adjusted to better reflect the characteristics of social media and the particular challenges they pose.

In the conclusion, I try to look into the future a bit, considering recent developments and what they might mean for the future of platform governance, for journalism, and for an informed citizenry.

Finally, a note about scope. Throughout the book, I focus primarily on the intersection of social media and news, with occasional references to related areas of concern such as political advertising and hate speech. But the primary concern here is with the role these platforms play in the news ecosystem and the governance issues and challenges related to that evolving role. Also, the focus here is very U.S.-centric, primarily because one of my motivations in writing this book was to explore the points of continuity and discontinuity between the rather idiosyncratic system of media regulation that has developed in the United States and the evolution of social media platforms. Also, it seems we have reached a point where the old notion that the global nature of the Internet makes the application of national-level legal or regulatory frameworks untenable is being dispelled, given recent regulatory interventions we have seen in countries such as Germany. Nonetheless, issues and examples from outside the United States will be touched upon at various points.

CHAPTER 1

The Taming of the Web and the Rise of Algorithmic News

t is still quite common to use the term "new media" in connection with the Internet. However, the Internet is almost forty years old. The web, as a component of the Internet, is more than twenty-five years old. This is a sufficient passage of time that any analysis of our contemporary media ecosystem needs to be grounded in the historical context of the evolution of online media.

As we look back on this history, it becomes clear that the initial structure of the web (Web 1.0, as it has been called)[1] was fundamentally incompatible with the economics of media and, in many ways, inhospitable to established—and perhaps intractable—dynamics of media usage. Thus, many of the characteristics we associate with the social media stage of Internet evolution (once widely referred to as Web 2.0) represent efforts to tame the web, to counteract fundamental Web 1.0 characteristics that were problematic for many stakeholders. Whether we are thinking about publishers seeking to provide content online, advertisers wanting to reach audiences online, or even audiences hoping to produce, transmit, and receive news and information, we can see ways in which the 1.0 version of the web represented a media system that was, to some extent, unsustainable—or at least undesirable.[2]

When we think about the web in its early incarnation, many characteristics, such as the information search and retrieval demands it placed on users, can be seen as incredibly—even debilitatingly—inefficient for many categories of stakeholders.[3] Embedded within the many undeniable advancements that we associate with the transition from the Web 1.0 to the Web 2.0 digital media ecosystem, however, are a number of less widely recognized *regressions* that can be interpreted as reestablishing elements of a more traditional, more manageable, more passive mass media framework for our digital media ecosystem.

Audience Disaggregation to Reaggregation

If there is one defining characteristic of the early web, it is the extent to which it represented a degree of fragmentation of both content options and audience attention that went well beyond any previous medium.[4] This fragmentation was a function of the extent to which the web provided lower barriers to entry to producing and distributing content than any previous medium, as well as the lack of channel or space constraints that characterized previous media. This fragmentation was widely lauded as a central component of the "democratization" of the media that the Internet represented, in which the opportunity to speak and be heard could extend well beyond the privileged few who owned or operated the relatively few media outlets.[5] This fragmentation represented, for many, the ideal in terms of providing an opportunity to serve the full gamut of audience tastes and preferences. No longer would a relatively limited number of gatekeepers (TV networks, cable systems, or local newspapers) wield so much control over the production and distribution of news, information, and cultural content. No longer would content catering to niche interests be unable to find distribution, and thus fail to reach those niche audiences.

However, there are a number of somewhat intractable problems inherent in a media ecosystem of unprecedented fragmentation, diminished gatekeepers, and exceptionally low barriers to entry. As the Internet grew, and evolved as a commercial medium, these fundamental problems became more pronounced.

AUDIENCE CHALLENGES

From an audience standpoint, effectively navigating the web was fairly labor intensive in comparison to other media. The number of choices available was astronomical. Fortunately, tools such as search engines and portal sites were available to assist in this process. Early search engines, however, were not nearly as comprehensive or efficient as Google, which did not arrive until the late 1990s and eventually came to dominate what was a fairly crowded search engine market.[6] Throughout the late 1990s and early 2000s, more than half of the top ten online destinations in terms of audience traffic were search engines or portals.[7] I recall a conversation during that period with a television industry professional, who made the point that this would be equivalent to six of the top ten television networks being various permutations of the TV Guide Channel, a TV channel that at the time featured a slowly scrolling list of all the programs currently airing on each available broadcast and cable network.[8]

In the early days of the web, there were even consumer magazines devoted exclusively to highlighting and reviewing websites of potential interest. There is of course something fascinatingly anachronistic about the idea of reading a print magazine to learn about which websites one might want to visit online.

Searching the web for content that interested you used to require a meaningful investment of time, along with the development of some basic search skills. The magnitude of these Web 1.0 search costs and the general unwillingness of online users to incur them were well reflected in the fairly limited channel repertoires that early web users developed. The term "channel repertoire" comes from television audience research; it refers to the extent to which television viewers tend to establish limited repertoires of channels that they consumed regularly.[9] Importantly, as the number of channels available to viewers increases, channel repertoires increase only slightly, not nearly in proportion with the increase in available channels. This pattern suggests a process of diminishing returns in terms of the relationship between the number of content options provided and the number of content options actually consumed.

When this analytical framework was applied to early web users, findings indicated that, despite the exponentially greater availability of content offerings, individuals' online channel repertoires (i.e., the number of websites they visited regularly) were not much bigger than their television channel repertoires.[10] While one person's online channel repertoire might be completely different from another's, the reality was that individual users tended not to incur the search costs necessary to take advantage of the diversity of content offerings online in the way that we might have expected. In many ways, this was a recurrence of what happened when cable dramatically expanded our television viewing options, and is perhaps indicative of an embedded characteristic of audience behavior. We simply do not take full advantage of diverse content offerings when they are made available to us.

ADVERTISER CHALLENGES

The fragmentation of the Web 1.0 world produced a different set of challenges for advertisers. To understand these challenges, it is first important to understand how the process of buying and selling audience attention (the key product advertisers need) has traditionally worked. The *audience commodity* (as it has often been called) was produced through content providers (television programmers, newspaper publishers, websites, etc.) attracting audiences to their content offerings.[11] The size and demographic characteristics of these audiences were determined by third-party audience measurement firms, who measured the media consumption behaviors of a very small sample of television viewers, radio listeners, or print readers. These samples by necessity tended to be small because the process of audience measurement has traditionally been quite expensive, given the costs associated with recruiting and training participants, as well as the costs associated with the measurement technologies. However, a small sample of media consumers was acceptable as long as it was representative of the population as a whole. Measurement firms could confidently make the claim that their ratings were generalizable to the population as a whole, and advertisers and content providers felt comfortable treating these ratings figures as the currency of exchange in the marketplace for audience attention.[12]

The web posed problems for this well-established dynamic. The first problem was that there were so many websites that needed to have their audiences measured. This meant that an enormous sample needed to be in place. Without an enormous sample, even for a website attracting a decent-sized audience, it can often be the case that none of the audience members in the sample are visiting this site. As a result, large swaths of audience attention can go unmeasured—and consequently cannot be bought and sold in the audience marketplace.[13] More choices in terms of content options means larger audience samples are necessary.

Fortunately, there was a solution to this problem. Instead of measuring the behaviors of a sample of audiences, audience measurement firms could "audit" the traffic of individual websites through the sites' server logs, thereby providing an objective accounting of how many people were visiting the site. Thus, instead of deriving audience estimates from a small sample of the total online population, these estimates essentially came from a census of that population.

There was just one problem. This system could not really tell you *who* was visiting the site. That is, audience ratings figures derived from website server logs could not provide advertisers with the demographic information that they tended to rely upon in deciding how to allocate their advertising dollars. Unless a visitor to a site voluntarily provided his/her demographic information, server log systems could only tell you how many different devices were visiting a site.

Given the different strengths and weaknesses inherent in these two approaches to online audience measurement, it is not surprising that what has emerged as the industry standard are hybrid measurement systems that utilize server log analysis and then supplement this approach with demographic information culled from very large online samples.[14] However, even these hybrid systems do not fully solve the problems described above.

So, another solution that emerged to address the problem of online audience fragmentation was ad networks. Ad networks started to come into being in the mid- to late 1990s as a way of pooling unsold ad inventory, in order to save advertisers the time and costs associated with dealing with individual websites. As digital intermediaries in the relationship between websites and advertisers, ad networks would distribute advertisers' ads across their network of member sites, in accordance with subject matter and/or audience criteria specified by the advertiser. For instance, advertisers might specify that their ads appear within/ alongside content that meets certain keyword criteria (e.g., women's fashion, car insurance). Or the advertiser could specify that the ads be directed at individuals who have demonstrated certain online behaviors (e.g., searching for an apartment, researching a car purchase) or who meet certain age, gender, or geographic location criteria. Ad networks helped to reaggregate audiences, to some extent, by allowing advertisers to more efficiently compile large aggregations of audiences without having to engage in transactions with each individual site.[15]

These networks had another important effect: they essentially decoupled advertisements from the media content in which they were displayed. Through ad networks, advertisers were purchasing the delivery of audiences without necessarily having to evaluate the content and/or content provider delivering those audiences, as the ad network—not the content provider—was now their point of contact. This tendency became more pronounced with the development of *programmatic advertising*, which essentially involves algorithms handling media-buying decisions that used to be handled by humans.[16] Because intermediaries increasingly handled the process of placing advertisements within sites, based on particular audience criteria, the content through which these audiences were delivered essentially became secondary—and somewhat marginalized—from advertisers' decision-making regarding how to reach audiences.

However, these ad networks still could not provide a completely effective means of targeting large aggregations of audiences according to detailed demographic criteria, given the limitations in the availability of audience demographic data for individual websites. If only there were some way in which audiences could be compiled into large aggregates online while at the same time voluntarily providing detailed demographic (and perhaps even behavioral and psychographic) data about themselves. . . .

CONTENT PROVIDER CHALLENGES

Content providers found the Web 1.0 scenario challenging as well. For starters, as has just been discussed, for sites with relatively small audiences seeking to monetize those audiences through advertising revenue, the available systems of audience measurement made this process challenging to say the least. Many sites found themselves unable to document the existence of their audience to advertisers in the audience size/demographics vocabulary that most advertisers preferred.[17]

A related problem had to do with the basic challenge of attracting audiences to a site in light of the unprecedented number of competitors for audience attention and the challenges associated with getting audiences to visit and (ideally) to integrate the site into their repertoire. As described in the previous section, the Web 1.0 environment imposed substantial search and navigation costs on users, which greatly limited the number of sites capable of attracting large audiences. It is not surprising that the rise of the web brought with it a flurry of both popular and academic analyses of the "attention economy," grounded in the notion that audience attention represented an increasingly scarce—and thus increasingly valuable—resource, relative to the growing number of competitors for a finite amount of available audience attention.[18]

As the web grew, it was common to hear audience attention (somewhat shortsightedly, it turned out) characterized as the "last bottleneck." Traditional media outlets have served as information bottlenecks because there has always been a fairly limited number of television/cable networks, radio stations, newspapers, and magazines—at least when compared with the range of media outlets online. These traditional media outlets served as bottlenecks through which only a limited amount of news, information, and entertainment could pass. As the web grew and content became available in such abundance, without the limited number of media outlets serving as bottlenecks for this content, the only real limit on consumption—the last bottleneck—was the availability of human attention. One of the contributing factors to the bursting of the dot-com bubble in the late 1990s was the extent to which so many digital start-ups burned through their capital by spending millions of dollars on television, radio, and online ads to drive traffic to their sites in an effort to overcome the attention bottleneck.[19] The bottom line, as Matthew Hindman convincingly demonstrates in his book *The Internet Trap*, is that aggregating audience attention online is incredibly costly.[20]

In light of the increasing challenges associated with attracting and monetizing human attention, one could easily imagine that content providers would find it valuable if there were someplace online that attracted huge aggregations of audiences, where sites could then present themselves to these audiences, and where these audiences could even help promote the sites to their friends and families.

THE LONG TAIL AND THE PATH FORWARD

The media and audience fragmentation scenario just described gave rise to the concept of the *long tail*—a term made famous by *Wired* editor Chris Anderson in his 2004 magazine article and subsequent book.[21] The long tail referred to how the Internet and digitization transformed the availability and consumption of media. Previously, storage and exhibition limitations meant that audiences had access to a relatively limited proportion of the totality of content being produced. Thus, a typical bookstore carried about 130,000 books; a typical video store carried about 3,000 videos; and a typical record store carried about 60,000 CDs. This may sound like a lot, but it represented a relatively small proportion of the available content.

These limitations in available offerings were born of the inherent constraints (and costs) of brick-and-mortar retailing and of media content being embedded in physical objects (books, discs, tapes, etc.), entailing production, shipping, and warehousing costs. These limitations constrained audience behavior to some extent, narrowing consumption to a relatively small subset of the content being produced. A key dynamic that emerged from this scenario involved exhibitors/retailers seeking to anticipate/appeal to audience preferences as accurately as possible to provide the mix of content options that would perform best—essentially trying to optimize the appeal of their offerings within the confines of the limited selection they were able to offer.

As more content moved online and, later, to digital distribution, the range of content options available to individuals increased, driving greater audience fragmentation. As Anderson famously asserted (and demonstrated with some compelling examples), the audience for niche content available in this fragmented media environment could, in the aggregate, be larger than the audience for mass-appeal content (the "hits"). Thus, the long-tail audience for niche content could be larger than the audience for mass-appeal content clustered in the "head."

Inherent in the long-tail scenario described by Anderson was the perhaps inevitable, and in some ways necessary, response to massive audience fragmentation: reaggregation. In his book, Anderson highlighted services such as Amazon, Netflix, and iTunes, which in many ways were the first generation of reaggregators of online audience attention. These platforms amassed, through licensing agreements, large quantities of content to make available to consumers (either à la carte or via subscriptions).[22] Unlike previous iterations of content aggregators (bookstores, record stores, cable systems, video stores, etc.) these aggregators did not concern themselves with identifying the subset of all available content offerings likely to perform best with consumers. Their model was to obtain and make available just about everything they could get hold of, since these aggregators did not operate under the same space constraints, and research showed that even the most obscure content attracted at least some audience attention.[23]

Though not all content aggregators have maintained this strategy (think, for instance, of the declining number of offerings available on Netflix),[24] these platforms demonstrated the importance of aggregation as a response to the digital media environment. Also, these platforms did not apply their aggregation processes to the totality of the web, but rather to certain categories of content. Where these early aggregators left off, social media platforms picked up.

THE SOCIAL MEDIA SOLUTION TO FRAGMENTATION

Social media platforms took this process of reaggregation further, and into a somewhat different realm, bringing the vast universe of online content providers, audiences, and advertisers together in a way that aggregators such as Amazon, Netflix, and iTunes, and search engines such as Google, did not. Social media platforms such as Facebook and YouTube essentially became aggregators of the web. In addition to their more apparent function as facilitators of social networks, they have become the place where audiences, advertisers, and content producers congregated, finding each other in a way that is less labor intensive and in many ways more efficient than in the Web 1.0 model.

This is not, of course, what these platforms were created to do. In fact, this increasingly important aspect of their functionality was, until recently, lost in the shuffle in the midst of the emphasis on the way these platforms connect individuals on an unprecedented, global scale.[25] The platforms themselves do not really emphasize this aggregation dimension of their functionality.[26] Facebook's Mark Zuckerberg has emphasized that Facebook is all about connecting people.[27] But Facebook, Snapchat, YouTube, and other social media platforms are also about streamlining how we access content online and providing a mechanism for content providers and advertisers to more efficiently reach otherwise scattered audiences. The fact that, despite not being what these platforms were created to do, this has become a big part of what they actually do, reinforces the idea that the 1.0 incarnation of the web was, to some extent, unsustainable in light of the constraints under which media audiences, content providers, and advertisers operate.

It is also important to emphasize that this audience aggregation function for content providers and advertisers—more than the social connectivity functionality—has served as the backbone of these social media platforms' business models. This dimension of their business model was seldom part of the original plan. Twitter, for instance, famously and publicly declared its lack of a clear business model as it rapidly grew and accumulated users.[28] The MO for many of these platforms was to focus

first on attracting large aggregations of users, and only after that to figure out a business model.[29] Of course, once a platform has achieved a
large aggregation of audience attention, a business model focused on
connecting content providers, advertisers, and audiences is more or less
an inevitability, given the value of large aggregations of audience attention to both content providers and advertisers.

There are important differences between the first-generation aggregators like Netflix and iTunes and second-generation aggregators like
Facebook and YouTube. Unlike Amazon, Netflix, and iTunes, social
media platforms do not own or license the content passing through
their hubs. They are not *curating* in the traditional sense; that is, they
are not making decisions and signing contracts about which content
to make available.

Social media platforms are much less discriminating. This is a
by-product of the scale and scope at which they operate. For these platforms, as media critic Jacob Silverman has noted, "scale is everything."[30]
These platforms do filter in an effort to weed out certain types of content, such as violence, hate speech, and pornography.[31] However, largely
absent from their business models are any deliberations as to whether
any of the content they make available will be sufficiently interesting to a
critical mass of users to be worth the licensing costs to make it available.
Their algorithmic curation systems make determinations about audience interest on a more individual basis. But the threshold to have one's
content distributed by social media platforms is much lower than with
any previous generation of media gatekeeper.

Social media platforms do seek to maximize audience interest (typically referred to as *engagement*) in the specific content options displayed
in an individual's feed. This is where the process of algorithmic curation
and prioritization comes into play. However, this process of rank-ordering
and filtering all content provided is very different from the process of
making decisions about which content to obtain and distribute. These
differences represent dramatic and significant reconfigurations of the
process of content curation, with wide-ranging repercussions that will
be discussed in subsequent chapters.

Government legislation played a role in encouraging and facilitating
social media platforms to operate as massive, somewhat indiscriminate,

content aggregators. To understand how and why this is, we must go back to a much-maligned piece of 1990s legislation called the Communications Decency Act of 1996.[32] The Communications Decency Act (CDA) was a subcomponent of the Telecommunications Act of 1996, which ultimately became a landmark piece of legislation in the communications sector.[33] The Telecommunications Act of 1996 represented the first comprehensive update to the Communications Act of 1934, the legislation that, somewhat incredibly, continued to guide media and telecommunications regulation more than sixty years after its initial passage.

Although the Telecommunications Act of 1996 was largely deregulatory in nature (for instance, relaxing media ownership regulations and removing restrictions on the types of products and services that different types of companies could provide), the Communications Decency Act most certainly was not. The CDA sought to impose harsh penalties on individuals and organizations that disseminated adult content online, essentially imposing a regulatory model more akin to that of broadcast regulation (where the broadcast of "indecent" content can result in fines from the Federal Communications Commission) on the Internet.

In so doing, however, Congress did not want to do anything to impede the rapidly developing Internet service provision industry, nor the emerging online content aggregation and curation industry. The key language of section 230 is: "No provider or user of an interactive computer service shall be treated as the publisher or speaker of any information provided by another information content provider."[34] Yet at the same time, these service providers were granted the authority to act as "good Samaritans" and restrict the distribution of obscene, violent, or other types of objectionable content as they saw fit.[35] Essentially, section 230 granted online platforms and service providers both the immunity from liability of common carriers (such as telecommunications companies) and the editorial authority of publishers. Like telecom companies, "interactive computer service" providers (a category that the courts have decided includes social media platforms) bear virtually no responsibility for the content that travels across their platforms, because section 230 says they will not be treated as the publisher or speaker of the content provided by their users. Nonetheless, they still have fairly broad rights to restrict the distribution of content they see as objectionable, but importantly, acting on these rights does not trigger any kind of liability or responsibility. It's the best of both worlds. The fact that these platforms operate with such a combination of protections and authority tells us quite a bit about how wary Congress was of doing anything to impede this powerful new engine of our economy. Whether the types of activities that these platforms now engage in continue to merit this kind of legal and regulatory carte blanche is the question we must now face, as these platforms continue to evolve and serve functions and have effects that policy makers did not anticipate back in 1996.

THE ALGORITHMIC IMPERATIVE

For these aggregators to operate at the scale necessary to effectively mediate online content, audiences, and advertisers, the imperative to automate much of their functionality became quite pronounced. Given the tech sector origins of these platforms (discussed in the introduction), the pursuit of algorithmic solutions was an inevitability.

The dynamics of this *algorithmic turn*[36] will be discussed in detail in the next chapter. For now, however, it is important to recognize that the algorithmically curated news feeds that have become a default characteristic of social media platforms were not there at the beginning. Facebook did not begin algorithmically curating its users' news feeds until 2009 (the platform was openly accessible by 2006). Prior to 2009, Facebook presented the news in reverse chronological order.[37] As Facebook abandoned this mode of presentation, the popularity of the individual posts was initially the driving factor determining if/where a post appeared in a user's feed.[38]

This process of algorithmic curation quickly became more sophisticated, leading to the well-known EdgeRank algorithm. In its early, relatively simple, articulation, the EdgeRank algorithm could be expressed as follows:

$$\sum = U_e \times W_e \times D_e$$

In this equation, U refers to "user affinity," an assessment of the relationship and proximity between the user and the individual post. So, for instance, the more shared friends between you and another user, the more likely that user's posts would be featured prominently in your news feed. W refers to the action taken by the user on the post, which in this case involved weighting different types of user posting activities differently (video and photos were weighted more heavily than link, links more heavily than plain text, etc.). D refers to what Facebook described as a "time-based decay parameter," the process of prioritizing more recent posts over older posts. By 2013, however, Facebook replaced EdgeRank with a much more sophisticated algorithm incorporating more than 100,000 factors into the process of curating users' news feeds.[39]

Other social media platforms followed a similar pattern. Twitter incorporated algorithmic filtering only in 2016, a full ten years after the platform's launch in 2006.[40] It was also in 2016 that Instagram (launched in 2010) began migrating from reverse-chronological presentation to algorithmic filtering for its news feed.[41] YouTube has evolved from a platform driven by search queries and individual subscriptions to channels to a platform driven by an algorithmically curated feed of recommendations. This transition did not begin in earnest until around 2012, seven years after the platform's launch in 2005.[42] By 2017, more than 70 percent of the time people spent watching videos on YouTube was being driven by algorithmic recommendations.[43]

What seems to have been forgotten already is that these decisions to move from chronological to algorithmically curated presentation of content generated a fair bit of resistance at the time. For instance, Twitter's decision to employ algorithmic filtering resulted in the immediate trending of the #RIPTwitter hashtag.[44] Some user groups even organized boycotts of these platforms in response to the transition to algorithmic filtering.[45] Even Instagram royalty Kendall Jenner was upset about Instagram's transition, tweeting that Instagram was attempting to "fix something that wasn't broken."[46] These protests represent the only really tangible consumer resistance we have seen so far to the insertion of content-curation algorithms into the relationship between media consumers and aggregations of content. For at least some consumers, the original model of cycling through unfiltered, unranked aggregations of content was preferable to algorithmic curation.

These platforms moved forward with algorithmic filtering regardless, and users seemed to quickly get over their initial anger. It should be noted that, in some instances, users have been provided the option of opting out of the algorithmic feed; or, in the case of Twitter, algorithmically curated selections are highlighted and then followed by the reverse-chronological feed. In Facebook's case, the opt-out option is difficult to locate, frequently reverts back automatically to the algorithmic option, and is sometimes unresponsive when you select it.[47]

Why has the imperative toward algorithmic filtering been so strong? Because in each of these cases, the transition to algorithmic filtering and recommendations was driven by one primary objective: to increase the number of regular users and the time that they spend on the platforms—to increase engagement.[48] Regardless of the protests and expressions of discontent from some users, the switch to algorithmic curation seems to systematically have this effect. For instance, according to Twitter, the algorithmic transition led to increases in key metrics such as monthly active users, impressions, and time spent on the site.[49] Even after the protest among Twitter users, only 2 percent of users opted to maintain their chronological feed.[50] As a former Facebook chief technology officer noted, algorithmic filtering "was always the thing people said they didn't want but demonstrated they did via every conceivable metric."[51]

THE GRAVITATIONAL PULL OF SOCIAL MEDIA

Eventually, these social media platforms came to exert an almost gravitational pull on content providers, advertisers, and audiences. Astrophysicists have speculated whether the ongoing Big Bang (the continued expansion of the universe) will be followed by a Big Crunch, in which the universe essentially contracts.[52] This theory provides an analogy for thinking about the evolutionary patterns online. If the low barriers to entry and virtually global reach of the web represent the massive expansion of the online universe, social media platforms represent the gravitational force that has initiated a process of contraction, in which more and more of the content and audience attention online gravitates to, and funnels through, these platforms. Today, six of the ten most popular sites online are social media platforms,[53] dominating the top ten in the same way that search engines and portals did in the late 1990s and early 2000s.

These platforms' aggregations of content and audiences served to attract more content providers and audiences. Content providers were going to where the audiences were, and audiences were going to where online content could be accessed and consumed in the most efficient and user-friendly manner. As a result, platforms such as Facebook, You-Tube, and Twitter have become not only where individuals accumulate to communicate with (and surveil) one another, but also where they can go to watch live NFL games, stream Bloomberg News 24/7, or read the *Washington Post*. Social media platforms have emerged as the most vital and influential media distributors and curators since cable television systems, but at a scale that utterly dwarfs cable. While cable systems operated at the local or regional level, social media platforms operate as global distribution systems.

These platforms were able to exert this gravitational pull through the reaggregation process they instituted, which helped to solve some of the most persistent problems of the web for audiences, content providers, and advertisers.

SOLVING THE AUDIENCE CHALLENGES

From an audience standpoint, as noted previously, compared to using other media, navigating the web was a fairly labor-intensive task. A user could either invest the time and effort necessary to locate the most relevant or satisfying content, or fall into a routine of relying upon a fairly limited "channel repertoire." Now, through social media platforms, algorithmic curation and filtering systems—operating with the guidance of users' expressed interests and preferences (through likes, follows, shares, etc.)—

simplified and largely automated the task of combing the web for interesting and personally relevant news and information.

This kind of aggregation of online content always held value for audiences. The earliest portal sites, such as Yahoo!, literally relied on human beings to surf the web and generate hyperlinked lists of websites for users to access. Needless to say, this soon became completely inadequate for the scope of content options available online. Search engines came to perform this function as well, in a more sophisticated, comprehensive, and personalized manner than the earlier portal sites. However, social media platforms represented a fundamentally different approach to content aggregation than could be found through search engines. Whereas search engines generate content aggregations in response to search queries, social media platforms provide a steady flow of curated, personalized content aggregations.

To better understand the service that social media platforms provide to audiences, we can return to the analogy of the TV Guide Channel mentioned at the beginning of this chapter. The existence of something like the TV Guide Channel seems hard to fathom today, in light of interactive electronic program guides and the continuing transition to on-demand, rather than linear, programming that characterize today's television environment. But the TV Guide Channel became necessary because, as the channel capacity of cable systems expanded and the "500-channel universe" became a reality, television experienced a similar (though much less extreme) fragmentation process to what took place online.[54]

We can think of what happened subsequently in television, with the rise of DVRs as an increasingly essential (and widely beloved) television viewing accessory, as providing similar functionality for television viewers as social media have come to provide for Internet users. With one's DVR fully informed as to one's program preferences, the device would be consistently full of a range of appealing content, freeing the user from having to actually navigate the increasingly cumbersome range of channel options, or even to keep track of which channels provided which programs.[55] More advanced DVRs, such as TiVo, could even learn your preferences and proactively record programs that matched your demonstrated interests.[56] This dynamic is not unlike how social media platforms act upon our demonstrated preferences to provide us with a curated feed culled from the enormity of content options available online, freeing us from having to incur the search costs associated with identifying, locating, and retrieving the desired content.

SOLVING THE ADVERTISER CHALLENGES

From the advertisers' standpoint, thanks to social media and the aggregations of audiences that they provide, advertisers no longer needed to chase down audiences across an array of online content options. With platforms such as YouTube and Facebook aggregating so much of the online content and audience attention, the Internet became a place—like traditional mass media such as television and newspapers—where advertisers could purchase large (and thus more easily measurable) aggregations of audiences in one fell swoop. However, whereas under the Web 1.0 model audience data were provided by third-party measurement firms, under the social media model, the provider of audience attention is also the provider of audience data, in a form of vertical integration that is perhaps unprecedented in the audience marketplace.

These platforms also provided the value-added proposition of targeting, within these large aggregations, specific audience segments, to some extent delivering on the audience-targeting promise that Web 1.0 had failed to deliver on because of the measurement challenges described previously. This targeting is possible because users of social media platforms unhesitatingly volunteer a wealth of demographic, behavioral, and psychographic data about themselves through their day-to-day usage of the platforms, making these platforms a virtually irresistible funnel through which advertising dollars can flow (which may explain why advertisers have accepted the vertical integration of the provision of audience attention and audience data).

The audiences that flow through social media platforms represent perhaps the most comprehensively measurable audiences in the history of media. This is well demonstrated by the recent revelations about the

degree of micro-targeting of voters that took place during the 2016 presidential campaign. As came to light in the wake of the 2016 election, the
Trump campaign, using the firm Cambridge Analytica, was able to identify individual target voters on the basis of behavioral, demographic, and
psychographic data gathered through social media (and other channels)
and then deliver individualized targeted messages to these voters.[57]

Thus, the efficiencies and low transaction costs of buying massive
audiences aggregated via traditional mass media have been married to
the demographic and behavioral targeting that were expected to be the
distinguishing characteristic of the online realm—an irresistible combination for most online advertisers. In this way, social media went a long
way toward making a somewhat inefficient advertising medium much
more efficient.

SOLVING THE CONTENT PROVIDER CHALLENGES

Finally, for content providers, these social media platforms represented
an opportunity to do more to reach audiences than simply post their
content online, advertise, engage in search engine optimization, and
wait for the audience to arrive. Social media platforms generated aggregations of audience attention that could not be found elsewhere online
and, irresistibly, offered content providers the opportunity to access
these audiences.

Much has been made of this Faustian bargain that online content
providers have entered into with social media platforms.[58] Social media
platforms help to deliver large aggregations of audiences to online content providers, but siphon off a substantial amount of the advertising
revenue in the process. To return to the TV Guide Channel analogy,
it is as if advertisers would rather advertise on the TV Guide Channel than on any of the networks displayed on that channel. In 2017,
social media platforms accounted for almost 35 percent of global digital
ad spending (up from 23 percent in 2013). Facebook is the dominant
force here, accounting for roughly two-thirds of all social media ad
spending.[59]

In some ways, the speed with which news organizations have embraced social media platforms as distribution mechanisms recalls what happened during the initial Internet boom of the 1990s. As Internet access diffused rapidly, news outlets rushed to establish an online presence, typically making the online content available for free.[60] These outlets were often motivated by the simple (and perhaps ultimately self-destructive) imperative that they needed to establish an online presence immediately because everyone else was doing it.[61]

Perhaps the destructive effects that the Internet has had on the business model for journalism were inevitable. Nonetheless, it remains worth considering whether, in their blind rush to get online, newspapers helped to sow the seeds of their own decline. Media analyst Jack Shafer asks, "What if, in the mad dash two decades ago to repurpose and extend editorial content onto the web, editors and publishers made a colossal business blunder?"[62] This question was prompted by research suggesting that, in their rush to abandon the print format for digital, newspapers essentially abandoned the platform with the greater long-term revenue potential.[63] From this standpoint, it seems reasonable to ask whether news outlets perhaps failed to learn an important lesson from their own digital history and have instead let history repeat itself in their rapid and unquestioning embrace of social media platforms.[64]

REAGGREGATION IN HISTORICAL PERSPECTIVE

The overarching point here is that online fragmentation compelled reaggregation. Reaggregation met the needs of a number of key stakeholders and helped to solve some of the intractable problems that the Internet had introduced.

It is worth noting that this process of reaggregation is not unprecedented. If we look back to the rise of cable television in the 1980s and 1990s, one of the prevailing narratives was the way in which the explosion in the number of channels steadily ate away at the massive audiences that the Big Three broadcast networks (ABC, NBC, CBS) controlled at the peak of their dominance.[65] However, what received less attention was the extent to which the corporate parents of all those broadcast networks were able to respond to these audience declines by acquiring and launching various cable networks, thereby replenishing the audiences they had lost. Thus, for instance, while the audience for the NBC broadcast network declined, the audience for the NBC *family* of networks (MSNBC, CNBC, Bravo, SyFy, NBC Sports, etc.) compensated for those losses with their own audiences.

This process of reaggregation through ownership concentration helped, to some extent, to solve the problem of declining audiences for the broadcast networks.[66] Reaggregation also helped solve some of the problems for advertisers associated with the fragmentation of television audiences. For instance, one media conglomerate famously offered, through its family of networks that each targeted different demographics, one-stop "cradle-to-grave" audience access opportunities.[67] Today's social media platforms have taken the process of reaggregating content and audiences a quantum leap further, but the factors compelling the process are essentially the same.

IMPLICATIONS: FROM *PULL* TO *PUSH, ACTIVE* TO *PASSIVE*

The scenario described so far affects another important dynamic in online evolution: the transformation of the Internet from more of a pull medium to more of a push medium. The terms *push* and *pull* have been around for quite some time to characterize specific media and how they are used.[68] A push medium typically refers to contexts in which users have a number of content options broadcast directly to them, from which they can make their own selections. So, for instance, traditional television was generally perceived as a push medium, with an ever-growing array of channels being pushed directly to one's television, providing a menu of readily accessible options from which one could make a selection. Correspondingly, the navigation process for traditional television was simple and limited (involving flipping through channels not unlike the way one scrolls through a news feed), lacking any kind of robust search functionality.

The evolution of television is helpful in illustrating the distinction between push and pull media. As television has become based around on-demand viewing (through cord-cutting and reliance on digital streaming services such as Netflix), it has become more of a pull medium. In this evolving context, television programs reside on a distant server, to be retrieved by the viewer through a process of search, browsing, and recommendations. The recommendation process in this context serves, to some extent, to reinstitute the push model (given that it obviates the need for searching), which parallels the transition from pull to push online.

In its original incarnation, the web represented the epitome of a pull medium. Indeed, the media evolution from push, as represented by most traditional media, to pull, as represented by the ascension of the web, was widely seen as one of the fundamental dimensions of the transformation of our media environment. Media futurist Nicholas Negroponte famously noted in 1995, in his influential book *Being Digital*, "Being digital will change the nature of mass media from a process of pushing bits at people to one of allowing people (or their computers) to pull them. This is a radical change."[69]

The conventional wisdom, then, was that, with some exceptions, "old" media tended to operate under a push model, while "new" media operated under more of a pull model. Embedded within this dichotomy are now-outmoded notions of the specific, distinct contexts in which television and web use take place, with television usage traditionally taking place while leaning back on a couch and web usage while learning forward at a desk (in the days before the widespread adoption of laptops and home Wi-Fi).

This "lean-forward" versus "lean-back" terminology had more or less drifted into the dustbin of media history. However, the terminology has recently been revived, through Facebook's announcement in June of 2017 of its new original video programming initiative. The programming being produced has been described to advertisers as fitting into one of three categories: "on-the-go," "lean-back," and "lean-forward."[70] Clearly, old media buzzwords never die; they just cycle through again. And while Facebook may assert a distinction between "lean-back" and "lean-forward" dimensions of its service, the argument here is that social media platforms have, on the whole, regressed the Internet and how we use it into more of lean-back medium, along the lines of traditional television.

To understand this argument, it is worth considering one more relevant dichotomy. These notions of push versus pull, and lean-back versus lean-forward, have crystallized within the academic literature on media technologies and audiences into an extensive body of research exploring the distinction between *active* and *passive* audiences.[71] A key aspect of this distinction is the extent to which users engage in active searching and retrieval (leaning forward to pull content), as opposed to being "programmed to" (leaning back and having content pushed at them).[72]

In a number of ways, our online experience is evolving into one that is more push than pull, more lean-back than lean-forward, and, ultimately, more passive than active. The ongoing transition from PC- and laptop-based Internet access to tablet and mobile device–based Internet access is one example. The share of online traffic accounted for by mobile devices has been rising steadily, increasing from 16 percent in 2013 to more than 52 percent in 2018.[73] Mobile's share of total Internet traffic will likely continue this dramatic upswing in the coming years. This pattern has meant that the providers of online content and platforms are increasingly designing their products and services primarily, if not exclusively, to accommodate the dynamics (and constraints) of mobile device–based access and usage. This means that the Internet is actually evolving in a way designed to accommodate—and thus, to some extent, dictate—more passive, lean-back forms of online behavior.

As I have argued in detail elsewhere,[74] this transition to mobile devices institutes a more prominent push/lean-back/passive relationship between audiences and the producers and distributors of content. The devices themselves are less conducive to dimensions of audience activity such as user-generated content. Research has shown, for instance, that when Wikipedia users transition from laptops/PCs to mobile devices and tablets, the volume of their content contributions to the platform diminishes substantially.[75] The late Steve Jobs even described iPads as "more like iPods than they are like computers."[76] Certainly, mobile devices would be even closer to iPods on this continuum.

Reflecting this positioning of tablets and mobile devices as primarily content-consumption devices, research tells us that, across a variety of categories, content-consumption activities (reading, watching, listening) are a much more prominent part of mobile usage than content-creation activities, particularly in comparison to the distribution of consumption versus creation activities on PCs and laptops.[77] Information-seeking similarly declines in the mobile context; the frequency, complexity, thoroughness, and duration of online searches all diminish in the mobile context, in comparison to the PC/laptop context.[78] I refer to this dynamic as the *repassification* of the media audience, because as online behaviors evolve in this way, they take on more of the characteristics that we have long associated with our traditional mass media—characteristics that the Internet, for a time, seemed to work against.

The ongoing mobile conversion and audience repassification provide some context for the primary argument here—that the transition to social media–based, algorithmically curated forms of online news consumption represents a similar regression to a push/lean-back/ passive dynamic. This regression is indeed central to the ascension of these platforms. To illustrate this point, it is worth recalling that early social media platforms such as MySpace—and Facebook in its original incarnation—operated purely as massive aggregations of individual pages. In that regard, they were just aggregators of the home pages that had become ubiquitous on the web for both individuals and organizations. If you wanted to know what was happening in your friend's life, you needed to search for and navigate to his/her MySpace/Facebook page, a process not very different from accessing that individual's personal web page.[79]

In a change that most likely sealed Facebook's triumph over then social media front-runner MySpace (the Betamax of social media platforms), even though it generated substantial user resistance at the time,[80] Facebook introduced its News Feed in 2006.[81] Now, news and information produced on the pages of members of your social network would get pushed to you, rather than you actively retrieving it. MySpace did not adopt this format until 2008,[82] at which point it was apparently too little, too late. Here, too, as was the case with the algorithmic filtering of news feeds, there was initially a fair bit of resistance to this change. Tech-sector publication *TechCrunch* ran a dramatic headline at the time, "Facebook Users Revolt," and detailed the widespread boycotts, petitions, and protest sites that emerged in the wake of the change—another example of at least a subset of users fighting to maintain more autonomy in how they engaged with their media platforms.[83] Today, of course, we take the scrolling-news-feed structure of pretty much every social media platform for granted. However, it is important to remember that this is not how social media platforms such as Facebook and MySpace originally operated—that they once required a more active, lean-forward orientation from their users than they do today.

The original dynamic was obviously much more of a pull dynamic than if the activity of everyone in your network is being cycled through a single, easily scrollable feed on the social media platform's landing page. Now, through social media, content can be pushed to those who have expressed an interest (this expression of interest through a Like/Follow being the last real remnant of the pull model), and—even better from the standpoint of content providers—these individual recipients can also push it further along. This shift from a pull to a push model of content access ultimately facilitated the tremendous reaggregation of content, audiences, and advertising revenues described above. As James Webster has noted, the greater choice and empowerment associated with a genuine pull-oriented media environment has resulted in an "ironic twist": the greater the extent to which such options are available, the greater the reliance on tools that "reinstate the features [of] push media."[84]

It is particularly important to consider the implications of this altered dynamic in relation to news. As I have argued, social media platforms institute a stronger push dynamic to online behavior than existed previously. This has facilitated the notion of "ambient journalism,"[85] in which news serves almost as ubiquitous background noise that can be easily accessed. Within this conceptualization, the news consumer would seem to be somewhat *passified*, no longer engaging in directed efforts at getting information.

There is perhaps no stronger illustration of this point than what has come to be the defining perspective on the nature of contemporary, social network–derived news consumption: "If the news is that important, it will find me."[86] This phrase, which, according to some analysts "has taken on a life of its own,"[87] has its origins in a statement made by a college student participating in a market research focus group back in 2008.[88] While the statement typically has been discussed within the context of the revolutionary degree to which sharing has come to play a role in news distribution, what has been less discussed is the level of passivity in news consumption reflected in this statement.

Social media platforms have enabled news consumption to become as passive as in any traditional mass media context—perhaps more so. At least in traditional media contexts, a decision was made to walk down the driveway and pick up the paper, or turn to the station airing a news broadcast. Now, the process of scrolling through a social media news feed—often not even with the intention of consuming news—has emerged as one of the most predominant ways individuals now become informed.[89] The process of getting informed is now seamlessly integrated with the processes of keeping up with family and friends, watching cat videos, and stalking exes. This is all a function of the extent to which social media platforms have imposed a push model on what was previously a pull medium.

The results may ultimately be damaging to the cultivation of an informed citizenry. As one recent study of the consumption of news on social media concluded, social media news consumers devote comparatively less time to news stories incidentally encountered on social media than to newspaper or television news consumption. As a result, news loses its privileged place in the hierarchy of available media content options, which undermines news consumers' ability to effectively contextualize the news stories that they consume.[90]

In the end, when we look back at earlier statements about the transformative effects of the Internet, it seems reasonable to ask how well they hold up today. A statement such as that made by media scholar Sonia Livingstone in 2003, that the Internet has facilitated the transformation of the audience "from passive observer to active participant in a virtual world,"[91] seemed virtually incontestable at the time. Now, however, such a generalization seems far less convincing. The reality is that the contemporary Internet user has—through social media—taken on at least some of the characteristics of passive observer.

IMPLICATIONS: THE REEMERGENCE OF WALLED GARDENS

There is another important way in which the process of reaggregation involves a regression to an earlier media dynamic. Specifically, we are seeing a reemergence of the walled-garden strategy that characterized the early days of commercial Internet access. The term *walled garden* was used most frequently in relation to onetime Internet powerhouse America Online (AOL). To fully understand the nature of the walled-garden model, it is important to revisit AOL's origins. Today, most of us remember AOL as the dominant provider of dial-up Internet access in the 1990s and, subsequently, as the instigator of the largely disastrous AOL–Time Warner merger in 2000. However, AOL began as what was known as a bulletin board service (BBS) in the 1980s. Unlike an Internet service provider (ISP), a bulletin board service did not provide access to the Internet. When BBS subscribers dialed in through their modems, their computers were not accessing the Internet, but rather were accessing proprietary content and services offered by the service provider and housed on their servers. Such services might include chatting applications, games, and news and information.

As the web developed, dial-up BBS services such as AOL evolved to provide subscribers with access to the Internet (and subsequently the web) as well. Of course, from an economic standpoint, it was preferable that these subscribers spend as much time as possible with the proprietary content and services, rather than drifting away to the web. Users that stayed within the proprietary content and services were more lucrative, as they could be better monetized through selling them additional products and services, and through selling their attention to advertisers.

Thus, the walled-garden strategy emerged, in which ISPs provided subscribers with access to the web but enticed these subscribers to stay within the array of content and service options that they offered. For a time, it was successful. Many AOL subscribers actually spent a majority of their online time within the walled garden rather than on the web.[92] Many users did not even understand the difference.

AOL's fateful merger with Time Warner was, to some degree, motivated by this walled-garden strategy. This marriage of "content" (Time Warner) and "conduit" (AOL) and of "old media" and "new media," as its supporters heralded it at the time,[93] was motivated in part by the desire to construct a more effective and lucrative walled garden. That is, if AOL's proprietary content included high-quality offerings from Time Warner's massive library of publications, music, television programs, and movies, then the company would be better able to contain its subscribers within its walled garden, and be able to grow its subscriber base and monetize these subscribers more extensively.[94] However, as the web continued to grow and offer more and more to users, the walled-garden model became increasingly untenable and more or less died with the failure of the AOL–Time Warner merger, a failure that left AOL as little more than a cautionary footnote in the history of the Internet.[95]

Now, as we look at the dynamics of how social media platforms such as Facebook, Twitter, and Snapchat are operating, we see a revival of the walled-garden strategy, albeit in a slightly different configuration.[96] While the original walled gardens sought to discourage users from accessing the web, these new walled gardens are web (or mobile app) based. The goal this time around is to keep users constrained within the particular platform, for the platform to serve as something of a one-stop shop for as many needs and interests as possible. This time around, the content contained within these social media platforms' walled gardens is not necessarily available exclusively through these platforms. However, to the extent that the content is hosted, licensed, or owned by—and accessed through—the social media platform, the effect is essentially the same, with the goal being to keep users on the platform as much as possible in order to monetize them as extensively as possible.

For instance, when Twitter signed agreements to stream content such as Bloomberg News or NFL football games,[97] or Snapchat licensed original news programming from CNN or Vice,[98] this was about funneling high-value content through the platform so that users would not need to access that content elsewhere. Facebook's recent foray into original video programming can similarly be seen as a way to enhance the scope (and thus the retention power) of its walled garden. Given that online video aggregators such as YouTube and Netflix attract a substantial amount of online audience attention, it is not surprising that Facebook would move in the video-programming direction, in an effort to retain some of that audience attention within its platform.

Facebook's introduction of Instant Articles provides a useful window into this approach.[99] Introduced in May 2015, Instant Articles would directly host content uploaded by media outlets, rather than these outlets' posts including a link to their home page.[100] This arrangement included a limited revenue-sharing model between Facebook and media outlets, with Facebook providing publishers the options of selling ads in their articles and keeping the revenue or using Facebook's Audience Network, the site's own targeted advertising product.[101]

Ostensibly, the primary appeal of—and rationale for—Instant Articles was that it would reduce load times (particularly on mobile devices).[102] However, the timing of the introduction of the Instant Articles program raises another possibility. In June 2015, a month after Facebook announced the Instant Articles program, the company announced an adjustment to its News Feed algorithm that would give greater weight to posts based on the amount of time users spent with the links within those posts.[103] Thus, more engaging content (as measured by time spent) would receive priority in a user's News Feed. This adjustment was the result of internal research begun in 2014 that showed that a key predictor of how positively a user was likely to evaluate a post was the amount of time the user spent with that content.[104] Thus, for instance, if a user followed a link posted to Facebook and returned to Facebook from that link in thirty seconds, the odds are that the user would rate that post as lower quality than a posted link that the user spent three minutes with. Facebook referred to this research when making the announcement about its algorithm adjustment, noting, "We've discovered that if people spend significantly more time on a particular story in News Feed than the majority of other stories they look at, this is a good sign that content was relevant to them."[105]

These results point to an interesting conundrum for social media platforms. User satisfaction with the platform positively correlates with the amount of time that users spend away from the platform, consuming content hosted elsewhere. The business model for most social media platforms depends on increasing the time spent on the platform (i.e., engagement). More time spent equals more ad exposures, which equals more ad revenues. However, a higher-quality user experience depends on providing users with more content that keeps them away from the platform for longer stretches of time. The obvious solution to this conundrum is to host the high-quality content directly.

The logic of Instant Articles raises a well-established concern—one that those who have followed the saga of network neutrality (or net neutrality) should quickly recognize. *Network neutrality* refers to the requirement that Internet service providers engage in no discrimination (in terms of access or download speeds) in any of the content traveling on their networks. Network neutrality proponents have long been concerned that ISPs might favor traffic in which it has an ownership stake, or provide higher speeds to content providers willing to pay a toll in order to enter the Internet's "fast lane." There has been enough evidence of such behaviors over the years, and enough evidence of its negative consequences, that network neutrality would seem to be something worth maintaining.[106] This is why the FCC under Obama imposed network neutrality requirements on ISPs, though the Trump FCC subsequently eliminated these requirements.[107]

How does network neutrality relate to a program such as Instant Articles? The reality is that a very similar dynamic could ultimately be at work here. Those content providers who take part in the Instant Articles program are, presumably, doing so at least in part to take advantage of a "fast lane" of sorts (i.e., faster load times). To the extent that Facebook wants to encourage content providers to take part in the Instant Articles program (and the previous discussion of walled gardens suggests that they have good reason to want this), it is perhaps not unreasonable to consider whether they might be incentivized to slow the load times for content operating outside of the Instant Articles system—to effectively widen the load-time gap between affiliated and unaffiliated content providers. One could imagine a scenario in which social media neutrality, or platform neutrality more broadly, becomes the next frontier for the net neutrality debate. The key point here, however, is that social media platforms have a variety of tools at their disposal to reconstruct the walled gardens that characterized the early days of the Internet.

CHAPTER 2

Algorithmic Gatekeeping and the Transformation of News Organizations

O ur ability to fully understand the operation—and thus the impact—of algorithmically controlled media platforms is inherently limited. One of the most common refrains over the past decade has been that the algorithmic systems that increasingly control the dynamics of how news is produced, disseminated, and consumed are "black boxes."[1] The term *black box* refers to any complex system in which the inner workings are unclear to its users. Within the context of algorithms, the key issue is that the decision outputs that they provide are generally the result of a complex, frequently evolving set of criteria and inputs—the bulk of which are kept proprietary for a variety of reasons, including competitive concerns and the need to try to minimize the extent to which these systems are "gamed" by third parties.[2]

Within the specific context of news, the key issue involves the uncertainty and concerns that arise when decision-making about the type of news that is produced, disseminated, and consumed is delegated, to some extent, to algorithmic decision-making systems. The internal workings of these systems are a mystery to most of the stakeholders who engage with them, and researching how they operate, and the implications of how they operate, is challenging.[3]

Over the past few years, however, we have learned quite a bit about how these systems operate and how their operation affects the news organizations and news consumers with whom they interact.[4] These algorithmic systems do not operate in a vacuum. Individual news consumers play a fundamental role in guiding the work of these systems. Similarly, human editors and decision-makers continue to play important roles, with algorithmic systems often operating in a supplementary or advisory capacity—though sometimes the role of human decision-makers is unclear or intentionally concealed.

In, this chapter I will focus specifically on the transformation that has taken place in the process of gatekeeping—the process by which news organizations make decisions about which news stories are presented to news consumers. Understanding contemporary algorithmic gatekeeping, however, requires that we first provide context in terms of how the gatekeeping process has traditionally operated.

Traditional Gatekeeping

Within the context of journalism, gatekeeping refers to the process by which news organizations make decisions as to which of the events taking place or issues being discussed receive coverage. Historically, this gatekeeping process has proven quite influential; a large body of research has shown that there is a strong correlation between the amount of coverage an issue receives in the news media and the extent to which news consumers perceive that issue as important.[5] More recent studies have shown, not surprisingly, that the traditional news media's agenda-setting power is in decline as a more complex and interdependent agenda-setting process has developed across both traditional and social media.[6]

A key question for gatekeeping is, what makes a story newsworthy? From this standpoint, it is worth revisiting one of the earliest gatekeeping studies, David Manning White's famous 1950 case study of "Mr. Gates," a wire services editor at a Midwestern newspaper.[7] As a wire services editor, Mr. Gates operated in a way that is actually similar to contemporary content aggregators like Google News or Facebook, though obviously on a much smaller scale. His job was to decide which of the many stories being produced by others (in this case, the three major wire services) to include in the day's paper. Mr. Gates was essentially curating third-party content for his paper's readers.[8]

While today we wonder about the factors that determine whether a story appears in our news feed, in 1950 David Manning White wondered about the factors that led to some wire services stories' making it into the paper and others' being rejected. In order to answer this question, White had Mr. Gates maintain a record of all the wire service stories that came across his desk and record the reasons for including or excluding each story.

One thing that White found was that Mr. Gates was a very stringent gatekeeper: 90 percent of the wire services stories that crossed his desk were rejected.[9] More importantly, White found that Mr. Gates's individual preferences often appeared to be the determining factor. For instance, Mr. Gates noted that he "didn't like" stories about suicides, which meant he generally rejected stories on that topic. Mr. Gates also had a preference for political news (with a decidedly conservative leaning) and a general distaste for sensationalistic news.[10]

The Mr. Gates study (and others that have followed in its wake)[11] helped to make more transparent the dynamics of a decision-making process that generally is not transparent at all. White's illumination of the combination of individual idiosyncrasies and more general news values that guide the gatekeeping process established a baseline that guided future research.

However, what is too often forgotten about this landmark study is the subsequent reanalysis of the original data that was conducted more than twenty-five years later by sociologist Paul Hirsch.[12] In this reanalysis, Hirsch found that different types of stories made it through the gatekeeping process in direct proportion to the frequency with which they were provided by the wire service. For instance, if 30 percent of what the wire services sent consisted of political stories, 30 percent of what Mr. Gates selected for inclusion in the paper was political stories as well. So what looked like individual autonomy at one level, on closer examination seemed a bit more like decision-making that operated within—and to some extent adhered to—parameters established by a preceding level of gatekeeper. This interaction between levels of gatekeeping becomes particularly important as we consider our evolving media ecosystem, in which the layers of gatekeepers have expanded.

Thus, a complex set of individual, organizational, and institutional factors have always been brought to bear in the gatekeeping process. [13] However, central to all of these levels of analysis is the notion of news values—the criteria for newsworthiness that guide decision-making. These values can vary across individuals, organizations, and institutional and cultural contexts. They can vary over time and can be affected by changing technological, economic, or political conditions. Clearly, they are not monolithic, universal, or necessarily stable. Nonetheless, they provide a framework for understanding why certain news stories make it through the gatekeeping process and others do not.

Commonly identified news values include the unexpected (stories that are in some way surprising), the power elite (stories that focus on powerful individuals, organizations, or institutions), timeliness (stories that have occurred recently), conflict (stories involving opposing individuals or forces), and proximity (stories that are geographically near the news audience).[14] More recent analyses have identified celebrity and entertainment as core news values, a reflection of the extent to which economic and competitive pressures have pushed the news values that drive many news organizations in less substantive, more sensationalistic directions.[15]

It is safe to say that news values have always been, to some extent, an amalgam of what news organizations believe is important for audiences to know and what these organizations believe these audiences would find most appealing. The extent to which these two different points of origin for news values can come into conflict has produced one of the defining tensions in the institution of journalism. This tension has been expressed in terms of giving the audience what it needs versus what it wants or, more broadly, whether news organizations approach audiences as citizens versus consumers.[16] To some extent, this is a false dichotomy, as there is certainly room for overlapping news values that serve audiences as both citizens and consumers.[17] Nonetheless, to the extent that they are not perfectly congruent, considering these concepts as opposing points on a continuum provides a useful way of thinking about the tension inherent in the simultaneous financial and civic imperatives that are central to the operation of news organizations.

One development that has affected the dynamics of this tension is that, until fairly recently, it was difficult for news organizations to have a detailed sense of what their audiences actually wanted. A newspaper or a news broadcast was a *bundled*[18] product—delivered as a packaged collection of assorted news stories. News organizations delivered this product through media that generally lacked interactivity, so there was no backchannel of communication. Because of this combination of characteristics, news organizations could not gather direct information about the relative audience appeal of individual stories or story types.

Of course, audiences provided feedback on individual stories through phone calls and letters to the editor.[19] However, this kind of feedback tends to represent the viewpoints of a very narrow spectrum of the audience and is therefore of limited value as a decision-making tool.[20] In addition, news organizations could engage in activities like market research surveys and focus groups.[21] However, asking relatively small samples of news consumers to self-report on the types of stories they consume—or would like to consume—does not provide as powerful or reliable a guide to formulating audience-centric news values as today's constant influx of granular data on how many people read /watched a particular story online, how long they spent with that story, how highly they rated that story, whether they shared or commented on the story, etc.[22]

Ultimately, predigital news organizations knew relatively little about their audiences' news preferences. This limited the extent to which audience preferences and behaviors could directly affect news values, allowing news organizations' own self-generated news values to hold greater sway and/or allowing more imagined or impressionistic notions of audiences' news values to affect their decision-making.[23]

Contemporary Gatekeeping

Now we switch gears to the contemporary news environment and the ways in which algorithmic and individual gatekeeping have intruded on a process once dominated by journalists and editors.[24] Increasingly, in our age of social media, individual users have taken on the role of gatekeepers. Individual news consumers now have the autonomy to disseminate news through social media by sharing stories.[25] In the aggregate, this is becoming an increasingly important gatekeeping function, as evidenced by the extent to which news organizations have become fixated on getting the stories they produce shared as widely as possible on social media (discussed in more detail later).[26] Indeed, research focusing on Twitter showed that social media sharing accounts for a larger percentage of visits to a news story than direct access through a user's news feed.[27] These sharing behaviors, along with other observable news-related consumption and engagement activities, also serve as key criteria informing the algorithmic systems that determine what news makes the cut and appears in an individual's curated news feed in the first place. In this way, individual gatekeeping activities are intertwined with the broader algorithmic systems in which they often take place.[28]

The role of algorithmic systems in gatekeeping runs counter to what many expected from the Internet. There was a time when the Internet's role as *disintermediator* was widely heralded.[29] In the 1990s and early 2000s, as we watched the Internet undermine traditional intermediaries such as record labels and, to some extent, newspapers, it was easy to get caught up in the notion that intermediaries were going to become a thing of the past. However, as chapter 1 illustrated, the nature of the digital transformation created needs and incentives for different types of intermediaries—intermediaries that could operate at an unprecedented scale and scope. Contemporary media platforms such as social media and search engines emerged to operate at a scale that has both compelled and been facilitated by a reliance on algorithmic decision-making systems.

We are also witnessing an unprecedented decoupling of the production and distribution functions of journalism. Historically, news organizations have been vertically integrated in terms of news production and distribution. Newspapers traditionally had their own distribution systems (archaic as they may seem now) in the form of fleets of trucks, home delivery and news racks. These vertically integrated distribution mechanisms operated alongside unaffiliated exhibition outlets such as newsstands, grocery stores, and bookstores. Each of these unaffiliated outlets could elect not to carry some or all newspapers, but there was generally no monopolistic or oligopolistic structure to this wide-ranging collection of partners, which minimized the risk of any widespread exhibition problem. And, of course, these exhibitors did not have the capacity to make curation decisions at the level of individual stories, only at the level of individual publications.

Television and radio stations were similarly vertically integrated, with stations producing news and broadcasting it directly to viewers/listeners over the airwaves. To some extent, national television and radio networks had to rely for distribution on their local affiliates, which could preempt national programming, but the contractual terms of network-affiliate relationships have always contained strong economic disincentives for preemption, and when such preemption does take place, it has tended to be for entertainment programming rather than news.[30]

The arrival of the Internet, however, represents the starting point of a dramatic change in the relationship between news production and distribution. The Internet itself did not effectively decouple production from distribution, since the Internet infrastructure has generally operated like a common carrier—essentially, a neutral, nondiscriminating, passive distribution platform.[31] Internet users could access news directly from the websites of the news producers, with no meaningful intermediary involvement. The decoupling of production and distribution begins in earnest with the applications and platforms that were layered onto the Internet, such as aggregators, search engines, and later, social media.

In many ways, the vertical integration of production and distribution is vital to the operation of a free press. Once an independent intermediary is integrated into the distribution process, opportunities arise to filter or suppress the news during its journey from news producer to news consumer. The ascendance of cable television in the 1970s and 1980s illustrates this point and, to some extent, foreshadows some of the issues we see today. Specifically, as local cable systems emerged as an intermediary between local broadcast stations and television households, conflicts arose around cable systems' rights and obligations when it came to carrying the signals of local television stations.[32] Cable systems had the ability (which they sometimes acted on) to drop local stations from their systems, making them unavailable to cable subscribers. The end result was the "must carry" rules, imposed by the Federal Communications Commission, essentially requiring local cable systems to carry local broadcast stations.[33] One reason for the imposition of the must-carry rules was to ensure that audiences continued to have access to local news (something that cable systems at the time generally did not produce).[34] Thus, the behavior of an emergent intermediary was regulated in an effort to assure that news still effectively reached audiences.

At the time, some stakeholders argued that the fact that a cable system did not carry a local station did not mean it was completely unavailable because households could still access local stations via the over-the-air antenna system that preceded cable. However, the FCC ultimately decided that the widespread adoption of cable represented a sufficient distribution enhancement (through improved reception) that broadcast-only distribution could not be considered equivalent. Cable reception of broadcast stations was generally so much better than over-the-air reception that stations available only over the air would be at a significant disadvantage in terms of their audience reach.

The FCC also decided that it was unreasonable to expect television users to toggle back and forth between cable and over-the-air signal inputs in an era when cable had become the norm for television viewing. Readers of a certain age may remember the A/B switch on the back of 1970s- and 1980s-era television sets, allowing the user to flip back and forth between cable and over-the-air inputs (requiring the user to actually get off the couch to do so). Such a system, according to the FCC's logic, fundamentally disadvantaged local stations available only via broadcast antenna.[35]

Both of these points offer parallels for today's relationship between news organizations and social media platforms. With regard to the FCC's first point, the reality today is that social media represent a monumental distribution enhancement over other means available to online news outlets. It is certainly the case that news consumers can still access news directly from news organizations, either through their home pages or through the mobile apps that many news organizations have developed. However, the size of the audience base on social media and the "push" mechanism (see chapter 1) to individual news feeds represent substantial enhancements over other available means of reaching audiences.

With regard to the FCC's second point, we may be approaching a point when it becomes unrealistic to expect news consumers to access online news through means other than social media platforms and news aggregators, given the efficiencies that these platforms represent for news consumers and the passivity in news consumption that they are cultivating (see chapter 1). However, recent trends (discussed later in this chapter) raise the possibility that we may have already witnessed social media's peak as a news intermediary.

Nonetheless, today's centrality of social media platforms and news aggregators as intermediaries between news producers and news consumers represents a far more dramatic departure from the historical norm than did the introduction of cable. News organizations generally have no ownership stake in this distribution mechanism (i.e., no vertical integration). Nor, at this point, have any must-carry-type regulations been imposed to assure that audiences have the opportunity to consume the news that news organizations produce. Rather, these intermediaries operate under regulatory safeguards (section 230 of the Telecommunications Act of 1996) that explicitly articulate their right to filter the content that passes through their systems in accordance with their own criteria.

Now, each individual story operates as its own entity, seeking the widest possible distribution from the algorithmic systems that guide the distribution/curation practices of news aggregators, search engines, and social media platforms. This shift introduces unprecedented, exponentially greater levels of complexity and opacity to the ways in which these new intermediaries can affect the consumption of news.

Researchers, however, are beginning to untangle this process. One natural point of focus has been on the algorithmic systems undergirding Facebook's News Feed. The News Feed's algorithmic system has evolved over time to take into account thousands of factors in making its decisions about which posts to place in a user's curated News Feed.[36] Because this system is proprietary, researchers have attempted to piece together the nature of the factors that power the News Feed through a variety of indirect approaches. One study, for instance, analyzed public-facing documents such as Facebook's News Feed FYI blog.[37] According to an analysis of this blog, the factors that serve as inputs into its ranking calculations appear to fall into six main categories: (1) content (story characteristics, such as picture or video, number of likes or comments associated with the story, etc.); (2) source (characteristics of the user or page that posted a story, such as friends/family or organization, or more granularly, the extent to which the source has posted clickbait headlines); (3) audience (consumption-related characteristics, such as frequency of video watching, frequency/context of use of Hide functionality, etc.); (4) action (individual behaviors in response to a specific story, such as liking, sharing, or time spent reading/watching); (5) relationship (relationship indicators between individuals/pages, such as frequency and nature of interactions between them); and (6) likelihood (probability that a user will engage in some future action, such as liking or commenting on a story).[38]

Another analysis, which drew upon Facebook patents, press releases, and SEC filings, identified nine values as the most prominent input factors associated with Facebook's News Feed algorithm.[39] Far and away the most prominent factor was friend relationships. Other prominent factors were user interest as determined by text mining of status updates, the age of a post (giving priority to newer posts), and the number of likes, comments, and shares generated by a post. It is interesting to note that content quality turned out to be by far the least prominent factor identified through this analytical approach.[40]

Of course, as with a recipe, just knowing the ingredients is insufficient. It is also necessary to know the relative quantities. Similarly, in terms of social media algorithms, knowing the criteria is only one piece of the puzzle; their relative priority is also important, but more difficult to ascertain.

The various ranking criteria associated with Facebook's News Feed algorithm have so far shown only slight connections to many traditional news values. There is a connection in terms of a prioritization of new stories (novelty), as well as in terms of recent efforts to prioritize local stories (proximity). Beyond that, connections are indirect at best, if we choose to think of the liking, commenting, and sharing activities of an individual's social network as a reasonable proxy for newsworthiness. As media and technology researcher Michael DeVito has noted, a key point of differentiation between the news values that guide Facebook's News Feed and the news values that have traditionally guided news organizations is that Facebook's News Feed values emphasize *personal significance*, whereas traditional news organization values emphasize *social significance*.[41]

Similarly, there has been a fair bit of disconnect between the professional norms and values that guide these organizations and the news values that have traditionally guided news organizations.[42] As one news app designer said, when queried about how journalistic values influenced his work, "I don't think that the people in this space . . . are familiar with these ideas of journalism . . . I don't think they believe they're important. . . . I think there are no ideals being pursued."[43]

In interviews conducted with executives at Silicon Valley firms such as Google, Facebook, and Twitter, journalism researcher Frank Michael Russell found a consistent failure to articulate any specific norms or values undergirding the design and implementation of algorithmic gatekeeping systems, but found that more general norms associated with disruption and innovation were quite prominent.[44] The primacy of engineers over other types of media professionals was also a recurring theme in these interviews. Ultimately, Russell concluded that these executives operated under "institutional values such as a belief in technocratic solutions for societal problems."[45]

For these reasons, it is perhaps not surprising to see a divergence between the news agendas as represented by news organizations and the news that is presented by algorithmically curated social media platforms like Facebook. One study compared the frequency of different story types that a set of Swedish news outlets posted to their Facebook pages with the quantity of sharing activity associated with each of these story types, finding significant disconnects between story-type prominence and sharing activity.[46] A comparative analysis of the algorithmically curated versus chronological (at the time) news feeds of Facebook and Twitter showed that Facebook's algorithmically curated feed failed to pick up on a significant news event at the time—the civil unrest in Ferguson, Missouri—while coverage and discussion of this event was appearing prominently on Twitter.[47] This pattern was also reflected in research showing that, of the news feeds of six social media platforms,[48] only Twitter's uncurated (at the time), chronological news feed exhibited a significant correlation between news story sharing/retweeting activity and the distribution of news items per section of both the *Guardian* and the *New York Times*.[49] Thus, in the case of these last two studies, the news agenda as represented by news organizations appeared more likely to be reflected in social media when the news feed operated without algorithmic curation. Thus, it would seem that social media users—when not subject to algorithmic curation—operate a bit like Mr. Gates in their news-sharing activities, taking their cues from the gatekeeping decisions of the news organizations.

The challenge in interpreting the findings of studies such as these is that they generally do not disentangle the individual user's sharing decision from the preceding algorithmic decision-making about which stories to feature in the user's news feed, or whether a story being shared was originally encountered on social media in the first place. As with Mr. Gates—whose gatekeeping decisions appeared to be a function of the decision-making of the wire services—the sharing decisions of individual social media users are, to some extent, a function of the curation decisions of the algorithmic systems underlying social media platforms. These curation decisions are a product of the user's previous sharing decisions, though they are also a product of independent priorities baked into the algorithmic curation systems.

Also complicating matters is that we do not know very much about the origins of sharing behaviors. How often is a story that a user shares on social media one that the user first encountered on social media, versus a story that the user encountered initially on the web and then shared via social media? The answer to this question matters in terms of deepening our understanding of the extent to which an individual's news-sharing activities on social media are affected by the platforms' curation decisions. It seems reasonable to expect that, over time, a growing proportion of social media sharing of news originates from social media–disseminated news stories. According to recent Pew Research, only 6 percent of social media consumers regularly post links to news stories they have encountered outside of their social media platforms.[50] These results suggest that the bulk of the news-sharing on social media is limited to the stories that news outlets have posted to those platforms.

As much as the focus here has been on the gatekeeping patterns and news values embedded in the algorithmic systems that guide social media, it is important to recognize that more traditional, human-centered editorial decision-making often comes into play. As was well publicized at the time (mid-2016), Facebook employed human editors to determine the content of its Trending feed that occupied the upper right corner of a user's Facebook page. The publicity came in the form of an exposé, in which former editors claimed that the staff regularly engaged in the suppression of conservative news stories that might have merited inclusion in the Trending list on the basis of the volume of social media activity they were generating.[51]

Looking back on the uproar that this revelation generated (conservative members of Congress were particularly up in arms),[52] along with the subsequent furor roughly six months later over how Facebook's algorithmic curation systems were failing to identify and prevent the spread of fake news,[53] we get a sense of the difficult tensions inherent in the scale at which these platforms seek to operate as gatekeepers. It's a bit of a damned-if-you-do, damned-if-you-don't situation.

These tensions are further highlighted by the fact that, in the wake of the conservative-news-suppression accusations, Facebook chose to rely more heavily on algorithmic curation for its Trending list (which, ironically, led to an uptick in fake news stories showing up in the Trending list, leading to the eventual cancellation of the Trending feature),[54] and yet, after the 2016 election, one of Facebook's most concerted efforts was to hire substantially more staff to review content posted to the platform.[55]

Going forward, then, it seems clear that a combination of human and algorithmic curation will be brought to bear on users' news feeds.

While the studies and examples discussed here provide useful insights, it is important to recognize that we are at the very early stages of trying to understand these new levels of gatekeepers. Decades of media sociology research have told us quite a bit about the inner workings of news organizations and the roles that individual, organizational, and institutional constraints and incentives play in affecting the nature of the news that is produced,[56] but this body of research touches only the tip of the iceberg in understanding gatekeeping in today's news environment. And while the types of organizations studied in this vast body of research still exist (e.g., the *New York Times* and network news), they are operating today in such a dramatically different environment that we should be wary of placing too much stock in the findings of this body of research.

Establishing a robust understanding of the contemporary gatekeeping process requires a detailed examination and understanding of (a) the generally opaque algorithmic systems that guide the curation activities of social media platforms, news aggregators, and increasingly, traditional news organizations; (b) the perspectives, values, and priorities of the individuals and organizations involved in the creation, maintenance, management, and application of these algorithmic systems and the platforms in which they are embedded; and (c) the priorities, preferences, and behaviors of the users of these systems, who not only engage in direct gatekeeping activities but also provide much of the data that feed into the algorithmic gatekeeping systems. The activities of all these entities intersect and influence one another to represent the contemporary, much more complex, gatekeeping process.[57]

Algorithmic Creep in News Organizations

The focus so far has been on the behavioral dynamics of algorithmic gatekeeping platforms. Equally important, however, is the extent to which the existence of these new gatekeepers—and the tools that they employ—is affecting the behaviors of the news organizations that increasingly depend on these gatekeepers for the dissemination of their work, as they struggle to achieve what technology scholar Tarleton Gillespie describes as *algorithmic recognizability*.[58] As noted earlier, news organizations are now dealing with complex systems making determinations regarding the relevance of each news story to each individual user—essentially billions of individualized gatekeeping decisions. Consequently, news organizations must strategically adjust what they do in response to the frequently changing and largely opaque algorithmic curation systems employed by social media platforms. One well-publicized example is the "pivot to video" that many news organizations engaged in as a result of adjustments to Facebook's algorithm that prioritized video content (particularly live video content).[59] Facebook based these shifts on data demonstrating high levels of user engagement with video content, and many news organizations shifted tactics and reallocated resources accordingly. The irony in this case is that the Facebook metrics that motivated this prioritization of video proved to be faulty, overestimating video consumption by as much as 60 to 80 percent.[60] This situation raises a host of questions about the appropriateness of the vertical integration the provider of audience attention with the provider of the audience data that quantifies that attention.

Needless to say, the rise of social media is not the first time that news organizations have been forced to evolve in the face of the Internet's changing distribution dynamics. When search engines emerged as the primary mechanism for navigating the web, search engine optimization (SEO) became a strategic imperative for journalism. News organizations sought to enhance their visibility in search returns in a variety of ways, including placing commonly searched-for words in their headlines or leads and adjusting their hyperlinking activities.[61] All of these activities reflected the criteria embedded in Google's search algorithms.

At the most extreme end of the influence continuum, search activity would, to varying degrees, dictate the stories that news organizations produced. This was a key part of the MO of "content farms," as well as of digital native news organizations such as the *Huffington Post*.[62] Under this model, news organizations mine search data for indicators of current demand for news stories, and produce stories that meet that demand. Responsiveness to search trends, and to the ever-changing dynamics of Google's search algorithms, remains an imperative for digital news organizations, as search returns continue to be one of the most important gateways through which news consumers access news stories.[63]

Social media distribution has compelled a similar recalibrating of the journalistic product. The *New York Times* provides a useful case in point. The *Times* publishes about three hundred stories per day. In order to effectively and strategically manage their social media presence (and not inundate their followers' news feeds with content), the *Times* posts a relatively small subset of these stories to its main Facebook page each day.[64] The question then becomes, which of the stories published each day merit inclusion on the *Times*' Facebook page? This becomes crucial given the increasing extent to which social media provide the point of entry for visitors to news sites, with the hope that once the visitors are there, the sites can then use various techniques to keep them there by recommending other stories they might find of interest.

The *Times*' approach to maximizing the effectiveness of its Facebook posts was to utilize a self-developed bot called Blossom, which "predicts how articles or blogposts will do on social [media]" and makes recommendations accordingly.[65] Blossom's algorithms analyze "enormous stores of data, including information on story content and performance metrics such as Facebook post engagement."[66] This approach appears to be achieving its desired goal. According data that the *Times* has made public, "Facebook posts recommended by Blossom on average have been getting 120 percent more clicks than non-Blossom-powered posts, and the median, or 'typical,' Blossom post gets about 380 percent more clicks than a typical non-Blossom post."[67]

The question that this scenario raises going forward is whether the characteristics of high-performing social media posts will ultimately drive the allocation of journalistic resources and gatekeeping decisions within news organizations in ways that compel a deviation from core news values. It is encouraging that recent research indicates that the stories news organizations post to social media platforms reflect established news values such as social significance and proximity.[68] Also encouraging is a study conducted at Duke comparing the front page, home page, and Facebook page stories provided by the *New York Times*, which found that hard news stories were equally prominent on the *Times*' home page and Facebook page (accounting for about 75 percent of total stories in both cases), with both lagging only slightly behind the hard news composition of the *Times*' front page (about 81 percent).[69] Of course one cannot generalize from the *New York Times* to journalism more broadly.

As the *New York Times* case illustrates, even large, relatively successful news organizations have found themselves somewhat beholden to the algorithmic systems and initiatives of dominant platforms such as Facebook, Twitter, and Google,[70] and their own home pages matter less and less as a means of attracting and retaining audiences.[71] Digital-native news outlets like the *Huffington Post*, *BuzzFeed*, and *Upworthy* led the way in this regard (with traditional news outlets following suit), in some cases structuring entire business models around relying upon, and maximizing, the distribution power and curation criteria of social media platforms.[72] Given the frequency with which the curation criteria (and the underlying algorithms) can change, this is a precarious business model at best.[73]

As a byproduct of Facebook's dominant position in aggregating online audiences, content providers have found themselves at the mercy of Facebook algorithms, which change frequently and can suddenly and dramatically affect a content provider's audience.[74] In mid-2016, Facebook adjusted its News Feed algorithms so that posts from friends and family members would have a higher priority than posts from organizations such as news outlets and brands.[75] This action was a response to the controversies that were arising at the time around the suppression of conservative news and the prominence of fake news, and represented a reversal of a previous adjustment designed to bring more news organization content into users' News Feed.[76] This adjustment meant a sudden and significant drop in audience access for many content providers relying on Facebook to deliver audiences to them.[77]

Facebook adjusted its algorithms again in January 2018 to further favor friends and family posts over "public content." In addition, Facebook announced that greater weight would be given to posts of all types that "encourage meaningful interactions between people."[78] In announcing this shift, Zuckerberg noted that "too often today, watching video, reading news or getting a page update is just a passive experience" and that "passively reading articles or watching videos—even if they're entertaining or informative—may not be as good [for our well-being]."[79] It remains questionable whether commenting on or sharing an article from one's news feed represents the kind of migration from passive to active that leads to a better-informed citizenry, but this adjustment creates an incentive for news outlets to try to figure out what types of stories consistently generate comments, and to produce those stories. By many accounts, the net effect of this algorithmic adjustment has been a dramatic reduction in Facebook-driven traffic to news sites.[80] Online news site *Slate* described the effect of the algorithmic adjustment as "The Great Facebook Crash," noting that it led to their receiving only 20 percent of the Facebook-generated traffic they had received before the adjustment.[81]

Social media distribution had, of course, become the lifeblood of many news organizations, a path to sustainability in an increasingly challenging economic and technological climate.[82] Social media have always represented a double-edged sword for news organizations: they can enhance audience reach, but they have also siphoned off online advertising dollars and have imposed opaque, ever-evolving dynamics of algorithmic intermediation upon news organizations.[83]

However, there may be an upside to this transition toward emphasizing friends and family (assuming Facebook maintains this commitment going forward). It may lead to a decoupling of social media usage from news consumption. As I argued earlier, a free press is enhanced when production and distribution are vertically integrated. Under such a model, the priorities and values of an unaffiliated distributor cannot intrude upon the gatekeeping decisions of news organizations. From this standpoint, any diminishment of social media intermediation is beneficial for reestablishing journalistic autonomy and authority. As one engagement editor at a U.S. news outlet noted, Facebook's announcement of its algorithmic changes provides an impetus for "building meaningful, authentic relationships with readers."[84] As this same editor noted, "let's put the nail in the coffin of chasing clicks and likes."[85]

PERSONALIZATION ON NEWS SITES

The personalization inherent in the algorithmic curation conducted by social media platforms is also spreading beyond these platforms and into the news organizations themselves.

Nicholas Negroponte's famous mid-1990s speculation about the inevitability (and desirability) of the *Daily Me* (an individual's personalized newspaper)[86] provides a useful starting point for the rise of personalization in digital media. Negroponte predicted that interactive media would allow each of us to craft our own individual news diets. What he did not predict, however, was the role of independent distribution platforms serving as the intermediate step on the way to direct, personalized news products—that platforms such as Facebook would emerge to try to become what Mark Zuckerberg described in 2014 (echoing Negroponte) as "the perfect personalized newspaper for every person in the world."[87] Driven, to some extent, by the operation of these platforms, personalization continues to work its way through the news ecosystem.

As news organizations personalize their presentation of the news, they are doing so within the framework established by personalization intermediaries such as social media platforms. This would seem to be the case of the well-documented "mimicking" strategy in media evolution, in which legacy media attempt to adopt the characteristics, and provide the functionality, of new media, but are fundamentally less equipped to provide this functionality.[88] Without the volume and diversity of content that funnels through social media, and without comparable troves of user and content data to feed into the personalization process, news organizations are unlikely to dislodge news aggregators and social media platforms as intermediaries, regardless of how effectively they personalize their own new products. They persist nonetheless, in an effort to wring more engagement from the audiences they attract.

For instance, once a news consumer reaches the *New York Times'* site, algorithmic recommendation systems go to work. Like many online news sources, the *Times* has a section containing a list of recommended news stories. The initial version of the *Times'* recommendation engine was a content-based system, in which keywords associated with original stories were the primary drivers of the recommendation process.[89] Thus, if your reading history contained a number of stories tagged with the "health care" keyword, then additional stories tagged with the "health care" keyword would be recommended to you.

Over time, the *Times* integrated collaborative filtering.[90] *Collaborative filtering* refers to a process in which the reading histories of similar users are taken into consideration. Thus, if users with similar reading patterns to yours gravitated to a particular article, that article would be recommended to you as well. Although in the *Times*' case, collaborative filtering was driven by users' reading patterns, collaborative filtering can be employed in ways that take into account a range of other factors, such as geography or demographics, or behavioral patterns such as product purchases or social media response/activity. This integration of content- and user-behavior-based inputs was ultimately integrated into an algorithm based on a technique called collaborative topic modeling,[91] which models content, adjusts this model by incorporating viewing signals from readers, models reader preference, and then makes recommendations based on the similarity between preference and content.[92]

In 2017, the *Times* announced that it was beginning to experiment with going beyond personalized recommendations to personalized story selection for its home page.[93] Home page personalization meant that sections of the home page would vary for individual users based on their demonstrated preferences, characteristics, and interests. Initial efforts have included personalizing sections of the home page based on a user's geographic location or prior reading behaviors.[94] Other approaches that the *Times* has been considering include adjusting home page content on the basis of the amount of time since a user's previous visit, as a way to foreground content that a user may have missed since last visiting the site.[95] As a result, the current *New York Times* home page is a mix of stories that all visitors see and stories that are algorithmically curated according to the demonstrated preferences of the individual user.[96]

These efforts by the *New York Times* reflect the broader transition that has taken place in journalism, with algorithmically driven personalization seen as fundamental to attracting, retaining, and engaging news consumers. The *Wall Street Journal*'s mobile application now incorporates a fully personalized My WSJ feed alongside its standardized news feed.[97] The *Washington Post* employs personalized newsletters and story recommendations,[98] as well as a host of algorithmic tools that do everything from predicting the virality of an article to determining (and implementing) the best combination of headline and image to automatically generating headlines based on story text.[99]

Generally, these initiatives appear to achieve their desired goal of leading users to spend more time with the site or application.[100] The *Washington Post*, for instance, has found that click-through rates for its personalized newsletters are three times the average, and that the overall open rate is double the average for the *Post*'s newsletters.[101] The *Wall Street Journal* has found that its personalized content does not cannibalize consumption of its standardized content, but rather is additive to the time spent with the standardized content.[102]

THE CASE OF TRONC

Some news organizations have sought to completely remake themselves through the integration of data and algorithmic decision-making systems. Even the BBC has recently announced an initiative to utilize "user data and apply algorithms to get marketing and media insights about audiences' preferences."[103] Perhaps the most high-profile—and most widely criticized[104]—transformation was Tribune Publishing's 2016 rebranding as tronc (meant to stand for tribune online content). This abrupt (and ultimately short-lived) rebranding was accompanied by a widely derided press release and accompanying employee video,[105] both of which managed to come across as near-parodies of contemporary tech-speak in their focus on harnessing the benefits of artificial intelligence and machine learning. At one point in the video, a tronc executive describes how a newly created "optimization group" would "harness the power of our local journalism, then feed it into a funnel, so we reach the biggest global audience possible." This description is accompanied by a visual of a number of tronc news outlets (including the *Chicago Tribune*, the *Orlando Sentinel*, and the *Baltimore Sun*), all represented as planets of various sizes orbiting around a large sunlike sphere (labeled "tronc"), with arrows coursing inward from the planets to the sun under the label "content optimization."

The video was eviscerated as the centerpiece of a segment on the precarious state of local journalism on HBO's weekly satire program *Last Week Tonight with John Oliver*.[106] The *Washington Post* described the press release announcing the rebranding[107] as the "worst press release in the history of journalism," with "the most concentrated mess of buzzwords that digital publishing has ever seen."[108]

Notably, a subsequent press release announced "Tronc Begins Trading on Nasdaq, Joins Leading Tech Firms."[109] Just as many tech companies have resisted acknowledging their evolution into media companies, so too are media companies seeking to characterize themselves as having evolved into tech companies. Even the *New York Times*, in recent job postings, describes itself as "a technology company committed to producing the world's most reliable and highest quality journalism."[110] It would seem that nobody wants to actually be a media company, which raises the specter of traditional journalistic news values' essentially being orphaned.

While the communication of the transition taking place within Tribune/tronc was handled a bit clumsily, very little was happening at Tribune/tronc that was not also taking place (if perhaps more effectively) at many other large news organizations.[111] The tronc case, however, seemed to bring to the surface the ways in which fundamental aspects of this transition were inherently disconnected from the mission and practice of journalism. One scathing critique, published in the *Harvard Business Review* by media executive and consultant Greg Satell, is worth quoting at length.

> So what I find most disturbing about the video isn't the buzzwords, but how it indicates that the company is failing to address the fundamental questions the company is facing: What is the role of a newspaper business in a digital media environment? How can we use technology to empower our journalists to collaborate more effectively and further our editorial mission? The role of a great publisher is not to predict

what readers may want to read, but to help them form their opinions through strong, authoritative journalism. You win in the marketplace not by chasing readers with algorithms, but by attracting them with a superior product. Yet great journalism can't be automated, because it is among the most human of endeavors.[112]

Contained within this critique is the essence of the concerns that reside at the core of the process of algorithmic creep affecting journalism.

In considering the implications of this transition, it would be easy to focus on issues such as the displacement of human decision-making or the lack of transparency associated with how many of these systems operate. Perhaps the most profound implication of this process, however, is that it represents the end of the long-standing tension in journalism over the appropriate role that the preferences of news consumers should play in journalistic decision-making.[113] The same digital media environment that undermined the economics of journalism and eliminated the luxury of maintaining a "church-state" separation between the editorial and the economic priorities of news organizations facilitated an influx of analytical tools and audience data that has empowered news organizations to capitalize on this fading distinction with a rigor that was never possible before.[114] Essentially, a perfect storm has ushered in a new norm of audience-centric approaches to journalism.[115]

Implications: Beyond the Two-Step Flow

A useful way to encapsulate the magnitude of the changes in gatekeeping is to revisit—and revise—one of the foundational theories of media effects: the two-step flow. For the purposes of this analysis, our concern is less with the origins and magnitude of media effects than with the dynamics of content flows.

The two-step flow theory was first articulated by sociologist Paul Lazarsfeld and his colleagues in a study of the 1940 U.S. presidential election[116] and subsequently refined by Lazarsfeld and Elihu Katz in their landmark book, *Personal Influence*.[117] The theory asserts that, for most people, media effects are filtered through interpersonal contact, with a select group of individuals (labeled "opinion leaders") serving as the mechanism through which ideas and news conveyed in the media reach—and influence—the rest of the population. That is, some people pay attention to media and are affected by the content they consume. These individuals, in turn, pass along news, ideas, or viewpoints they have been exposed to through their media consumption to individuals in their social network through interpersonal communication. Within this process, the substance of what is being disseminated by the media may be altered somewhat to reflect the interpretations and perspectives of the opinion leaders.

Applying the two-step flow to our contemporary media ecosystem is both fascinating and problematic.[118] For starters, the clear line distinguishing "interpersonal" from "mass" communication that existed in the 1940s and 1950s has become somewhat blurred;[119] an individual's social network today is much more media dependent than it was in 1945.[120] Communication campaigns that once relied heavily on traditional interpersonal communication (that were essentially dependent on the two-step flow) now typically count on social media–based communication to operate in a similar manner, but at a much greater scale. To illustrate, as an undergraduate, I worked for a public relations firm that serviced the motion picture industry. One of our primary tasks was to recruit individuals to attend advance screenings of upcoming films. Our goal was to recruit individuals who would be most effective at disseminating positive word of mouth (movie studios only hold advance screenings for films they think are actually good)—individuals with extensive social networks. To do this, we recruited from lists of taxi drivers, hair stylists, and receptionists—people with occupations that put them in conversation with large numbers of people throughout the day. This, of course, seems rather antiquated and ineffectual by today's standards. Today the goal is to target social media influencers, who reach far more people than taxi drivers, hair stylists, or receptionists ever did.

A number of researchers have characterized social media as reasserting the relevance of, or magnifying the scope of, the two-step flow.[121]

Notions of opinion leadership certainly continue to resonate in a socially mediated context in which a relatively small proportion of the online population appears to have disproportionate influence.[122]

However, I would argue that social media platforms have done much more than give us a case of the two-step flow on steroids. Yes, there are still individuals who can be identified as opinion leaders, and yes, other individuals frequently learn about issues and topics being covered in the media through these opinion leaders. However, if we try to apply the two-step flow framework to the social media gatekeeping context, we see an undeniable need for expansion and refinement.

The top portion of figure 2.1 presents a model of the traditional two-step flow, with a focus on news. As the figure illustrates, news originates at a news organization and is then transmitted to opinion leaders (referred to here as direct news consumers). Once processed by these direct news consumers, news is then further disseminated (through interpersonal contact) to indirect news consumers. The key shortcoming of this traditional model of the two-step flow in relation to algorithmic media platforms is that it does not account for the number of contexts in which the news is processed and redisseminated in its journey from news organization to indirect news consumer. Specifically, the many instances in which algorithmic processing intervenes in the relationship between news producers and news consumers are missing.

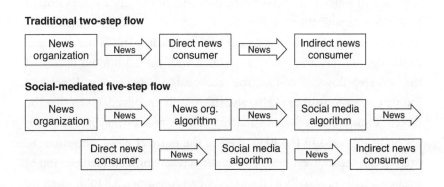

FIGURE 2.1 Beyond the Two-Step Flow

A more accurate representation of the contemporary flow of news is depicted in the bottom half of figure 2.1. Here, we introduce social media and algorithmic gatekeeping into the equation. As a result, the traditional notion of the two-step flow becomes much more complicated. We still start with the editorial decisions made by news organizations. We need to recognize that, within a social-mediated context, the outcomes of these editorial decisions are not conveyed directly to news consumers. Rather, as noted earlier in discussion of the *New York Times* and Blossom, it may be the case that a subset of the day's news stories gets disseminated via social media in accordance with an algorithmic recommendation system that is focused on identifying those stories likely to perform best on social media. In addition, any news consumers who follow the *New York Times* on social media are having their news feeds curated by the social media platforms' news-feed algorithms, which produce individualized decisions as to whether individual stories make it into each user's curated news feed. Once posted to social media, stories must make their way through the algorithmic filtering and curation employed by these platforms in order to reach the direct news consumer. Essentially, there are two algorithmic intermediaries operating between the news organization and what we are calling the direct news consumer. The term *direct news consumer* begins to feel a bit less accurate in light of these two stages of algorithmic curation.

Next, we move on to the relationship between the direct news consumer and the indirect news consumer. Our focus now is on the sequence in which one social media user encounters a news story posted by a news organization in her social media feed and then makes the decision to share the story with her social network. This is the analogue to the opinion leader activity associated with the traditional notion of the two-step flow. Of course, the relationship between the direct and indirect news consumer is also algorithmically mediated, given that the direct news consumer's news-sharing activity may or may not show up (or be prioritized) in the news feed of the indirect news consumer. In this regard, the indirect news consumer is receiving a curated version of the news-sharing activity of the direct news consumer. All told, when we account for these instances of algorithmic intermediation, the two-step flow essentially expands to a five-step flow—a transition that introduces many additional layers of gatekeeping into the gatekeeping process.

■ ■ ■

Perhaps the greatest irony in how news organizations have transformed themselves in response to the increasing centrality of social media platforms as gatekeepers is that recent trends suggest that the prominence of social media platforms as gateways to news is in decline. For instance, according to a late-2018 analysis of news consumption through mobile devices by online audience measurement firm Chartbeat, Facebook-driven traffic to news sites has dropped 40 percent since 2017. According to Chartbeat, these decreases in traffic have been compensated for by increases in visits driven by search engines and by direct visits through the web or mobile apps.[123] Also, for the first time, survey data showed no year-to-year increase in self-reported reliance on social media platforms for news. According to a 2018 study by the Pew Research Center, the percentage of Americans who get at least some of their news from social media held steady at 68 percent from 2017 to 2018.[124] International research has documented similar patterns in other countries, even finding declines in some cases.[125]

Whether these patterns represent a brief anomaly in response to the various issues and concerns that have plagued social media platforms, or the beginning of a longer-term reversal in the prominence of social media platforms in the news ecosystem, remains to be seen. In any case, social media platforms' position as gatekeeper in the contemporary news ecosystem remains volatile. Consequently, understanding the impact of these platforms' position on the news ecosystem—and the implications for how we think about core communications policy principles such as the First Amendment, the marketplace of ideas, and the public interest— remains vital. The next three chapters explore these issues.

CHAPTER 3

The First Amendment, Fake News, and Filter Bubbles

When new communications technologies arise, law and policy makers generally respond in ways that reflect two ends of a continuum. One end involves treating the new technology as revolutionary and unprecedented, and therefore in need of a new legal and regulatory framework. So, for instance, when radio broadcasting developed, Congress viewed the technology as fundamentally different from (i.e., more influential than) previous communications technologies, and thus developed a legal and regulatory framework that introduced an unprecedented level of regulatory oversight and restrictions on free speech. We therefore ended up with a system of federal licensing of broadcast outlets, indecency regulations, and various public-interest obligations that required broadcasters to air certain types of content (such as news and public affairs programming).[1] This was a dramatic departure from the government's much more arms-length relationship with the print media.[2]

The other end of the continuum involves treating the new technology as an extension of an existing technology, and thus applying the legal and regulatory framework developed for the existing technology to the new technology. So, for instance, when television came along, the entire legal and regulatory framework that had been established for radio simply migrated to television.

Other technologies have fallen somewhere in the middle of this continuum. Cable television, for instance, has been regulated to some extent like broadcast television, but without as many content regulations. The Internet persists as a place where the question of the appropriate legal and regulatory framework remains in a state of flux. In its early years, the Internet was a largely unregulated space. By the mid-1990s, Congress had tried (and failed) to regulate the Internet much like broadcasting. And in recent years, we have seen the pinballing back and forth between the imposition and elimination of net neutrality regulations. Trying to place the legal and regulatory framework for the Internet on this continuum thus involves a moving target. The situation is further complicated by the rise of social media and the associated concerns about fake news and disinformation that have prompted new discussions about appropriate legal and regulatory frameworks.

A key factor determining the nature of the relationship between a communications technology and government policy makers is the First Amendment. As will be discussed in later chapters, different communications technologies and services are treated differently under the First Amendment. And, as will be discussed in this and later chapters, the role and function of the First Amendment in regulating communications technologies and services can be subject to different—sometimes conflicting—interpretations.

For these reasons, this chapter begins with an exploration of the relationship between social media and the First Amendment. Because one of the key functions of the First Amendment is to facilitate an informed citizenry, the analysis will focus in particular on the intersection of fake news, filter bubbles, and the First Amendment. In combination, filter bubbles and fake news represent perhaps the most challenging and troubling dimensions of how social media platforms and algorithmic curation may be affecting the media ecosystem.[3] These phenomena interact in ways that have raised significant concerns about the nature of the relationship between contemporary news and information flows and the effective functioning of the democratic process.[4] As a result, policy makers have begun to pay attention.[5] Countries such as Germany have been particularly proactive.[6] In the United States, however, despite a number of congressional hearings and reports,[7] we have not yet seen much concrete policy action. (Various policy interventions will be discussed in more detail in chapter 6.)

The relative inaction in the United States can be explained, at least in part, by a First Amendment tradition that has valorized the notion of *counterspeech*. A central tenet of First Amendment theory is that more speech is an effective remedy against the dissemination and consumption of false speech.[8] This counterspeech doctrine was first explicitly articulated by Justice Louis Brandeis in *Whitney v. California* (1927).[9] Since then, the effectiveness of counterspeech has become an integral component of most conceptualizations of an effectively functioning "marketplace of ideas," in which direct government regulation of speech is minimized in favor of an open and competitive speech environment in which ideas are free to circulate, and truthful speech is presumed to be inherently capable of overcoming false speech.[10]

However, in the age of filter bubbles and fake news, the logic of the counterspeech doctrine is worth revisiting. In this chapter, I argue that fundamental assumptions about how the First Amendment is supposed to work need to be called into question in the context of social media.

I'll begin by unpacking the assumptions about the dynamics of the production, dissemination, and consumption of news that are embedded in the counterspeech doctrine. If these assumptions are no longer viable within the evolving structure and operation of the contemporary media ecosystem, we need to rethink contemporary media law and policy. Specifically, I argue that structural and economic changes in the news media, increased fragmentation and personalization, and algorithmically dictated content dissemination and consumption, affect the production and flow of news and information in ways that may make it more difficult to assume that legitimate news will systematically win out over misinformation. Just as it has been asked whether the assumptions underlying the Second Amendment right to bear arms (written in the era of muskets and flintlocks) are transferrable to today's technological environment of high-powered, automatic assault weapons,[11] it may be time to ask whether this fundamental assumption of First Amendment theory, crafted in an era when news circulated primarily via interpersonal contact and print media, are transferrable to today's radically different media environment.[12]

Counterspeech and the First Amendment: Assumptions, Applications, and Critiques

According to Justice Brandeis in *Whitney v. California*,[13] "If there be time to expose through discussion the falsehood and fallacies, to avert the evil by the processes of education, the remedy to be applied is more speech, not enforced silence."[14] This perspective is in many ways a natural outgrowth of the "marketplace of ideas" metaphor,[15] which has served as a fundamental principle in communications law and policy[16] but has also been subject to substantial critique.[17] In his famous articulation of this metaphor, Oliver Wendell Holmes asserted, "The ultimate good desired is better reached by free trade in ideas—that the best test of truth is the power of the thought to get itself accepted in the competition of the market."[18] Under this formulation, the ideas marketplace is inherently capable of distinguishing between truth and falsity; it can be counted on to accept and act upon true information and reject what is false. This process is fundamental to the well-functioning democracy that, according to many interpretations, the First Amendment is intended to protect.[19] Looking at Holmes's statement today, we can see it echoed in more contemporary notions such as the "wisdom of crowds"[20] or the "wealth of networks"[21] that have been central to some of the more enthusiastic views of our evolving media ecosystem.

Given the metaphor's assumption (explicitly articulated by Holmes) that the marketplace is capable of effectively distinguishing between truth and falsity,[22] a speech environment that facilitates as much speech as possible is an effective way of assuring that truth prevails over falsity, and that good ideas prevail over bad ones. "More speech" (i.e., counterspeech) thus becomes an effective, First Amendment–friendly approach to assuring that individuals have the information they need to be informed participants in the democratic process. It is important to emphasize that, for better or for worse, the marketplace-of-ideas metaphor has traditionally been applied quite broadly—to news, information, and facts as well as to less verifiable concepts such as opinions and ideas. In this regard, the marketplace-of-ideas concept reflects the fact that the journalistic sphere encompasses the full continuum, from facts to opinions/ideas.

A number of assumptions underlie this perspective. First, of course, is the assumption that individuals are capable of distinguishing between true and false information, and between good and bad ideas.[23] The logic here is that, just as participants in the traditional product market are capable of distinguishing between high-value products and low-value products, participants in the idea market are, in the aggregate, similarly capable of distinguishing between true and false news and information, and between good and bad ideas. A second, related assumption is that participants in the idea marketplace place greater value on true news and information, or good ideas, than they do on false information, or bad ideas. This assumption strikes at the core of what the marketplace actually values.[24] A third assumption is that, as the late Supreme Court Justice Antonin Scalia stated, "Given the premises of democracy, there is no such thing as too much speech."[25] According to this assumption, the market is capable of managing any information-processing or information-overload problems. A fourth assumption that underlies the counterspeech doctrine is that a sufficient number of those exposed to false information or bad ideas also will be exposed to the countervailing true information or good ideas. Of course, if the previous assumptions hold true, then this exposure to true and accurate information will have its desired effect of contributing to an informed citizenry. However, each of these assumptions is contentious, and all have been critiqued from a variety of perspectives.[26] Economic and technological changes in the media ecosystem have led to conditions that further challenge many of these assumptions.[27]

THE COUNTERSPEECH DOCTRINE IN PRACTICE

Applications of the counterspeech doctrine have been wide ranging in media law and policy.[28] It is worth noting a few applications that have particular relevance to the structure and operation of contemporary social media and their relationship to a well-functioning democracy.

The well-known (some might say notorious) Fairness Doctrine is a rare instance in which the counterspeech doctrine has been utilized to justify government regulation.[29] The Fairness Doctrine required broadcast licensees to devote news coverage to controversial issues of public importance.[30] In providing such coverage, broadcasters were further required to devote time to competing perspectives on an issue. So, for instance, if a news broadcast ran a story on new research asserting a link between cigarette smoking and cancer, the tobacco industry was entitled to demand that time be devoted to the perspective that the causal link between cigarette smoking and cancer had yet to be determined. Importantly, this competing perspective needed to air during a day/time when a number of viewers comparable to the audience for the initial broadcast could be reached.

To the extent that the Fairness Doctrine compelled additional, most likely contradictory, speech, it embodies the counterspeech doctrine and its commitment to "more speech." The irony is that the Fairness Doctrine was eliminated in the late 1980s under the logic that the requirement to provide counterspeech "chilled" broadcaster coverage of controversial issues,[31] essentially resulting in less speech rather than more. So, for instance, rather than air a story about a new study linking cigarette smoking to cancer (and then having to deal with accommodating the Fairness Doctrine complaint of the tobacco industry), a broadcaster might choose to avoid the headache and not run the original story at all. The Nixon White House made aggressive use of the Fairness Doctrine to try to counteract reports that reflected negatively on the administration's Vietnam policies.[32]

In the case of the Fairness Doctrine, counterspeech served to justify speech regulation. More often, it has been used to reject speech regulation. For instance, in the realm of political campaign advertising there has been a history of efforts to impose restrictions on the dissemination of false information.[33] As one example, the State of Washington sought to impose a regulation that allowed a state agency to determine the veracity of campaign statements and to fine campaigns found to disseminate false statements. The Washington Supreme Court overturned these regulations for a host of reasons.[34] The court rejected the state's contention that protecting the integrity of elections represented a sufficiently compelling government interest.[35] It held that prohibiting "arguably false, but non-defamatory, statements about political candidates to save our elections conflicts with fundamental principles of the First Amendment."[36] In addition, the court explicitly argued that counterspeech represented the more appropriate approach to coping with falsity in political campaign communications. "Our constitutional election system already contains the solution to the problem that RCW 42.17.530(1) (a) is meant to address. . . . In a political campaign, a candidate's factual blunder is unlikely to escape the notice of, and correction by, the erring candidate's political opponent. The preferred First Amendment remedy of 'more speech, not enforced silence,' thus has special force."[37] "In other words," the court concluded, "the best remedy for false or unpleasant speech is more speech, not less speech."[38]

These examples reflect how the First Amendment to some extent facilitates the dissemination of false news and information. However, the importance of the circulation of diverse ideas and viewpoints is so great that such falsity must be tolerated. This tolerance is accompanied by the confidence that a robust speech environment will allow truthful and accurate news and information to triumph over falsity. This position is well reflected in the Supreme Court's statement in the case of *Gertz v. Robert Welch, Inc.*, which ruled that the First Amendment requires protecting "some falsehood in order to protect speech that matters."[39]

Compared to less protected categories of speech such as commercial speech, the First Amendment protections for political false speech are at their most pronounced.[40] Journalism represents the most explicitly protected category of speaker (as reflected in the "of the press" clause of the First Amendment), given the political implications and potential effects of journalistic output.[41] For news organizations, legal liability for falsity has been largely limited to intentional and malicious falsities directed at individuals or organizations that are damaging to the individual's or organization's reputation.[42] This reflects the Supreme Court's position that "false statements of fact [can] cause damage to an individual's reputation that cannot easily be repaired by *counterspeech*, however persuasive or effective."[43] No such liabilities exist for the production and dissemination of falsities for the remaining vast swath of political issues and concerns that might be disseminated by media outlets, given the broad protections given to the press and its role in maintaining "uninhibited, robust, and wide open"[44] political discussion. These include older examples such as AIDS conspiracy theories or Holocaust denial,[45] or more recent examples such as the nature of the scientific evidence surrounding climate change.

Similarly, the journalistic presentation of falsities about individuals or organizations that enhance rather than damage reputations is fully protected. Therefore, while a news outlet that runs a story that implicates a political figure in running a child sex ring out of a Washington, DC, pizza parlor could, in theory, be vulnerable to a (still difficult to win) libel lawsuit, a news outlet that knowingly reports falsely inflated figures for a candidate's net worth or charitable donations (thereby enhancing the candidate's status with voters) is in the clear, even if it is subsequently proven that this information was published with knowledge of its falsity, because the candidate's stature or reputation has not been damaged by the false information.

The bottom line is that, beyond libel, "any test of truth" when applying the First Amendment to the work of journalists has been rejected.[46] According to the Supreme Court, "factual error affords no warrant for repressing speech that would otherwise be free."[47] The burden, therefore, for addressing such falsity falls heavily on counterspeech. From this standpoint, we can assume that the prevailing First Amendment response to fake news is more news.

It is important to note that social media platforms have integrated the notion of counterspeech into their operational philosophies. Facebook, for example, in 2015 commissioned a series of studies that highlighted the prominence of counterspeech on its platform within the context of a variety of controversial issues across different countries.[48] In addition, in 2016, the company launched the Online Civil Courage Initiative, which has as its mission "to promote the civil courage displayed by organizations and grassroots activists carrying out valuable counterspeech work online."[49] Facebook's commitment to counterspeech is reflected in its description of this initiative: "We believe that engagement is more powerful than censorship in reforming prejudiced and bigoted opinions and voices, and are committed to amplifying campaigns which encourage positive dialogue and debate."[50] Thus, Facebook seems to be suggesting that the platform will work to enhance (via "amplifying") counterspeech that addresses prejudiced and bigoted opinions and voices. Along similar lines, Twitter has organized online forums where participants can discuss strategies for producing and disseminating counterspeech through social media.[51] Google, in its 2017 testimony before the Senate about its initiatives to combat extremist content and disinformation on its platforms, highlighted that the company is "creating new programs to promote counterspeech on [its] platforms."[52] These programs include efforts to redirect consumers of extremist propaganda toward content that counters those narratives, as well as efforts to encourage YouTube content creators to speak out against hate speech, xenophobia, and extremism.[53]

CRITIQUES OF COUNTERSPEECH

To some extent, critiques directed at the counterspeech doctrine overlap with those directed at the overarching marketplace-of-ideas metaphor. This is particularly the case for those critiques that emphasize fundamental human characteristics and tendencies that could lead to the embracing of false news and information over true news and information. In light of the concerns that have arisen in the wake of the 2016 election about the potential influence of fake news, there is a renewed interest in the vast literature, across fields such as communication, cognitive psychology, and behavioral economics, that highlights how established behavioral patterns, such as selective exposure, confirmation bias, heuristics for coping with information overload, and directionally motivated reasoning, explain the acceptance of false news or information.[54] Legal scholar Frederick Schauer has noted, "That people believe things that are false comes as no surprise. That large numbers of people believe things that are false despite being told the truth is also hardly a revelation."[55] The bottom line is that the notion of the "rational audience"—capable of processing speech from diverse sources and of effectively and rationally assessing the truth, quality, and credibility of speech—which permeates First Amendment theory, is much more an ideal-type than an empirical reality.[56] What may be different today, however, is the extent to which our media system may be exacerbating these tendencies to an unprecedented degree.

Other critics have explored specific speech contexts in which the counterspeech doctrine is particularly ineffective. They have noted that the efficacy of counterspeech can depend upon a wide range of circumstances related to the character of the speech at issue.[57] Hate speech, for instance, has been singled out as being particularly resistant to the effects of counterspeech.[58] Hate speech may have a silencing effect on would-be speakers, inhibiting their ability to engage in counterspeech, or it may impose unfair or dangerous burdens on those who express differing opinions.[59] Further, to the extent that hate speech is directed at marginalized groups, these groups may lack the access and resources to reach all of those exposed to the initial speech.[60] One study of hate speech on Twitter found that counterspeech from a white speaker could discourage racist hate speech, but if that same opinion originated from a black speaker, the amount of hate speech was not affected at all.[61] Such a finding suggests that targets of hate speech may be uniquely powerless to utilize counterspeech.

Largely absent from these critiques of the counterspeech doctrine—and even of the broader marketplace-of-ideas metaphor—are detailed considerations of how technological and structural changes in the media and information environment may affect the extent to which factual speech can overcome false speech.[62] As BuzzFeed's Nabiha Syed has noted, "too often we analyze the problem of fake news by focusing on individual instances, not systemic features of the information economy."[63] From this perspective, how might the technological changes affecting the news ecosystem affect the integrity of the counterspeech doctrine? As I will argue, social media platforms have affected the news ecosystem in ways that undermine the likelihood (however slim it already may have been) that true and high-quality news and information will overcome false and low-quality news and information.

How Technological Change Undermines the Counterspeech Doctrine

The impact of filter bubbles and fake news on social media is represented in figure 3.1. There are six basic changes at work that either diminish the relative prominence of legitimate news or enhance the prominence of false news.

This analysis starts from the premise that it is possible to make valid distinctions between "real" and "fake" news. Some have argued that the widespread use (and misuse) of the term *fake news* has rendered it meaningless.[64] Certainly, as with all dimensions of speech classification (e.g., commercial versus noncommercial speech, libelous versus nonlibelous speech), there will be areas of ambiguity and disagreement, but such ambiguity and disagreement do not invalidate the viability, legitimacy, or importance of maintaining the distinction.[65]

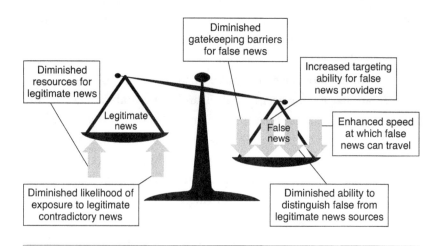

FIGURE 3.1 Impact of the Changing Media Ecosystem on the Relative Prominence of Legitimate Versus False News and the Effectiveness of Counterspeech

DIMINISHED RESOURCES FOR LEGITIMATE NEWS

In considering the changes that have affected our news ecosystem over the past two decades, it makes sense to begin with the changing dynamics of news production. The technological and economic changes that have transformed the news ecosystem have had a number of intersecting effects that have undermined the production of legitimate news, while having no such negative effects on the production of false news.[66] This relationship is reflected in figure 3.1, in the pressure being exerted on the production of legitimate news.

The ongoing economic crisis in journalism has been well documented.[67] Key consequences of this crisis include a decline in the number of newspapers across the country, the size of television newsrooms, and the number of professional journalism positions.[68] Some observers have viewed the rise of various online news outlets and the new opportunities that technological change has fostered for "citizen journalism" as adequate countervailing forces to the declines in traditional journalism.[69] The reality, however, is that these developments have not been able to fully replace the loss of news workers and news reporting that has resulted from the economic declines affecting traditional media.[70] The troubling paradox here is that the increase in the number of media outlets and channels has contributed to the decrease in the production of genuine journalism.

While it is difficult to reconcile this position with the apparent abundance of online news, it is more understandable when we take into consideration a seldom discussed, and (at this point) insufficiently researched, phenomenon in the realm of digital journalism that is perhaps best described as parasitic journalism.[71] *Parasitic journalism* refers to news stories that have as their origins and foundation reporting produced by another media outlet. If one examines news stories produced by digital media outlets through this analytic lens, the proportion of the online news reporting that merits classification as original journalism declines dramatically. Indeed, this kind of parasitic journalism (or "vampire web pages," as they are sometimes called) has emerged as a thriving business model. In some cases, this can just be a matter of a news site relying primarily on links to stories produced elsewhere (a very common online business model). Parasitic journalism can go further, however, with outlets utilizing social media platforms and online analytics software to identify popular news stories. These stories are then downloaded and reposted, typically retitled, perhaps only slightly rewritten, often utilizing the same photos and graphics as the original story. These recycled stories ultimately drain the audience (and thus, revenue) away from the outlets that produced the original story.[72]

Just as the explosion of television channels created an exaggerated perception of variety and diversity that masked a reality of repeats and repurposing, so too does the explosion of online news outlets mask a news ecosystem in which original reporting is recycled and circulated by scores of underresourced news outlets incapable of (or uninterested in) engaging in original reporting.[73] In many ways, this may be the true online echo chamber[74]—the process by which the same reporting ripples through outlet after outlet, often reconfigured and resummarized in ways that sometimes disguise the story's true origins and that provide opportunities for original commentary and/or interpretation—but *not* original reporting. The result is that the bulk of the news produced continues to originate from a relatively small number of media outlets, most of whose economic capacity to produce news is in a continuing state of decline.

Original reporting is costly to produce and, given the degrading economics of journalism, this production is in decline. Fake news, on the other hand, is far less costly to produce. Fabricated news stories require no rigorous research, no verification processes, and no trained professionals. This is why fake news has an extensive history—one that certainly predates the Internet and social media.[75] Changes in communications technologies have affected the dynamics of how fake news is produced, disseminated, and consumed,[76] so that today fake news can be easily and effectively produced (and monetized) by a Macedonian teenager in his bedroom.[77] The evolution of the media ecosystem, then, has made the production of fake news and information easier than ever. As a result, from the standpoint of the counterspeech doctrine, the relative production of legitimate news and information compared to false news and information is in the midst of perhaps an unprecedented decline.

DIMINISHED GATEKEEPING AND DISTRIBUTION BARRIERS

This shift in the relative prominence of legitimate versus false news and information is also a function of the fact that the gatekeeping barriers that have traditionally curtailed the dissemination of false news (and thus discouraged false news production) have been dramatically reduced. The mass media era was defined by gatekeeping bottlenecks, in which freedom of the press was "guaranteed only to those that own one."[78] Effective distribution was confined to outlets such as broadcast stations, cable networks/systems, newspapers, and magazines, all of which were relatively scarce for technological and economic reasons, and thus operated as news and information bottlenecks that wielded substantial gatekeeping power.

The Internet and social media have provided the opportunity to circumvent these bottlenecks. As a consequence, as has been noted, the economic incentives for producing legitimate journalism have been undermined, even as, paradoxically, the opportunities to distribute news have increased and the costs of distribution have decreased. Conversely, given the low costs associated with producing fake news, the diminished gatekeeping barriers and minimal distribution costs have enhanced the economic incentives for producing fake news.[79]

Even the gatekeeping to advertising dollars has been transformed in ways that enhance the opportunities for online fake news outlets. Today, given the overwhelming number of ad-placement options, the allocation of online advertising dollars is increasingly handled by algorithmically driven ad-placement networks.[80] Often advertisers do not even know (or perhaps even care) exactly where their advertisements are being placed.[81] Recall the discussion in chapter 1 about the decoupling of content and advertisements that has been a defining characteristic of the evolution of our digital media ecosystem. This situation stands in stark contrast to the mass media era, when information about when and where advertisements were being placed was common knowledge. Today, the criteria embedded in the ad-placement algorithms place fake news sites on a more or less equal footing with other online content providers that attract advertising dollars through automated media buying systems.

In the wake of the 2016 election, companies such as Google and Facebook have initiated a number of efforts to address this problem, even going so far as to ban known fake news outlets from their ad networks. The goal is, as Facebook has stated, to "disrupt the economic incentives to create false news."[82] Initial analyses have raised questions about whether these efforts have been effective.[83] Moreover, as will be discussed later, producers of fake news are not always motivated by ad revenues.

Previously, the distribution (and thus monetization) of fake news would be prevented to some extent by the limited number of gatekeepers. Given their limited number, these gatekeepers had both the incentive and the opportunity to curb the dissemination of fake news. The incentive came from the fact that, in a far less fragmented media environment, neutral and objective (and thus less likely to be false) reporting represented a potentially effective approach to attracting and retaining the largest possible audience.[84] The opportunity came in the form of the substantial economic resources these outlets had to research and verify stories—resources that were a function of the economic health of these outlets prior to the damaging effects of an increasingly fragmented media environment.

This scenario of diminished bottlenecks and gatekeepers represents a tremendous opportunity for the production and dissemination of fake news. As has been well illustrated in the time since the 2016 election, many of those engaged in the production and distribution of fake news did so purely because of the tremendous economic opportunity it presented, not out of any ideological motivations.[85] Economic incentives to provide false news have always existed, given the appealing economics of false news production. However, the diminished barriers to entry (and thus diminished institutional gatekeeping) afforded by the Internet have enhanced these incentives.

These economic incentives have been further enhanced over the past few years by social media distribution, and the associated regression from a "pull" to a "push" model of media consumption discussed in chapter 1. Social media provide means to more effectively capitalize on the diminished gatekeeping barriers on the Internet by providing previously unprecedented paths to low-cost distribution and large aggregations of audiences. Research indicates that social media referrals are a more crucial component of story distribution for hyperpartisan and fake news sites than they are for legitimate news sites.[86] This is because fake news stories are constructed with the overarching purpose of being shared as widely as possible, so the producers will always try to capitalize on what they know about the types of stories most likely to go viral at any particular time. Legitimate news stories are, of course, more constrained in their viral potential by their need to conform to the realities of current events. Reflecting this difference, one study found that 30 percent of fake news traffic linked back to Facebook, compared with only 8 percent of legitimate news traffic.[87]

Underlying this argument is the assumption that, regardless of motivation—whether it be purely economic, overtly political, or simply an unintended outcome of a more partisan approach to producing factual journalism—sources of news and information with more partisan orientations produce more false news than journalistic sources that adhere to more traditional notions of neutrality and objectivity. While perhaps controversial, this assumption is grounded in compelling empirical evidence.[88] For instance, in an analysis focusing on the prevalence of mass shooting–related conspiracy theories on Twitter, researcher Kate Starbird found that "alternative" news sites associated with extreme partisan orientations were much more likely to promote conspiracy theories related to mass shootings.[89]

In sum, within the counterspeech doctrine's valorization of "more speech," the point here is that, in today's news ecosystem, more of this "more speech" is likely to be false speech.

INCREASED ABILITY TO TARGET
THE MOST IMPRESSIONABLE

Within the context of the distribution of news, it is also important to take into consideration the changing dynamics of the distribution process, particularly the ways in which the distribution of false news can now be more effectively targeted at those individuals most likely to be—or most important to be—affected by the misinformation. As chapter 2 illustrated, interactivity provides a stream of audience data that facilitates audience targeting to an unprecedented extent.

Within the context of counterspeech, this means that those with an economic and/or political interest in the dissemination of false news are now far better equipped than in the past to deliver their content to those they most desire to reach. Targeting exclusively right- or left-leaning news consumers (or more radical factions within these ideological categories) has never been easier, as observable social media activity provides a host of reliable indicators of an individual's political orientation.[90] In these ways, the magnitude of the "evil" (to use Brandeis's term) that false speech can achieve is amplified.

As was widely reported in 2018, the Trump campaign employed a consulting firm, Cambridge Analytica, which drew upon massive amounts of social media data to construct detailed psychological, demographic, and geographic profiles of individual voters, then used these data to deliver microtargeted political messages through social media platforms such as Facebook.[91] According to whistle-blower Mark Wylie, the bulk of these messages cultivated and preyed upon recipients' political paranoia and racial biases.[92] The revelation that Cambridge Analytica had obtained these data improperly seems to have pivoted policy makers' focus away from the issue of fake news and toward the more familiar issue of user privacy. Indeed, there has been relatively little discussion of whether Cambridge Analytica used the data to deliver overtly false news or claims in campaign messages (though this is not uncommon in political advertisements). The key point here, however, is that the technological capacity to target citizens with tailored messages or information based on their unique characteristics appears to have taken yet another substantial leap forward, beyond what was possible through previous communications channels.[93] Hundreds of Russian Facebook accounts were similarly engaged in purchasing and placing such microtargeted political ads during the 2016 political campaign, highlighting the unprecedented accessibility to this capacity to microtarget. Congress recently released data on the ads' content, target audience segments, and reach,[94] which should lead to a much deeper understanding of the dynamics of contemporary social media–based audience-targeting strategies.

From a false news perspective, according to a U.S. Senate investigation, the army of a thousand Russian trolls working to spread fake news stories specifically targeted voters in swing states such as Wisconsin, Michigan, and Pennsylvania,[95] with this geographic targeting facilitated by social media data. A recent study on this kind of election-focused targeting activity found that in the ten days leading up to the election, voters in eleven swings states received more "fake, junk, and hyper-partisan" information than reliable, professionally produced news.[96]

Further, according to the testimony of cybersecurity expert Clint Watts, some of these fake news outlets explicitly targeted Donald Trump, tweeting fake news stories directly to his Twitter account during time periods when he was known to be online, under the presumption that he has shown himself to be particularly susceptible to disinformation.[97] Obviously, this is an extreme example of how today's highly personalized media environment enhances the opportunities for purveyors of fake news to reach those most likely to be affected by the disinformation.

Some recent analyses of the fake news phenomenon have demonstrated that the reach of, and/or the frequency of exposure to, election-related fake news stories was relatively limited.[98] Within the context being discussed here, one could argue that this is virtually irrelevant. In a typical general election, a relatively small percentage of the voting population is undecided, or could potentially "flip" to an opposing candidate. It is also the case that the margins separating winners from losers can be quite small. From these standpoints, it is not the reach, but the precision with which a relatively small group can be targeted, that matters most. And even if it were shown that tremendous precision was not achieved in 2016, it would seem reasonable to assume that precision could improve with experience and the inevitable advances in available tools and technologies.

One could argue that these dynamics provide comparable opportunities for accurate news to target those news consumers most in need of legitimate news, or most vulnerable to fake news. Legitimate news outlets generally do not engage in aggressive, targeted news dissemination campaigns over social media that are structured around reaching those most vulnerable to fake news, or most politically influential if affected. In addition, any notions of equality are further undermined when we factor in (as we do in the next section) the ways in which this process of personalization can reduce the likelihood of exposure to counterspeech that directly addresses the false speech that has been consumed.

DIMINISHED LIKELIHOOD OF BEING EXPOSED TO FACTUAL COUNTERSPEECH

As legal scholar Vincent Blasi has emphasized, one of the key conditions that influences the effectiveness of counterspeech is the extent to which "the counter-message comes to the attention of all the persons who were swayed by the original idea."[99] The dynamics of the contemporary media environment to some extent explicitly prevent this type of exposure to counterspeech. This is the essence of the filter bubble phenomenon, in which the intertwining of individual and algorithmic content personalization[100] on social media and other news aggregation platforms works to deflect news sources and content that do not correspond to the user's established content preferences and political orientation.[101] This process of deflection can work in different ways. One's filter bubble might deflect fake news that contradicts previously consumed legitimate news, or it might deflect legitimate news that contradicts previously consumed false news.

Here again is where the extent to which the filter bubbles have a partisan orientation comes into play. Given the empirical connection between partisanship and falsity,[102] to the extent that one's filter bubble has a partisan orientation, the likelihood of fake news making it through the filter bubble increases,[103] and the likelihood of consuming legitimate news that counteracts that fake news decreases.[104] This pattern is reinforced by the finding that those with a strong partisan orientation engage in significantly more sharing of fake news stories.[105]

The current situation is perhaps best termed the *spiral of partisanship*.[106] In this scenario, the increased media fragmentation and personalization that began in the 1980s with the development of cable television, then accelerated through the 1990s and 2000s with the rise of the Internet and social media (see chapter 1), facilitated the mutually dependent phenomena of more partisan news outlets and selective exposure to more partisan news. These are mutually dependent in that partisan news outlets require an audience to justify their existence and more partisan news consumption requires the availability of more partisan news outlets. As the media environment grows ever more fragmented, its ability to both sow and satisfy partisanship is amplified.[107] It is likely no coincidence that the upswing in self-reported partisanship began in the 1980s, at the same time that media fragmentation began in earnest.[108] In addition, research indicates that consumers of partisan news not only are more likely to consume false news (see above), but may also be inherently more resistant to counterspeech that might correct it.[109] Recent research tells us that "fact checks of fake news almost never reached its consumers."[110] Once again, the net effect is likely one in which the dynamics of the contemporary media ecosystem tilt the balance toward the consumption of fake news to an extent that was not the case in the pre–filter bubble era.

This dynamic is particularly damaging to traditional applications of the counterspeech doctrine. Traditional approaches to counterspeech have essentially operated under a broadcast-era model of media distribution. Assumptions such as those built into the Fairness Doctrine, which made the counterspeech available on the same platform and at roughly the same time as the original speech in order to produce equivalent exposure, seem at best quaint when applied to today's media environment of intertwined individual and algorithmic content filtering. From this standpoint, it seems reasonable to conclude that the ability of counterspeech to reach those it needs to reach has been diminished as a result of the technological changes that have affected the news ecosystem.

DIMINISHED ABILITY TO DISTINGUISH BETWEEN LEGITIMATE AND FALSE NEWS

It also appears to be the case that technological changes are undermining citizens' abilities to distinguish between legitimate and false news.

In illustrating this point, it is important that we begin with the unique challenges associated with evaluating news. Economists generally recognize three categories of goods: (1) search/inspection goods, whose quality can be readily determined through examination; (2) experience goods, whose quality can be determined only after usage for a period of time; and (3) credence goods, which must be consumed on faith, as quality is difficult to ascertain.[111]

Journalism can sometimes fall into the second category (say, for example, when the local newscast reports rain for tomorrow, but it ends up snowing instead). More often, it is likely to fall into the third category, with news being consumed, and potentially being put to use in decision-making, in ways that do not result in the kind of observable feedback that allows for a post hoc evaluation of the veracity or quality of that news.

When we talk about the evaluation of any kind of product, the notion of *bounded rationality* comes into play.[112] This is the idea that individuals make rational decisions, but within the confines of the information they have processed to aid them in that decision. So, individuals can be fully rational, but still make the wrong decision, if they have not processed all of the information necessary to reach the optimal decision.

As should be clear from the previous description of news as a product, news consumers typically lack the necessary information to make fully informed determinations as to the quality of the product they are consuming. This is a reflection of the fact that "by definition, news is what the public does not know."[113] Thus, it is likely the case that the consumption of false news is, to some extent, a function of inadequate information (interacting with the various cognitive biases discussed previously). Consumers of fake news are likely do so under the misperception that it is truthful. The challenge of accurately distinguishing between true and false news is further exacerbated by the dramatic increase in available news and information sources online,[114] which puts a greater information-processing burden on the news consumer.

Of particular importance is the extent to which the traditional mechanisms for combating this sort of uninformed behavior have been undermined by technological change. For instance, the reputations of news outlets long have served as a way for consumers to distinguish between truth and falsity.[115] Reputations serve as an important (though certainly imperfect) factor in facilitating efficient markets for experience and credence goods.[116] The reputation of the *New York Times* for truth and accuracy has generally been better than that of the *National Enquirer*.

This important heuristic, however, has been undermined as news consumption migrates to social media platforms. This is most compellingly demonstrated by research showing how seldom social media news consumers know the actual source of the news they are consuming. Research by the Pew Research Center indicates that individuals who consume news via social media are capable of identifying the originating source of a story only about half the time.[117]

This traditional reputation-based mechanism for evaluating the likely truthfulness of a news story is being replaced by a new heuristic—the trustworthiness of the individual who shared the story on social media.[118] Thus, an article shared by a trusted member of an individual's social network, but written by a source unknown to that individual, will be evaluated as more trustworthy—and thus be more likely to be consumed—than an article produced by a reputable news source but shared by someone viewed as less trustworthy.[119] This halo effect extends to news brands as a whole, with individuals more likely to follow and recommend news outlets that were referred to them by trusted members of their social network.[120] These tendencies may help explain why, according to one study, the majority of news stories shared on Twitter were not even clicked on (i.e., read) before being shared.[121] Given that the filter bubble, discussed earlier, is to some extent a function of the ideological homogeneity that characterizes many individuals' social networks,[122] we find once again that the likelihood of exposure to counterspeech is being undermined by the social media context in which news consumption is increasingly taking place.

These dynamics help to explain recent findings that trust in mainstream news outlets is much lower than the trust that news consumers place in the news outlets catering to their own ideological orientation.[123] The distribution of trust in news organizations is essentially being reallocated in ways that favor the consumption and acceptance of fake news over legitimate news, which works against the effectiveness of the counterspeech doctrine. Ultimately, if news consumers are increasingly unable to gauge accurately whether a news source's reporting is likely to be true or false, then more speech (e.g., counterspeech) does nothing to assure that truth prevails and that democratic decision-making is well informed.[124]

On top of all of this, we need to consider the intentional misrepresentation of news sources. Propaganda research tells us that a key means of enhancing the effectiveness of false propaganda involves disguising the source.[125] Propaganda presented under the guise of journalism has proven to be particularly effective.[126] Today, the opportunities to effectively disguise propaganda as legitimate journalism have increased tremendously.[127] This is a function of the diminished barriers to entry and diminished institutional gatekeeping, which operate in concert with the enhanced distribution capacity of social media and their users' diminished awareness of news sources. The extent to which propaganda operations can masquerade as news outlets is much greater in an environment in which legitimate and illegitimate news outlets can all exist side by side on social media platforms.[128] This is well illustrated by the report that, during the 2016 election, as many as a thousand Russian trolls were actively engaged in the production and distribution of fake news through social media.[129] An analysis of these online propaganda efforts emphasized Russia's utilization of a multiplicity of online sources that were often disguised as news outlets.[130] Russia's Internet Research Agency went so far as to establish "sleeper" local news sources on Twitter. These social media accounts had names that sounded like local newspapers (MilwaukeeVoice, Seattle_Post, etc.), and in one case adopted the name of a Chicago paper (*Chicago Daily News*) that had actually existed at one point but went out of business in 1978. These Twitter accounts spent years disseminating legitimate local news (and thus gaining audience trust) in order to then be "activated" to spread various types of disinformation in the lead-up to the 2016 election.[131] In a similar (though less extreme) vein, highly partisan local news sites are emerging around the country, "with names and layouts designed to echo those of nonpartisan publications," but which often conceal their ownership, staff identities, and sources of financial support.[132] According to one critic, this is an example of outlets trying to "adopt the forms of journalism without the norms of journalism," which "makes it very hard for citizens . . . to navigate this information environment."[133]

This issue of source misrepresentation bears directly on the effectiveness of counterspeech. In a 2012 television interview on the influence of money on political campaigning, an interviewer asked the late, conservative Supreme Court Justice (and vocal counterspeech enthusiast) Antonin Scalia how Thomas Jefferson would likely have viewed the contemporary political communication environment. Scalia replied, "I think Thomas Jefferson would have said 'the more speech the better.' That's what the First Amendment is all about."[134] He followed that statement, however, with this important caveat: "So long as the people know where the speech is coming from."[135] Thus, even from a traditionalist First Amendment perspective, the counterspeech doctrine is not absolute, and it is particularly vulnerable when the true source of news or information cannot be determined.

It is important to note that even mainstream news outlets have been unable to distinguish between legitimate news and fake news, and thus have contributed to the dissemination of fake news.[136] As noted previously, parasitic journalism is an increasingly prominent dimension of the news ecosystem, with news outlets facing diminished resources to produce their own reporting or, for that matter, to rigorously verify the reporting of other news outlets. These patterns increase the likelihood that legitimate news outlets will facilitate the dissemination of fake news and thereby legitimize it for some news consumers. Thus, it is not surprising that research has shown that the false news stories emanating from hyperpartisan right-wing news sites have been able to influence the agenda of the mainstream news media.[137] Another study found that tweets from Internet Research Agency–linked accounts could be found in the comments sections of news stories in thirty-two of the thirty-three mainstream media outlets that were studied, which the authors take as evidence of "the deep penetration of IRA content into news media."[138] From a counterspeech perspective, this means that even the key providers of the legitimate news that is intended (according to the counterspeech doctrine) to overcome false news are not only operating at a diminished capacity to counteract false news, but are sometimes even complicit in its perpetuation.

Then there is the question of how well our new distributors of news (i.e., social media platforms) are capable of distinguishing between true and false news, now that they seem to have reached a point that making such a distinction actually matters to them. In the wake of the 2016 election, these platforms ratcheted up their efforts to identify and curtail the spread of fake news stories (discussed in more detail in chapter 6).[139] In the lead-up to the 2018 midterm elections, social media platforms shut down "inauthentic" accounts in an effort to prevent a recurrence of what took place in 2016. Facebook shut down 583 million fake accounts in the first quarter of 2018;[140] among them were false accounts specifically focused on disseminating fake news and disinformation related to the 2018 election.[141] Twitter similarly purged its platform of tens of millions of fake accounts, including many engaged in coordinated dissemination of election-related disinformation.[142] Twitter deleted more than nine million accounts a week, on average, including accounts masquerading as Republican party members.[143] The platforms' tools for identifying organizational misrepresentation are clearly advancing, as is their willingness to use them to take action.

Whether these efforts have been successful remains a focus of debate.[144] The bottom line, however, is that when we compare previous content distributors (cable systems, broadcast networks, book distributors, etc.) to today's social media platforms, social media platforms know far less about the sources and content they are distributing (given the massive scale at which they operate) than any previous generation of content distributor.[145] In this regard, their limited ability to distinguish between fake and legitimate news stories/sources—their bounded rationality—gets passed right along to the news consumer.

THE ENHANCED SPEED AT WHICH FALSE NEWS CAN TRAVEL

Finally, it is important to consider how changes in media technology have altered the speed with which fake news can travel. Brandeis, in his original articulation of the counterspeech doctrine, noted that it provided the appropriate remedy to false speech only "if there be time."[146] This would seem a very important qualification to take into consideration in the context of today's news ecosystem, in which news can suddenly "go viral."[147]

Advances in media technologies have compressed the "news cycle" and facilitated ever-greater immediacy in the delivery of news.[148] The latest development in this process[149] is the role that social media can play in accelerating the distribution of a news story. An emerging literature on "digital wildfires" documents the speed at which false news can travel and seeks to explain the factors that can affect its diffusion.[150] The speed of diffusion can be enhanced by technological advances such as bots (certainly something Brandeis did not have to consider), which can operate at a scale and pace that human false news disseminators cannot.[151] The use of bots appears to have been an important component of Russia's efforts to rapidly distribute fake news in their efforts to influence the 2016 election.[152]

Presumably, legitimate news has the capacity to travel at the same speed as false news today, just as it did in Brandeis time. However, while the underlying technological capacity is the same, the troubling reality is that social media's capacity for rapid dissemination appears more likely to be brought to bear for false news stories than for true ones. Research indicates that false news stories are more likely to be shared—and are thus likely to spread faster (and farther)—than legitimate news stories.[153] The explanation for this disparity takes us back to the role of partisanship—in this case, the role that partisanship plays in increasing the likelihood of sharing a partisan news story[154]—in combination with the increased likelihood that a partisan news story is a false news story. The key implication here, once again, is that social media disproportionately favor fake news over legitimate news.

Given that news has never been able to travel faster and farther than it can today, it seems reasonable to conclude that the likelihood that "there be time" to rely upon counterspeech to counteract false news is less today than it was in Brandeis's era. Indeed, there may be less time to rely upon counterspeech today than has ever been the case before, particularly given the other technologically imposed challenges that counterspeech faces in counteracting disinformation.

■ ■ ■

The end result, then, is a compounding set of conditions that contributes to a news ecosystem that encourages and facilitates the production, dissemination, and consumption of false news in ways that the traditional media ecosystem did not. From the standpoint of the First Amendment, this means that counterspeech—a key component of the very efficacy of the First Amendment—is being undermined. What this ultimately may mean for the effective functioning of the marketplace of ideas is the focus of the next chapter.

CHAPTER 4

The Structure of the Algorithmic Marketplace of Ideas

Chapter 3 ended with the possibility that the First Amendment's core principle of counterspeech may, within the social media context, no longer be effective in assuring that the marketplace of ideas works effectively in cultivating an informed citizenry. This potential failure is due, in large part, to the technological and economic changes affecting the media ecosystem. It is also the result of the particular dynamics of how social media platforms have operated and been used. We can think, then, of social media platforms as a somewhat distinct algorithmic marketplace of ideas.

Given that the marketplace of ideas is fundamentally an economic metaphor, if we extend this metaphor a bit further, then these potential failings compel us to confront an issue that is central to the analysis of markets—the possibility of market failure. With this possibility in mind, I focus in this chapter on a structural analysis of the algorithmic marketplace of ideas. In so doing, I establish an analytical framework that both borrows and departs from how economists analyze traditional product markets. Needless to say, an idea market is not the same as a traditional product market in terms of how it operates, the type of products it produces, or what we expect it to achieve. However, these points of departure provide an opportunity for considering how we can assess the algorithmic marketplace of ideas. Once again, I focus primarily on journalism as the key input into this marketplace, providing both facts and opinion/ analysis that are consumed by, shared by, and influence other participants.

What are the causes of market failure, and do they apply to the algorithmic marketplace of ideas? What might market failure in the algorithmic marketplace of ideas look like? Have we perhaps already witnessed such a market failure? My discussion of these questions will use the structural analysis of the algorithmic marketplace of ideas as a baseline from which to consider the 2016 presidential election. Thus, whereas the focus in chapter 3 involved a legal perspective on issues of socially mediated fake news and disinformation, the focus here is more economic. The goal is to apply the concepts and criteria associated with the analysis of product markets to the idea market.

Causes, Indicators, and Outcomes of Market Failure in the Marketplace of Ideas

In laying the necessary foundation for this analysis, an important starting point is to consider some key causes and indicators of market failure, and how they require modification within the marketplace-of-ideas context. In a traditional product market, an effectively functioning market is determined by assessing economic efficiency and its underlying criteria such as consumer welfare, productivity, and competition. Market failure occurs when the allocation of goods and services is inefficient. Essentially, this means that the market is not operating in such a way as to serve the aggregate best interests of those participating in the market. Economists have thoroughly investigated the causes, indicators, and consequences of market failure within a wide range of product marketplaces, which will be brought to bear in this analysis.

Marketplaces of ideas, however, and the possible causes, indicators, and consequences of market failure within them, have received relatively little attention.[1] Economist Ronald Coase, in his classic comparative analysis of regulatory perspectives on the market for goods and the market for ideas, briefly noted that the results achieved by our political system suggest that there is a good deal of market failure in the marketplace of ideas, though he deemed the topic "a large subject on which I will avoid comment."[2] Unfortunately, few analysts in the forty-five years since Coase made this observation have explored this possibility. In light of the recent and dramatic changes that have affected our media ecosystem, the time has come to explore this territory with a new sense of urgency.

I begin by considering the ways in which idea markets have some fundamentally different characteristics from traditional product markets. Moreover, media markets and products also differ from traditional markets and products in some important ways that need to be taken into consideration when trying to develop a framework for evaluating market failure in a marketplace of ideas. Understanding these differences requires a brief detour into the unique economics of media.

THE DISTINGUISHING CHARACTERISTICS OF MEDIA MARKETS

When we are talking about an idea marketplace such as that reflected in the operation of our journalistic institutions, we are typically looking at what is described as a dual-product marketplace.[3] A *dual-product marketplace* is one in which two interconnected products are sold simultaneously. Most media organizations are selling (or giving away) content to audiences (product marketplace #1) and, at the same time, selling audiences to advertisers (product marketplace #2). The interconnectedness comes from the fact that audiences, who are the consumers in the first market, are actually the product in the second market.[4] Thus, success or failure in one market is interconnected with success or failure in the other. Attracting larger (or more valuable) audiences to one's content facilitates greater success in the audience marketplace. Attracting more valuable audiences provides revenues that can be used to create even more appealing content. This is the essence of the dual-product marketplace.

Different media organizations and industry sectors navigate this dual-product marketplace differently. So, for instance, some media organizations (such as many online news outlets) choose to give their content away rather than charge for it, in an effort to attract a larger audience and thus earn more through the sale of audiences to advertisers.

Facebook has long proclaimed that its service is free "and always will be,"[5] choosing to rely almost exclusively on advertising revenues, when even a nominal subscription fee of only a dollar a year could potentially earn the company nearly another two billion dollars in annual revenue (assuming every current user was willing to pay the fee).

Only in the wake of the Cambridge Analytica scandal,[6] and the accompanying criticisms of Facebook's user data–driven business model, did Facebook executives begin to float the possibility of adding a subscription version of the platform alongside the free version.[7] Presumably, a subscription model would diminish the extent to which Facebook's revenues are dependent on gathering and analyzing the user data that are so central to maximizing advertising revenues, and would diminish the incentive for Facebook to try to keep users on the site as long as possible (thereby maximizing their advertising exposure).

Other companies, such as Netflix, opt to charge their audience for content and choose not to try to sell their audience to advertisers. And, of course, some organizations (many cable networks, newspapers, some online news sites) choose to simultaneously charge audiences for their content and advertisers for their audiences.

As should be clear, there are many strategic approaches to navigating the media sector's dual-product marketplace. Often, an organization's (or an entire industry's) strategy will evolve over time. The *New York Times*, for instance, has gone back and forth in the use of paywalls for its online version and has adjusted the configuration of its paywall a number of times.[8] These dual-product marketplace dynamics are important when considering the operation of the contemporary algorithmic marketplace of ideas.

THE DISTINGUISHING CHARACTERISTICS
OF MEDIA PRODUCTS

We turn now from media markets to media products. In considering the relevant distinguishing characteristics of media products, we start with content. Media content is what economists call a *public good*. This term is somewhat misleading in that it does not mean that a product is inherently beneficial to the public (as quality journalism certainly is). Rather, it means that a product is not used up in consumption. That is, one individual's consumption of the product does not diminish its availability to others. In economic parlance, then, public goods are *nonexcludable* and *nondepletable*.[9]

Consider, for instance, an episode of a television program. The episode is produced once, and whether half a million people or twenty million people watch it, the costs to create and distribute the episode are essentially the same. Compare this to a traditional product such as a car (a classic example of a private good). Whether half a million people or twenty million people want to buy a particular make/model of a car matters quite a bit, because either half a million or twenty million individual cars need to be produced, and there are substantial costs associated with producing each car. And once I buy my car, that specific car is not available to another consumer; an additional car must be produced for the next consumer. Not so with an episode of a television show.

Indeed, all media content is a public good. Content is produced once and then can be sold and resold and repurposed in a variety of different ways, sometimes for long periods of time.[10] Consider, for instance, classic pop songs that continue to earn royalties decades after their recording, not only through radio airplay and sales, but through other channels such as licensing to television programs, commercials, movies, and even videogames. Journalism is a classic example of a public good. News organizations invest substantial resources in producing news stories; but once produced, these stories are widely available for consumption. Of course, news stories generally do not have the long, valuable shelf life of a hit song, a classic movie, or an episode of the *Simpsons*. Thus, journalism is not able to capitalize as extensively as other media sectors can on one of the key benefits of dealing in public goods.

It is important to recognize that, in many cases, content (the public good) has been embedded in a private good to facilitate distribution. So, for instance, books, movies, music, and news were traditionally embedded in "hard copy" formats. However, relative to the costs associated with producing the content (the public good), the costs associated with producing the physical object (the private good) are negligible. Paper and discs are very cheap compared to the costs of actors, directors, authors, musicians, and journalists. One of the defining characteristics of our increasingly digital media ecosystem is the extent to which such embedding of public goods in private goods is declining dramatically, as books, music, movies, and journalism all move from hard-copy versions to digital versions accessible online (goodbye record stores, bookstores, Blockbuster, and newspapers). This is the transition to a pure public good model for media distribution.

This primer on the economics of public goods is necessary because markets for public goods such as journalism have proven to be uniquely prone to market failure.[11] This vulnerability to market failure stems in part from the fact that public goods have a tendency to be underproduced relative to their full value, because of the ease with which they can be shared or consumed without payment.[12] Referred to as the "free rider" problem, it is the idea that there are more people who value the product than are paying for it. As a result, the economic incentives (and associated resources) to produce the product do not reflect the actual level of demand, in that some of those people getting the content for free would presumably have paid for it. If we think about how many times a single copy of a printed newspaper can be "passed along," or the ease with which one can copy and repost a story from a subscription news site, or share one's access password to a paywalled news site, then we begin to a get a sense of the economic challenges facing producers of public goods. These issues also tie in to the prominence of parasitic journalism discussed in chapter 3, with news outlets essentially repurposing the stories (and "free riding" on the significant investment in content creation) of other news outlets. These challenges are certainly part of what has compelled news outlets operating in the digital space to try to rely more heavily on the audience side of the dual-product marketplace.

To compound the problem, journalism also produces value for society as a whole that often is not captured in the economic transactions between news organizations and news consumers, and/or between news organizations and advertisers.[13] As noted previously, it is often the case that news is made available to news consumers for free, with the costs of producing the content being shouldered exclusively by advertisers. The societal benefits of an informed citizenry are not likely to be reflected in the prices that advertisers pay to reach news audiences. Economists typically refer to benefits that are not reflected in the costs paid in economic transactions as *positive externalities*.

The situation described here reflects market inefficiency in the form of the underproduction of journalism,[14] both because consumers are paying less than they would likely be willing to pay (given that it is often accessible for free) and because the amounts being paid by consumers for news and by advertisers to reach news consumers do not fully take into account the broader social, political, and economic value associated with an informed citizenry. These conditions are exacerbated by the more challenging economic environment for journalism discussed in the previous chapter. From this standpoint, the market for journalism is inherently vulnerable to market failure.

Turning, then, to audiences as a product, we need to start with the recognition that the purchasing of audiences essentially involves the purchasing of human attention (certainly a unique product). The dynamics of what has been termed the *marketplace of attention*,[15] or the *attention economy*,[16] have received a substantial amount of analysis. For the purposes of this discussion, there are a number of relevant takeaways. The first is that the value of audiences is increasingly defined in terms of their level of engagement, with *engagement* often being defined in terms of the time audiences spend with content (more time equals more ad exposures) and/ or the extent to which they interact with the content (likes, shares, posts, etc.).[17] Such interactions provide data points that facilitate better attracting and retaining of audiences, and serve as criteria for enhancing their value to advertisers by facilitating better-informed message targeting.

It should be noted that there have been some troubling applications of this increasingly data-driven approach to targeting and valuing audiences. For instance, in 2017, Facebook received a substantial amount of criticism when it was revealed that its ad-targeting platform allowed advertisers to target audiences along criteria such as "Jew Hater," and also allowed housing and employment advertisements to be placed in ways that they would avoid reaching minority users.[18] Such discrimination in housing and employment advertising is a violation of federal law. This kind of targeting is facilitated by the detailed data that individuals contribute to these platforms through their interactions with them. Although these revelations resulted in promises by Facebook to overhaul its ad-targeting system, in 2018 it was revealed that one could use the platform to target individuals with an interest in "white genocide conspiracy theory"—a theory, associated with the alt-right and white nationalists, that activities such as mass immigration and racial integration represent a form genocide against the white race.[19] This targeting category represented about 168,000 Facebook users.

These examples also highlight a vitally important way in which social media platforms have advanced beyond earlier media. Unlike traditional media such as television, newspapers, or radio, social media allow for spectacularly well-informed targeting of individual media users, thanks to the troves of data that users systematically contribute to these platforms through their interactions with them. The old media model of purchasing audiences on the basis of broad demographic characteristics garnered from a small sample of media users is woefully inefficient and ineffective by comparison.

In sum, what social media platforms want in order to maximize the value of their "audience product" is for these audiences to: (1) be as large as possible; (2) spend as much time on the platform as possible; and (3) interact (i.e., provide data) on the platform as much as possible. The nature of these sources of value for audiences is important to keep in mind as we assess the structure and operation of the algorithmic marketplace of ideas.

ASSESSMENT CRITERIA FOR A MARKETPLACE OF IDEAS

From an economic theory perspective on the marketplace of ideas, an informed citizenry and an effectively functioning democratic process are positive externalities. They are ancillary benefits of an effectively functioning market. From a democratic theory perspective, however, these characteristics are not peripheral; they are fundamental. Thus, an effectively functioning marketplace of ideas needs to be assessed according to different standards, with an informed citizenry and an effectively functioning democratic process moving from the periphery to the center.

How do we assess, then, whether an idea marketplace is effectively contributing to these outcomes? A useful starting point is to consider the nature—essentially, the quality—of the products being produced. Antitrust experts Maurice Stucke and Allen Grunes have argued in their analysis of the role of antitrust in the marketplace of ideas, "If a market is plagued with falsities or material omissions reflecting the media's self-interests, this may be evidence of market failure."[20] Fleshing out this perspective in a bit more detail, legal scholar Tamara Piety suggests that market failures in the marketplace of ideas can be exemplified by characteristics such as "(1) the proliferation and acceptance of false ideas, (2) the suppression of truthful information, (3) the failure to produce truthful information, and (4) limitations on choice, and the channeling of the exercise of preferences within those limitations."[21]

Many of these conditions recall the issues discussed in the previous chapter. All appear to be increasingly likely outcomes of the changing technological and structural characteristics of our media ecosystem. Items one and two reflect the increasing prominence and influence potential of fake news and the role of filter bubbles in inhibiting exposure to legitimate news. Item three reflects the diminishing journalistic capacity of legitimate news organizations. Item four again takes us back to the operation of algorithmic filter bubbles, noting how they have tended to constrict, rather than expand, news and information consumption within a narrower range of options determined by demonstrated preferences.

To the extent that these conditions contribute to the increased production, dissemination, and consumption of false news, we once again find ourselves in the economic realm of externalities. That is, from an economic perspective, fake news can be thought of as a negative externality[22] produced by a marketplace of ideas. Negative externalities are the (often unintended) costs associated with the operation of a product market. For instance, a negative externality associated with a factory manufacturing cars is the pollution produced by that factory. Or, as media economist James Hamilton has compellingly shown, a negative externality of advertisers' desires to reach young adult television viewers is children's exposure to violent programming intended for adults.[23] Under this model, children's exposure to violent programming is akin to a more traditional negative externality such as pollution.[24]

Within this tradition of thinking about the dynamics of our media ecosystem through the lens of negative externalities, it seems reasonable to consider false news production and consumption as a negative externality of the algorithmic marketplace of ideas—as a social cost that is a by-product of social media platforms' efforts to effectively navigate the dual-product marketplace. The strategy that social media platforms have chosen—relying entirely on advertising revenue—means that their focus has been on attracting as many users as possible and hosting as many different content providers as possible, in an effort to engage audiences on their platform as long as possible and provide advertisers with the highest-value "audience product"[25] possible. The presence of such a negative externality is particularly important given that negative externalities are accepted indicators of market failure.[26] A market is not operating efficiently if the benefits of the market are accompanied by substantial costs.

ALTERNATIVE PERSPECTIVES

It is important recognize that there are alternative interpretations of the presence and impact of fake news within the algorithmic marketplace of ideas. Some might argue, for instance, that the increasing production, dissemination, and consumption of fake news is a reflection of the ways that technological changes have allowed the market to more efficiently identify and meet consumer demand for falsity (the marketplace of ideas essentially becoming more efficient in serving consumer demand for fake news, or at least for news and information that confirms existing beliefs, regardless of its veracity), rather than a reflection of consumers' diminished ability (as was asserted in chapter 3) to accurately distinguish between true and false news.[27]

In considering this possibility, the notion that consumer demand for fake news is now being better met is cynical in that it reflects a grim view of the citizenry. According to this perspective, citizens possess a conscious desire to be misinformed. Even the bulk of the literature discussed in chapter 3 delineating the various cognitive biases that can lead to the consumption and acceptance of false news and information does not suggest that individuals are consciously and intentionally seeking false information, but rather that their cognitive biases lead them to mistakenly embrace false news and information as true.

The notion that individuals desire true and accurate information, but are not always capable of making the distinction for the reasons discussed above, reflects a less cynical view of the citizenry and a reasonable sense of how an idea marketplace actually functions, given the recognized prominence of bounded rationality (see chapter 3) in limiting marketplace efficiency. Further, this perspective represents the more optimistic (and perhaps naive) normative principle that an effectively functioning marketplace of ideas facilitates informed democratic decision-making—something that is presumably incompatible with decisions based on false information. Legal scholar Larissa Lidsky argues, "The ideal of democratic self-governance . . . makes no sense unless one assumes that citizens will generally make rational choices to govern the fate of the nation. If the majority of citizens make policy choices based on lies, half-truths, or propaganda, sovereignty lies not with the people but with the purveyors of disinformation. If this is the case, democracy is both impossible and undesirable."[28] Reflecting this position, my analysis will proceed (perhaps naively and optimistically) from the perspective that consumers generally prefer legitimate to false news.

Looked at this way, the unintentional consumption of fake news is a reflection of the bounded rationality of the news consumer that was discussed in chapter 3, which is a function of inadequate information for determining the accuracy and reliability of available news sources. This challenge becomes particularly pronounced because of the various forms of deception and misrepresentation that fake news purveyors employ in order to be perceived as legitimate news outlets. Inadequate information (sometimes referred to as an *information asymmetry*) is a recognized cause of market failure.[29] A market cannot operate efficiently if consumers lack the information necessary to make well-informed decisions about the relative value of the products and services available to them. In a market made inefficient by inadequate information, consumers end up unintentionally consuming undesirable or low-quality products—essentially buying lemons.[30] When individuals consume fake news, they are essentially buying lemons in the marketplace of ideas, from sellers who often are operating with substantial troves of behavioral, demographic, and geographic information about news consumers. This scenario represents the essence of an information asymmetry.

Structural Characteristics of the Algorithmic Marketplace of Ideas

MONOPOLY AND MARKET FAILURE

Two important characteristics that have long been associated with market failure are monopoly (a single provider of a product or service)[31] and oligopoly (very few providers of a product or service).[32] The primary concern in these scenarios is that a monopolist, or oligopolists, can potentially charge inflated prices, scale back production, or stifle competition, leading to substantial inefficiencies in how the market operates.

When we translate this concern to the marketplace of ideas, however, the situation is a bit different. For starters, content (the key product in the marketplace of ideas) is often made available for free (often due to the choices content providers make about how to navigate the dual product marketplace discussed earlier). From this standpoint, a focus on pricing is of limited relevance to our understanding of monopoly or oligopoly power in the marketplace of ideas. Of much greater concern, traditionally, has been the extent to which monopolistic or oligopolistic situations in the marketplace of ideas affect the availability of "diverse and antagonistic sources" that is at the core of the marketplace-of-ideas metaphor.[33] This is the underlying source of long-standing concerns—both within the United States and around the world—with concentration of ownership in the media.[34] These concerns have been as much political as they are economic.[35]

The extent to which media concentration is an issue that extends beyond traditional economic concerns is reflected in the fact that, in the United States, proposed media mergers generally undergo a separate public-interest assessment by the Federal Communications Commission. The public-interest assessment is intended to extend beyond the narrower economic parameters that either the Justice Department or the Federal Trade Commission (they share jurisdiction over media mergers) brings to the analysis. Embedded in this concept of the public interest, discussed in greater detail in the next chapter, is the concern that ownership concentration in the media can have not only damaging economic effects, but also damaging effects on the marketplace of ideas. Not surprisingly, then, a substantial body of research has sought to quantify various performance dimensions of the marketplace of ideas, such as diversity, quality, and social responsibility, and to determine if, or to what extent, ownership concentration affects these dimensions.[36] Many of these studies have found compelling evidence that increases in ownership concentration can lead to decreases in socially valuable dimensions of media content such as quality and diversity.[37]

These concerns, which have traditionally been focused on contexts such as group ownership and cross-ownership of local television stations and newspapers, or the creation of massive multimedia conglomerates (think AT&T/Time Warner or Comcast), have only recently begun to emerge within newer contexts such as the Internet and social media.[38] It is worth noting that some analyses have suggested that platform industries such as social media may even be *natural monopolies*—cases in which the most efficient, and thus inevitable, market structure is one in which a single firm dominates the market.[39]

From an economic standpoint, it seems increasingly plausible to make a case that, at minimum, an oligopolistic structure has taken hold in the audience component of the online dual-product marketplace. Facebook and Google have established incredibly dominant positions in the online advertising space, capturing more than 63 percent of U.S. online advertising revenue, according to recent estimates.[40] Globally, these two companies are estimated to account for 84 percent of all digital advertising outside of China.[41]

In terms of the content market, however, things are a bit more complicated. These dominant platforms have generally refrained (so far) from taking a prominent role in content creation. In this regard, they do not generate exactly the same concerns that have arisen around increased ownership concentration within news-producing media outlets. The question in this case is whether they represent substantial distribution bottlenecks, and are thereby able to exert monopoly/oligopoly power. If so, what does this exertion of monopoly/oligopoly power look like, and what are its implications for the marketplace of ideas?

In considering these questions, we need to recognize that any news outlet can, via its online presence, make its content directly available to audiences without relying on social media platforms such as Facebook, YouTube, and Twitter for distribution. In this regard, the barriers to entry to becoming an online content provider remain lower than they were in the traditional media context. The question is, however, given the way the Internet has evolved, does the traditional approach to attracting audience attention online (post your content, engage in some advertising, hyperlinking, and search engine optimization, and hope for the best) represent a reasonable substitute for the access to massive aggregations of algorithmically directed audience attention that social media platforms provide?

Let's assume for the moment that the answer is no.[42] Given that Facebook and Google combined account for 75 percent of all Internet traffic referrals in 2017,[43] this seems like a reasonably defensible position. The next question is, how does having very few of these platforms playing a prominent role in curating online access to news and information affect—or potentially affect—the nature of the news and information that audiences receive? That is, how can the monopolistic/oligopolistic distribution structure characteristic of contemporary social media contribute to market failure in the algorithmic marketplace of ideas?[44] Certainly, the potential to act as an influential gatekeeper is there, as it is generally within the rights of social media platforms to curate the content they disseminate as they see fit. This happens all the time, as these platforms work to stifle the distribution of hate speech, violence, and pornography.[45]

They have also, however, frequently gone beyond these protective measures. Facebook, for example, intentionally manipulated the news feeds of almost 700,000 users in order to test the hypothesis that social media could facilitate "emotional contagion."[46] Specifically, Facebook adjusted the news feeds of these users so that some received a higher concentration of more upbeat items and some received a higher concentration of more downbeat items. Then, the posting activities of these groups were analyzed to see if alteration in the emotional tenor of one's news feed influenced the tenor of one's own posting activity (the answer was yes). This well-publicized, and controversial, activity raised larger questions about Facebook's potential for intentional political influence.

Facebook, Google, and Twitter have all been the subject of accusations that their filtering and curation activities have involved intentional, directed efforts at favoring or obscuring certain political viewpoints, issues, or candidates.[47] A few studies have provided compelling evidence that such activities could produce effects of sufficient magnitude to affect election outcomes.[48] The point is that if we see the social media space as monopolistic or oligopolistic, the opportunity to exert monopoly or oligopoly power over the marketplace of ideas is certainly there.

The magnitude of this potential power became apparent during congressional hearings in October and November 2017 that focused on the possibility of Russian interference in the 2016 presidential election.[49] As Facebook's general counsel revealed in his testimony, the number of users exposed to Russia-sponsored misinformation was not ten million, as Facebook had originally estimated, but rather 126 million.[50] In this case, it appears that Facebook's role in manipulating public opinion was not intentional. Nonetheless, when algorithmic distribution power is highly concentrated, the magnitude of the impact of any flaws, shortcomings, or intentional or unintentional biases in the small number of influential algorithmic curation systems can be tremendous.[51]

In this way, Facebook's failure can beget market failure in the algorithmic marketplace of ideas.

What is particularly important about the nature of this power is the way it can be utilized in a targeted manner. In *Virtual Competition: The Promise and Perils of the Algorithm-Driven Economy*, antitrust analysts Ariel Ezrachi and Maurice Stucke focus on the threats of algorithmic platforms to traditional product marketplaces. Their analysis illustrates the ways in which these platforms can engage in behavioral discrimination, using behavioral data to charge different prices in ways that can lead to the exploitation of certain groups.[52] For instance, one study they discuss found that residents of communities with high Asian populations were 1.8 times more likely to be charged higher prices for Princeton Review's online college test prep services, regardless of income.[53]

If we consider this dynamic within the context of the algorithmic marketplace of ideas, we should be similarly concerned about the ways in which the behavioral discrimination facilitated by social media platforms facilitates the targeting and exploitation of those most susceptible to false news and information and/or those whose succumbing to such falsity would have the greatest impact (e.g., swing voters in battleground states). Particularly relevant in the marketplace-of-ideas context is the way in which the monopolistic/oligopolistic position held by social media platforms can be exploited by third parties (e.g., false news purveyors), utilizing these platforms for their particular ends.

This prospect brings us to the notion of "too big to fail," a phrase that emerged in the wake of the late 2000s financial crisis and has reemerged in discussions about Facebook and its dominant position.[54] Facebook, it has been argued, has reached such a size that its size alone can sustain the company's viability in perpetuity.[55] Social media, like many other communications platforms, possess *network effects*:[56] the service they provide becomes more valuable to the individual user as the network of users grows. Thus, the fact that so many people are on Facebook can have a "lock-in" effect, compelling people to stay with the platform even if alternatives are available, thereby insulating the platform from the threat of competition.

Within the context of the financial crisis, the notion of "too big to fail" meant that certain financial institutions were so large and so important that their failure would be unthinkably catastrophic for the country, and thus needed to be prevented at all costs. Similarly, one could argue, Facebook has reached such a size that the broad ripple effects of its failure (from a performance standpoint) would be so far-reaching and significant, and the reverberations so disastrous, that such failure must be prevented at all costs. This scenario is perhaps where we find ourselves today. Facebook has established such an unprecedented degree of gatekeeping power in the distribution of news and information that the implications of any failure to do so properly (e.g., to effectively police disinformation) could be catastrophic to the algorithmic marketplace of ideas.

RUINOUS COMPETITION AND MARKET FAILURE

At the other end of the continuum from monopoly, market failure has also been found to result from market structure conditions that are too competitive. Economists have referred to this situation as *ruinous competition*[57]—a scenario in which there are so many competitors in a marketplace that they ultimately drive each other out of business.[58] The result is either the end of the industry or the survival of a single monopolist—either of which takes us back to the market-failure scenario. Along the way, product quality can suffer because of the economic hardships the firms are enduring in this highly competitive environment—hardships that impede their ability to invest in quality products.[59] Antitrust regulators and the courts have generally been skeptical of the idea of ruinous competition because of the frequency with which concerns about ruinous competition are put forth by industry players seeking to engage in mergers, price-fixing, or other activities that are generally viewed as anticompetitive.[60]

From a marketplace-of-ideas perspective, competition can perhaps be ruinous without the industry collapsing or a single monopolist emerging. In the idea marketplace, participation is not always driven purely by economic motivations. Participation can often be politically motivated as well—or instead. In fact, the extent to which individuals create content for reasons other than direct financial reward is a defining characteristic of media markets.[61] Thinking specifically about journalism, for much of their early history, U.S. newspapers were operated by political parties and were used to distribute the partisan viewpoints of those parties.[62] Profit-making was not a priority; political influence was.

More recently, as the economics of journalism have become increasingly challenging, the economic motivations for owning news organizations have, to some extent, diminished, allowing political motivations to reemerge as a more significant factor. From this standpoint, it is somewhat telling how much recent media acquisition and merger activity in the United States has seemed to have an overtly political dimension. Consider, for instance, the attempted merger between Sinclair Broadcasting and Tribune. This merger would have created the country's most far-reaching television station ownership group, reaching more than 80 percent of U.S. television households. This merger appears, by many accounts, to have been motivated in large part by the very conservative Sinclair ownership's desire to obtain a much wider audience reach for its local television newscasts.[63] These newscasts often contain highly partisan (and often inaccurate) segments that are produced centrally and their dissemination mandated across all Sinclair-owned local TV stations.[64] Similarly, Meredith Corporation's acquisition of magazine publisher Time, Inc. has been backed by billionaire conservative activists the Koch brothers. Their backing of this acquisition has raised questions as to whether their investment is an effort to utilize publications such as *Time* magazine to better disseminate conservative viewpoints.[65]

The point here is that as the economic motivations for producing journalism diminish, political motivations remain, can increase in relative prominence, and can sustain journalistic output even when it is unprofitable. This dynamic once again raises questions about the quality/veracity of the journalism that is produced, given the relationship between partisanship and accuracy discussed in chapter 3. Thus, in an idea market, ruinous competition need not lead to producers exiting the market; it may instead lead to dramatic declines in overall quality (if we associate more partisan journalism with lower-quality journalism).

From a marketplace-of-ideas perspective, we need to ask whether there is so much competition that the overall quality is being driven down to the point that the products do not function effectively. In this case, it would mean that a substantial amount of the news and information being produced is not of sufficient accuracy or quality to facilitate informed decision-making. Some analyses of journalism have found that, as competition increases, journalistic quality can decline dramatically across a range of vectors that are relevant to the effective functioning of the marketplace of ideas. These studies have found relationships between dramatic increases in competition and increases in sensationalistic and trivial news output, and decreases in diversity and locally oriented content.[66]

Let's consider this modified approach to ruinous competition within the context of the algorithmic marketplace of ideas. If we think about the thousands of news and information outlets that are accessible online, this certainly looks like a marketplace that is, at minimum, highly competitive. This competition has been facilitated by the very low barriers to entry and the elimination of geographic impediments to content distribution that were described in chapter 1. Thanks to the Internet, everyone is, essentially, competing in everyone else's market.

Of course, one could argue that these outlets are not all competing with one another, that they operate in different product markets (local, regional, national, international; sports, political, entertainment, etc.). This perspective brings to the forefront long-standing, and largely unresolved, media policy debates about how the parameters of media markets should be defined.[67] Regardless of whether one favors expansive or narrow media market definitions, the reality today is that the Internet has facilitated an environment in which more news and information providers are in more direct competition with one another than was the case with traditional media.

However, the key here is that this competition has become more direct and more pronounced as news consumption and distribution have migrated to social media platforms. In the old "pull" model of the

Internet, your news consumption needed to be self-directed, to some extent. Thus, your particular interest/need would guide your online news- and information-seeking behaviors. If you needed or wanted local news at that particular moment, your behaviors would be guided accordingly, and national or international news outlets would not factor into your behaviors. In the "push" model of social media, all types of news outlets (including fake news outlets) compete for algorithmic prioritization and audience attention within the same individual news feeds. Audience attention can be more easily diverted from one news source to another. This is a fundamentally different dynamic than the traditional web model, in which variation in user needs and intentions created greater separation across different content markets. With the increased centrality of social media news feeds, online news sources compete head to head in a more direct way than they did on the pre-social media web.

Given the nature of contemporary news media, the end result of this ruinous (or at least near-ruinous) competition scenario need not be the demise of most (if not all) marketplace participants or the shutdown of news organizations. Rather, the organization is in jeopardy of becoming a shell of its former self, surviving on the public-good nature of media and information products, operating in the realm of parasitic journalism, and focusing its increasingly limited resources on repurposing content produced elsewhere. In this scenario, a media organization focuses on less resource-intensive content such as commentary rather than reporting, or simply publishes the types of news stories that generate the most audience attention and revenue. In these ways, the high fixed costs that traditionally lead firms in ruinous-competition scenarios to exit the market are, to some extent, circumvented in the digital media space.

A MODEL OF THE ALGORITHMIC MARKETPLACE OF IDEAS

The algorithmic marketplace of ideas represents a complex and potentially troubling scenario. This scenario is presented in figure 4.1. As represented in the figure, from a production standpoint, the algorithmic

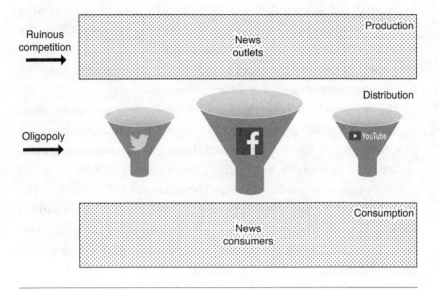

FIGURE 4.1 Structure of the Algorithmic Marketplace of Ideas

marketplace of ideas may be suffering from a case of ruinous competition. That is, we have a virtually uncountable number of news outlets (along with other content options), with tremendous variation in audience size, geographic location, ideological orientation, financial resources, and motivations. The low barriers to entry afforded by the Internet have made possible this massive number of producers participating in the algorithmic marketplace of ideas. The lack of geographic distribution barriers has facilitated more direct competition between news producers based in, or oriented around, specific geographic regions than was ever the case via traditional media. Because the public-good nature of content makes it possible to participate in this market while incurring relatively low fixed costs (by repurposing content produced elsewhere), and because the motivations for participating in this marketplace can be political instead of (or in addition to) economic, ruinous competition in the algorithmic marketplace of ideas context does not take the traditional form of all firms (or all but one) exiting the market. Rather, it takes the form of a decline in the overall quality of the products being produced to levels that essentially make them incapable of serving their intended purpose—cultivating an informed citizenry. Given the bounded rationality of news consumers, consumers are not necessarily aware of this massive deficiency in much of what is available to them. All of this contributes to a market-failure scenario.

This situation is compounded in an ironically converse manner when we consider the distribution dimension of the algorithmic marketplace of ideas. Here, as figure 4.1 illustrates, instead of ruinous competition, we have the opposite: a monopolistic/oligopolistic situation, in which relatively few social media platforms (represented by the funnels in the figure) play a dominant role in collecting and disseminating to consumers the news and information produced in the hypercompetitive production layer. Facebook plays a particularly dominant role in this distribution process, given the size of its user base, as is reflected in the model.

The 2016 Presidential Election as a Market-Failure Case Study

The preceding scenario has laid out a set of conditions that characterize the algorithmic marketplace of ideas in a way that would seem to raise red flags about potential market failure. This section seeks to take this analysis one step further by considering the possibility that the results of the 2016 presidential election represent compelling evidence of market failure in the algorithmic marketplace of ideas. Perhaps this is a way to make sense of an election outcome that baffled and blindsided most journalists, political analysts, and many voters—and that took place within a media ecosystem that had changed significantly in the four years since the 2012 presidential election. Certainly there are other, equally (and perhaps even more) plausible explanations for this outcome. The question being posed here is whether market failure in the algorithmic marketplace of ideas represents one potentially plausible explanation.

Let's start by considering what we know about how voters make decisions. Many political analysts have defined well-informed voting decisions in terms of the extent to which citizens vote in ways that reflect their best interests.[68] Economic approaches, in particular, have emphasized the role of self-interest—that voters will vote for those candidates whose policy positions are likely to benefit them the most.[69] It should be emphasized that this notion of self-interest has been conceptualized not purely in terms of narrow, short-term economic self-interest, but more broadly as well, to accommodate family and social network affinities.[70]

Not every theoretical perspective on voting behavior embraces the centrality of voter self-interest. Other theoretical perspectives emphasize the "expressive" dimension of voting,[71] or the inherent irrationality of voting that is a function of the negligible likelihood of rational voting behavior's having a meaningful impact.[72] The market-failure argument being put forth here in reference to the 2016 election does not reflect these theoretical perspectives, but is instead grounded in the self-interested-voter hypothesis. This hypothesis, it should be noted, has received strong empirical support in recent research.[73]

Similarly, a variety of competing (sometimes contradictory) perspectives have been offered to explain the results of the 2016 presidential election. Some of these explanations have emphasized the likelihood that voters were motivated primarily by informed self-interest.[74] Others have emphasized factors such as frustration with the entirety of the political system (a desire to "blow up the status quo" in protest)[75] or prejudices such as racism[76] and sexism.[77]

All of that being said, an additional possibility being put forth here is that the 2016 election represents a case of market failure in the algorithmic marketplace of ideas. Under this scenario, some segment of self-interested voters was sufficiently ill informed because of the changing conditions in the media ecosystem—conditions that reflect established causes and indicators of market failure—that they failed to vote in a way that reflected their best interests.

The underlying foundation of this assertion is the substantial body of analysis produced since the election indicating that many categories of voters who voted for Donald Trump were actually those most likely to be harmed by his policies.[78] These analyses have concluded, for instance, that elderly voters and rural voters (two demographics that were strong Trump supporters) faced the greatest economic harms from Trump policy initiatives such as the repeal of the Affordable Care Act, the abandoning of the Trans-Pacific Partnership, and dramatic cuts to Medicaid and agriculture subsidies.[79] A similar flurry of analyses arose in the wake of the unveiling of the Trump administration's tax plan.[80] As these analyses have indicated, many strong Trump supporters were in fact in those demographic categories that would fare the worst under the administration's tax plan.[81]

Such patterns of voting against apparent self-interest may reflect that the role of partisan affiliation in contemporary voting decisions has become largely disconnected from the associated policy positions of the candidates.[82] This pattern takes us back to the spiral-of-partisanship phenomenon discussed in the previous chapter.

In any case, if we accept the conclusions of these postelection analyses, and thus conclude that the 2016 election demonstrated an apparent decline in self-interested voting behavior, this could reflect the possibility that a segment of voters lacked adequate information to accurately determine the voting decision that best reflected their self-interest. In a politically oriented analysis of the operation of the marketplace of ideas, such indicators of voters' failing to vote in their best interests, possibly as a result of false or inadequate information (through the spread of fake news), can be interpreted as evidence of market failure.

Implications

Recent efforts to analyze all of the available evidence about whether fake news and disinformation disseminated over social media influenced the outcome of the 2016 election can only offer informed speculation, given the limitations in available data.[83] Renowned political communication scholar Kathleen Hall Jamieson, however, ultimately concludes that the election outcome was affected.[84] It is interesting that Facebook has launched an initiative to provide data and support for research into the impact of social media on elections,[85] but no data related to the 2016 election have been made available.[86]

Whether or not one accepts this proposed explanation for the results of the 2016 election, it still seems worth considering the ramifications of the possibility of market failure in the algorithmic marketplace of ideas. Regardless of whether one accepts that the election outcome was evidence of market failure, the analysis presented in this chapter does identify a number of characteristics of how this marketplace is structured and functions that have long been associated with market-failure scenarios in traditional product markets. The algorithmic marketplace of ideas is an environment of ruinous competition and monopoly/oligopoly operating in tandem, where consumers increasingly lack adequate information about the products they are consuming and the risks of negative externalities, such as poorly informed decision-making, appear to be growing.

While one might still resist the market-failure argument, at the very least it seems increasingly dangerous and misguided to maintain confidence in the notion that the marketplace is inherently oriented toward assuring that truth will effectively overcome falsity in the way that traditional First Amendment theory and normative conceptualizations of the marketplace of ideas would have us believe. Certainly, as chapter 3 illustrated, there have always been reasons to doubt this assumption. However, as that chapter and this chapter have shown, it may be that our media ecosystem is now evolving in such a direction that the gap between normative theory and empirical reality is no longer just a gap, but something much greater and more dangerous.

This brings us to the question of what is to be done. Are these problems that can be effectively addressed by policy makers? Can established regulatory principles and frameworks be brought to bear? Or can the platforms themselves, and the stakeholders with which they work (including users), effectively address these issues? Do they operate under the relevant professional norms and values to respond effectively to these problems? The next two chapters seek to make some headway on these questions.

CHAPTER 5

The Public-Interest Principle
in Media Governance

Past and Present

The problems that have arisen from, and are associated with, media platforms are of a type and potential magnitude that governments are increasingly exploring a variety of regulatory responses. The question of if or how a regulatory response might proceed, or whether there are alternative solutions, is particularly complicated and rife with uncertainty.

A useful starting point for addressing these questions is to revisit a concept has been relegated to the margins of the governance of our digital media sector—the public interest. The concept of the public interest has established traditions as a guidepost for media policy makers in their formulation and assessment of policies. It has emerged as a professional norm for certain categories of media organizations and professionals (particularly news outlets and journalists), and as an evaluative and rhetorical tool for civil society organizations in their assessments of media performance and their advocacy efforts on behalf of the broader public.[1] As this description indicates, the broad applicability of the public-interest concept connects with the similarly broad scope of the notion of media governance.

As noted in the introduction, media governance is broader and more inclusive than traditional notions of regulation or policy, particularly in the range of stakeholders that are seen as participating in the process. These stakeholders include not only policy makers, but also industry organizations, NGOs and civil society organizations, and even the media audience.[2] Importantly, from a governance perspective, "these actors are addressed as equal partners in shaping and implementing public policies and regulations."[3] Put simply, media governance can best be encapsulated as regulatory deliberations, processes, and outcomes that take place both within and beyond the state.

The governance concept has become increasingly prominent in the discourse surrounding digital media.[4] It has emerged as a reflection of, and response to, the distinctive characteristics of the Internet as a medium in which (a) national legal and regulatory jurisdictions are more difficult to define and enforce;[5] (b) the very origins of the technology and how it operates reflect a somewhat decentralized, interconnected, collectivist undertaking of governmental, commercial, and nonprofit stakeholders; and (c) the traditional rationales for government regulation often lack clear applicability and relevance. This third point is particularly relevant to this chapter.

While the public-interest concept has, for a variety of reasons, been diminished and marginalized within the context of the governance of social media platforms. I will make the case that the public-interest principle is just as relevant—if not more so—to today's digital media environment. As media scholar Tarleton Gillespie has noted, "like the television networks and trade publishers before them," new media platforms such as Facebook and Twitter are "increasingly facing questions about their responsibilities: to their users, to key constituencies who depend on the public discourse they host, *and to broader notions of the public interest*."[6]

I begin with a brief introduction to the public-interest principle and its traditional role in media governance. I then explain how and why the public-interest principle has been diminished and marginalized within the digital media realm in general, and within the context of social media governance in particular. Finally, I will illustrate some of the specific repercussions that make clear the need for a more robust public-interest framework for social media governance.

Revisiting the Public Interest

The public-interest principle has a long, contested, and sometimes con-voluted history in the realm of media governance. One of the defining characteristics of the concept is the extent to which its meaning has often been perceived as unclear, or "vague to the point of meaninglessness."[7] With this in mind, a useful starting point for this (re-) introduction is to review how the principle has been defined and put into practice both in the operation of media organizations (the public interest as *institutional imperative*) and in the realm of media regulation (the public interest as *regulatory mandate*).

THE PUBLIC INTEREST AS INSTITUTIONAL IMPERATIVE

Let's first consider the public interest as a guiding principle within the operation of media outlets—particularly news organizations. As has been well documented, the institution of journalism (regardless of the technology through which news is disseminated) is infused with an eth-ical obligation to serve the public interest.[8] Consequently, the various sectors of the news media have traditionally maintained self-designed and self-imposed behavioral codes that embody the public-interest principle to varying degrees.[9] For instance, many of the components of the press's public-interest obligations are reflected in Article I (titled "Responsibility") of the Statement of Principles of the American Society of Newspaper Editors:

> The primary purpose of gathering and distributing news and opinion is to serve the general welfare by informing the people and enabling them to make judgments on the issues of the time. . . . The American press was made free not just to inform or just to serve as a forum for debate but also to bring an independent scrutiny to bear on the forces of power in society, including the conduct of official power at all levels of government.[10]

This statement represents a clear articulation of the public service objectives of aiding citizens in their decision-making and protecting them against governmental abuses of power. We find similar values reflected in the preamble to the Code of Ethics of the Society of Professional Journalists, which states "that public enlightenment is the forerunner of justice and the foundation of democracy."[11] Here, the tie between the activities of the press and the effective functioning of the democratic process is made even more explicit.

These statements exemplify the way public-interest values are intended to guide news organizations (i.e., the operational level). How are the values expressed in these behavioral codes actually applied? If we look, for instance, at the Statement of Principles of the American Society of Newspaper Editors, we find a number of specific behavioral guidelines, including independence, truth and accuracy, and impartiality.[12] Comparable behavioral obligations are also outlined in the codes of ethics of the Society of Professional Journalists[13] and the Radio Television Digital News Association.[14] Explicit in all of these codes are not only sets of values, but also the appropriate behaviors for maximizing the extent to which the news media serve the political and cultural needs of media users.

THE PUBLIC INTEREST AS INSTITUTIONAL IMPERATIVE FOR SOCIAL MEDIA

Can the public interest as institutional imperative be effective within the specific context of social media platforms? Presently, the key theme that emerges is a diminishment in the scope of the public-interest principle. Specifically, a fairly narrow, individualist model of the public interest has taken hold. Under this formulation, social media platforms primarily provide an enabling environment in which individual responsibility and autonomy can be realized in relation to the production, dissemination, and consumption of news and information. Missing here are any broader, explicitly articulated institutional norms and values that guide these platforms, along the lines of those articulated by the various professional associations operating in the journalism field.

In many ways, the dynamics of social media design and usage have fundamentally been about this transfer of responsibility to individual media users. Within the context of social media, individual media users—working in conjunction with content recommendation algorithms—serve a more significant gatekeeping function for their social network than is the case in the traditional media realm.[15] Through social media platforms, individuals are building, maintaining, and (potentially) helping to inform social networks of much larger scale than typically could be achieved through traditional secondary gatekeeping processes such as word of mouth. In other words, individuals are increasingly performing the filtering and mediating, taking on roles that are integral to the practice of journalism, and are doing so on a more expansive scale.[16] Individuals have always possessed this capability to some extent, through traditional means of secondary gatekeeping such as word of mouth. However, within the context of social media platforms, the flow of news and information is much more dependent upon the judgments and subsequent actions (liking, sharing, retweeting, etc.) of the individual users of these platforms (see chapter 2).

This contrast with traditional news media reflects the nature of platforms and how they operate. However, it also reflects something of a public-interest vacuum at the institutional level that characterizes how these platforms have been designed and how many social media companies have operated. As Facebook, for instance, notes in its very brief mission statement, the platform's mission is to "give people the power to build community and bring the world closer together."[17] This statement is a modification (made in 2017) of the previous, less directed mission statement, to "give people the power to share." In both, the focus is clearly on individual empowerment, but in the postelection revised version we see a narrowing in terms of the types of activities the platform is seeking to empower. Twitter's similarly brief mission statement focuses on giving "everyone the power to create and share ideas and information."[18] The overarching goal, clearly, has been to empower individual users; the service of any broader public interest must emerge from them.

This formulation reflects the valorization and empowerment of the individual media user that has been such a prominent theme in the discourse of Silicon Valley, and social media in particular.[19] The extent to which social media platforms empower individuals or communities emerged as a powerful frame of reference, particularly in the aftermath of the Arab Spring, in which social media platforms were being credited with facilitating successful revolutions.[20] Those who valorized the individual media user in this way also tended to have tremendous faith in these users (whether individually or in the aggregate) and their ability to serve the public interest.[21]

Social media companies built on these perceptions to project themselves as tools for empowering individual autonomy.[22] Greg Marra, the Facebook engineer who led the coding for the platform's News Feed, told the *New York Times* in 2014: "We try to explicitly view ourselves as not editors. . . . We don't want to have editorial judgment over the content that's in your feed. You've made your friends, you've connected to the pages that you want to connect to and *you're the best decider for the things that you care about*" (emphasis added).[23] This description at best understates the role that algorithms play in the dissemination and consumption of news. At worst it misrepresents the true power dynamics between social media platforms and users in terms of the distribution of editorial authority. Geert Lovink has argued in his critique of social media that we are in a "paradoxical era of *hyped up individualism* that results precisely in the algorithmic outsourcing of the self" (emphasis added).[24]

Users, however, have tended to cling to this misrepresentation. As Jeff Hancock, co-author of Facebook's controversial "emotional contagion" study (discussed in chapter 4) observed, much of the negative reaction to the study reflected the fact that many users had "no sense that the news feed [was] anything other than an objective window into their social world."[25] This observation was supported by research in 2015 that found that more than 60 percent of study participants were unaware that Facebook engaged in any kind of curation/filtering of their news feeds.[26] A more recent (2017) study of college students (whom we expect to have above average digital media literacy) found that only 24 percent of respondents were aware that Facebook prioritizes certain posts and hides others.[27]

Thus, through the discourse of individual autonomy and the inherently obscured nature of algorithmic editorial authority, the individualist notion of the public interest took hold and has, to this point, persisted in the realm of social media governance. This situation raised the question, as one critic of Facebook's emotional contagion study suggested, "Is there any room for a public interest concern, like for journalism?"[28]

This privileging of individual choice and empowerment has affected the approach that social media platforms have taken to preventing the spread of fake news. The fact that these platforms have implemented a variety of initiatives to combat the dissemination of fake news certainly represents the adoption of a stronger public-interest orientation than we saw before the 2016 election. However, in many aspects of implementation, the strong individualist orientation persists.

One of the most aggressive aspects of Facebook's response to the fake news problem has been to adopt a system in which the evaluations of users as to the trustworthiness of individual sources plays a prominent role in determining whether individual news sources feature in users' news feeds. According to Mark Zuckerberg, the key challenge was the development of an objective system of assessing trustworthiness.[29] Among the various options available to them, the company "decided that having the community determine which sources are broadly trusted would be most objective."[30] The system has been described as follows: As part of its regular user surveys, Facebook asks users whether they are familiar with individual news sources and whether they trust those sources. Individuals who are not familiar with a source are eliminated from the sample of users used to determine the overall trustworthiness of the source. Thus, "the output is a ratio of those who trust the source to those who are familiar with it."[31]

In terms of the specific methodological approach, it seems reasonable to ask whether this approach can succeed in its intended goal, which is presumably to weed out fake news as much as possible. The reliance on self-reported familiarity and trustworthiness raises some concerns. The approach, as described, applies the aggregate trustworthiness score to everyone's news feed. That is, your news feed will not more fully reflect the sources that you (or your social network) have identified as trustworthy. Rather, the system will "shift the balance of news you see towards sources that are determined to be trusted by the community."[32]

Obviously, this approach puts those individuals selected to take part in the surveys in an incredibly influential position—not unlike the way that those selected by the Nielsen Company to be part of its television audience measurement panel play an incredibly influential role in determining the fate of individual television programs. Just as with audience measurement, the dynamics of how this panel of Facebook users is constructed becomes incredibly important; and an inherently vulnerable point of critique.[33]

How big is it? According to a 2016 report, Facebook's "feed quality panel" was only about a thousand people.[34] What's the response rate to invitations to take part in the panel surveys? Is the sample demographically and geographically representative of the population of Facebook users? Initially, the feed quality panel participants were all in Knoxville, Tennessee.[35] Obviously, proper geographic representation is important when a panel is being used to evaluate the trustworthiness of the nation's news sources. Adam Mosseri, then head of Facebook's News Feed (now head of Instagram), described the survey that serves as the basis for this evaluation as coming from a "diverse and representative sample of people using Facebook across the U.S.,"[36] but further details have not been forthcoming. This sample will also need to be protected from coercion and manipulation efforts by third parties, just as Nielsen has had to police its samples to assure participants are not acting on behalf of any vested interests they might have in specific programs or programmers.

One also cannot help but wonder what could happen to mainstream news outlets, such as the *New York Times*, CNN, and the *Washington Post*, that have become the focus of President Trump's nonstop assault on the press. This dynamic would seem to assure that a substantial component of any Facebook user sample will consider themselves very familiar with these sources (even if they do not use them), and will label them as untrustworthy. In contrast, intensely partisan sources, with their smaller, ideologically homogenous user bases, are likely to demonstrate a stronger correlation between familiarity and trustworthiness.[37]

"Familiarity"—especially of the self-reported variety—would seem potentially problematic as a baseline for eligibility for assessing trustworthiness. One could certainly imagine a scenario in which some outlets are affected very differently than others, in ways that might not correspond with any kind of reasoned evaluation of those outlets' trustworthiness. Readers who consume a steady diet of partisan reporting bashing CNN as fake news, for instance, may feel sufficiently familiar with CNN to offer an assessment of its trustworthiness without ever actually consuming its reporting.

The broader philosophy reflected in Facebook's approach to evaluating trustworthiness fits squarely within the individualist approach to the public interest. Again, we can see the ways in which Facebook places tremendous faith—and responsibility—in the hands of individual social media users. These users must essentially make the determination as to which news outlets are serving the public interest. In this scenario, the public interest is being conceptualized according to one classic interpretation—as the aggregation of individual interests.[38]

The bottom line is that a user base that has already become more politically polarized than at any point in recent history, in part because of the continually evolving dynamics of media fragmentation and personalization, seems a questionable authority to rely upon to make determinations as to the trustworthiness of individual news sources. The fact that Facebook began hiring "news credibility specialists" within a few months after launching this program[39] is perhaps an indication that relying upon individual community members to effectively identify trustworthy news sources proved problematic.

All of this being said, there have been some initial efforts to establish and potentially institutionalize a stronger, more principles-based public-interest orientation in the digital media realm. Academic and professional organizations such as Fairness, Accountability, and Transparency in Machine Learning (FATML) and the Association for Computing Machinery (ACM) have developed and released statements of principles related to algorithmic accountability and transparency. FATML's statement includes as core principles responsibility, explainability, accuracy, auditability, and fairness.[40] The ACM's statement of principles also includes auditability, along with awareness (of possible biases), accountability, explanation, and access and redress.[41]

In late 2016, a collection of companies, including Facebook, Google, and IBM, formed an industry consortium called the Partnership on AI, which has begun to formulate broad tenets around fairness, trustworthiness, accountability, and transparency.[42] It remains to be seen whether these principles become institutionalized values that meaningfully guide the behavior of social media platforms and the way that algorithms are created and implemented.[43]

THE PUBLIC INTEREST AS REGULATORY MANDATE

Now we turn to the public interest as a regulatory mandate that guides the decision-making of policy makers and, consequently, the behavior of media organizations. The public interest as regulatory mandate supplements the public interest as institutional imperative, translating the principles of public service and commitment to the democratic process into regulatory policies and government-imposed requirements.[44]

During the seventy-plus-year history of the Federal Communications Commission and its predecessor, the Federal Radio Commission, specific sets of guiding principles have been associated with the public-interest principle. These began to take shape as early as 1928, and over the years, five key components of the public interest emerged: (1) balance of opposing viewpoints; (2) heterogeneity of interests; (3) dynamism, in terms of technology, the economy, and the interests of stakeholders; (4) localism; and (5) diversity, in terms of programming, services, and ownership.[45]

This is not to say that, historically, there has been strong and stable consensus in the regulatory realm as to how to operationalize or apply the public-interest principle. Rather, the evolving, contested meaning of the public-interest standard has been one of the defining characteristics of media regulation and policy in the United States.[46] Consider, for instance, the well-known "marketplace" approach to the public interest typically associated with Reagan-era FCC chairman Mark Fowler:

Communications policy should be directed toward maximizing the services the public desires. Instead of defining public demand and specifying categories of programming to serve this demand, the Commission should rely on the broadcasters' ability to determine the wants of their audiences through the normal mechanisms of the marketplace. The public's interest, then, defines the public interest.[47]

This conceptualization of the public interest takes a majoritarian approach—one in which market forces, rather than a coherent scheme of values, dictate what is in the public interest. In contrast, adherents of the "trustee" approach to the public interest[48] advocate placing policy makers in the position of identifying and defining specific values and then establishing specific criteria for media organizations to meet in pursuit of those values.

This is where the notion of public-interest obligations comes into play. These are affirmative requirements that regulated media outlets must meet. For instance, broadcast television stations have had to provide minimum levels of educational children's programming. Cable and broadcast stations have had to make ad time available to political candidates at discounted rates. At one point, broadcast and cable channels had to provide balanced coverage of controversial issues of public importance (the well-known Fairness Doctrine; see chapter 3). The history of U.S. media regulation is filled with many other examples of public-interest obligations that have come and gone.[49]

As might be expected, differences between the marketplace and trustee approaches become particularly pronounced at the level of application, where the key question involves what specific regulatory requirements to impose in the name of the values associated with the public interest. This applicational component of the public interest as a regulatory mandate is in a nearly constant state of flux, not only because of changes in the hierarchy of values held by different administrations, but also because of changes in the media environment and regulators' perceptions of how best to pursue those values.[50] This is well illustrated by the FCC's sudden reversal on the issue of network neutrality. In 2016, the FCC voted to impose network neutrality regulations on Internet service providers.[51] In 2018, a new FCC administration eliminated those regulations. And yet, perhaps not surprisingly, both the adoption and the elimination of the net neutrality regulations were couched in public-interest rhetoric.[52]

TECHNOLOGICAL PARTICULARISM
AND THE PUBLIC INTEREST

The nature and specifics of the public-interest regulatory framework applied to legacy media has varied as a function of the technological characteristics of each medium. For instance, broadcast radio and television, given their use of publicly owned and allocated broadcast spectrum, have been subjected to more intensive FCC-imposed public-interest regulations and obligations than other electronic media, such as cable television, mobile, or direct broadcast satellite (DBS), which utilize a different (or differently allocated) transmission infrastructure. However, even these media have been subject to a variety of public-interest-motivated FCC regulations premised on different, sometimes intersecting, regulatory rationales. And, of course, all of this stands in stark contrast to the print media, which operate almost completely outside of the U.S. framework for media regulation. We call this *technological particularism*, meaning that the distinctive characteristics of individual communications technologies serve as the basis for the construction of distinct regulatory models for each technology.

Motivations Versus Rationales in Media Regulation

Given the United States' strong First Amendment tradition, compelling public-interest-based motivations to apply regulatory oversight to the media must be grounded in compelling technologically derived rationales capable of overcoming assertions that any regulatory oversight represents an infringement on the First Amendment rights of media organizations. What may seem on the surface like a semantic distinction between motivations and rationales is, in many ways, key to understanding the current disconnect between digital media and the public interest.

Within the context of this analysis, the term *motivations* refers to the underlying needs and objectives that create the impetus for the imposition of a public-interest regulatory framework. In the United States, these motivations have taken the form of core (and often contested) public-interest principles such as diversity, localism, competition, and universal service that are generally seen as facilitating the effective functioning of the democratic process.[53] They have also included less politically oriented concerns such as protecting children from adult content.

The term *rationales* refers to the way that the pursuit of these objectives is justified when confronted with a First Amendment tradition that, when interpreted strictly, stands in opposition to any government intervention into the media sector. These technologically derived rationales are built on the premise that characteristics of certain media technologies or services compel public-interest oversight that, in some instances, necessarily infringes on the speech rights of media organizations. The key point here is that public-interest-minded motivations are, on their own, insufficient to justify regulatory interventions. There must be a distinctive characteristic of the technology that can justify such interventions, well intentioned as they might be.

The well-known, and widely criticized, spectrum-scarcity rationale provides a useful illustration of the distinction between the motivations and rationales for media regulation. According to the scarcity rationale, because there is insufficient broadcast spectrum to accommodate everyone wishing to broadcast, it is necessary for the government to provide regulatory intervention. The scarcity rationale is well articulated in the Supreme Court's response to an early (1943) challenge to the FCC's authority to regulate media ownership. In *NBC v. United States*, in which the Court heard NBC's challenge to an FCC order that the company divest itself of one of its national broadcast networks, the Court noted "certain basic facts about radio as a means of communication—its facilities are limited; they are not available to all who may wish to use them; the radio spectrum simply is not large enough to accommodate everybody. There is a fixed natural limitation upon the number of stations that can operate without interfering with one another."[54]

This spectrum scarcity allowed the FCC to be "more than a kind of traffic officer of the airwaves," but to also play a role in "determining the composition of . . . traffic."[55] In this way, the scarcity of the broadcast spectrum became the primary justification upon which the entire system of broadcast regulation—the regulatory model that allows for the greatest degree of public-interest oversight over the structure and behavior of media companies—has been built. The spectrum-scarcity rationale has persisted despite the fact that it is riddled with logical flaws. As economists have noted, for instance, all goods are scarce to some extent.[56] Certainly, when a valuable good is being given away (as is the case with broadcast spectrum), the demand is likely going to exceed the supply. Other critiques have noted that, as other communications infrastructures have developed (cable, Internet, etc.), it is difficult to make the argument that the logic of the scarcity rationale still holds up at all.

Why, then, has such a flawed rationale persisted? The answer may lie in the relationship between regulatory rationales and motivations. According to many accounts, spectrum scarcity was not the reason for government regulation of broadcasting, only the *rationale* that provided a justification capable of withstanding First Amendment scrutiny.[57] Media economist Eli Noam, for instance, counters the conventional wisdom that spectrum scarcity provided the federal government with the mechanism to regulate broadcasting. According to Noam:

> the opposite was the case. TV spectrum was scarce because governments chose to make it so, by allocating frequencies only grudgingly. One reason was the fear of the power of private broadcasting over politics and culture. State controlled radio had played a major role in the internal and external propaganda efforts before and during the Second World War and in the emerging Cold War. The extension of such power to private parties was seen as quite dangerous.[58]

According to Noam, this situation illustrates the reality that "each society has its concerns, problems, issues, traditions and priorities. The main purpose of media regulation is to advance such goals. . . . It seems unlikely that societies will simply give up on their societal priorities just because the . . . information now takes a different path, or is encoded in a different way."[59]

Ultimately, specific and evolving social and political concerns represent the true motivations for media regulation, with the rationales providing the technologically derived justifications for acting on these motivations. These motivations may or may not be affected by technological change, but the technologically grounded rationales likely will be. Thus, Noam concludes, "none of these objectives will vanish"[60] when the devices or infrastructure used to send and receive news and information change. Nor should they.

Like the scarcity rationale, a number of other regulatory rationales are determined by technological characteristics. There have been few, if any, efforts at this point to apply these rationales to the social media context. For this reason, it is worth briefly reviewing each of these rationales, and then considering whether any of them may be applicable to social media.

The extent to which a communications technology relies upon a *public resource* has served as a distinct regulatory rationale.[61] Often this rationale is linked with the scarcity rationale (i.e., broadcasters utilize a "scarce public resource"). In this way, the scarcity and public-resource rationales operate hand in hand. However, it is important to consider the public-resource rationale separately, because compelling arguments can be—and have been—made that public ownership of the airwaves justifies the imposition of a public-interest regulatory framework, independent of whether the public resource is uniquely scarce.[62] Obviously, broadcasting meets this public-resource criterion; as do cable television systems, which require access to public rights-of-way (telephone poles, public land for laying cable). Such access has served as the grounds for a quid pro quo regulatory model. Broadcasters have been required to abide by a variety of public-interest obligations in exchange for their use of the spectrum. It should be noted that, unlike mobile telecommunications service providers, broadcasters have not purchased their spectrum via auction (and thus have no claims of property rights); it is provided to them essentially for free through the licensing process. Similarly, cable systems have been required to provide channels dedicated to public, educational, and government programming in exchange for access to the public rights-of-way necessary for building and maintaining a cable system.[63]

Pervasiveness is another technologically derived regulatory rationale that has been brought to bear in the media sector. Certain media (broadcasting and cable in particular)[64] have been deemed "uniquely pervasive" in terms of the ease with which content can be accessed (even unintentionally) and the reach they can achieve. Pervasiveness has therefore provided the logical foundation for regulatory interventions such as restrictions on indecent programming.[65] Congress made a failed effort to extend the pervasiveness rationale to the Internet back in the mid-1990s, when it attempted to restrict the dissemination of adult content online through the Communications Decency Act.[66] In this case, however, the Supreme Court concluded that the Internet failed to meet the pervasiveness standard of broadcast or cable television, noting that "the receipt of information on the Internet requires a series of affirmative steps more deliberate and directed than merely turning a dial" and that "the Internet is not as 'invasive' as radio or television."[67] If, after reading this passage, you're still unclear why broadcasting and cable are uniquely pervasive and the web and social media are not, then you are beginning to understand the tenuous, ambiguous nature of regulatory rationales in the media sector.

Regulatory interventions have also been based on the rationale that some technologies are *reasonably ancillary* to other regulated technologies. Specifically, certain cable television regulations have been enacted because cable has traditionally played an intermediary role in the delivery of broadcast television signals. According to this perspective, cable is sufficiently "ancillary" to broadcasting that the regulatory authority already established for broadcasting can, to some extent, be extended to cable.[68] This rationale was first established in a Supreme Court decision that focused on whether the FCC had the authority to regulate cable television,[69] a technology that the FCC had previously determined could not be classified as either common carriers or broadcasters[70]— the two technology categories over which FCC jurisdiction had been established. Subsequently, the FCC proposed regulations that, among other things, prohibited cable systems from importing out-of-market broadcast signals.[71] These regulations sought to protect local broadcast stations and thus reflected the commission's long-standing objective of fostering localism.[72] When the Supreme Court considered the challenge to the FCC's authority to impose such regulations, it upheld the FCC's authority, in part on the basis that such authority was "reasonably ancillary to the effective performance of the Commission's various responsibilities for the regulation of television broadcasting."[73]

THE PUBLIC INTEREST AS REGULATORY
MANDATE FOR SOCIAL MEDIA

The key point in reviewing these regulatory rationales has been to illustrate how particular technological characteristics have provided the basis for regulatory interventions. To the extent that these rationales do not apply—or have not yet been attempted to be applied—to the realm of social media, public-interest regulatory frameworks remain sidelined. In some cases, however, there is some potential for traditional regulatory rationales to translate to the new context.

Consider, for instance, the public-resource rationale. As noted previously, the fact that certain components of the spectrum belong to the public has provided a key rationale for imposing a public-interest regulatory framework on broadcasters. Social media platforms do not utilize spectrum. However, they have built their business model upon monetizing large aggregations of user data. Many privacy advocates have argued that our user data should be thought of as our property— an argument that was revitalized to some extent in the wake of the Cambridge Analytica scandal. However, this perspective has never really taken hold in the United States, in terms of either policy or industry practice.[74] But building on this perspective, perhaps another way to think about aggregate user data is not as private property but as public property. Perhaps aggregations of user data (such as those utilized by social media platforms) should be thought of as a public resource, akin to spectrum.

Such an argument echoes the core premise of the scarcity rationale—that the public "owns" the airwaves, and this public ownership confers a certain amount of public-interest regulatory authority. If we think about aggregations of user data in a similar vein—if the public has some ownership stake in their user data—the large-scale aggregations of data accumulated by social media platforms can perhaps be seen as representing a similar collective public resource, thereby triggering public-interest regulatory oversight.

This perspective represents a shift from the traditional policy arguments around user data, which tend to focus on the need for limitations on data gathering and sharing, and granting users greater control over the data that are gathered and how they are used. Legal scholar Jack Balkin, for instance, has compellingly argued that digital platforms should be categorized as *information fiduciaries*—individuals or organizations that deal in information and thus are required by law to handle that information in a responsible manner (think, for instance, of doctors and lawyers).[75] A data-as-public-resource argument does not necessarily conflict with this argument. Rather, it builds upon it by creating a rational basis for the imposition of public-interest obligations on platforms that rely on the gathering and monetizing of large aggregations of user data for their business model. These obligations could operate alongside any privacy regulations directed at the gathering and use of data. When large aggregations of user data become the lifeblood of a platform's business model, then this information-fiduciary status could expand into a broader set of social responsibilities.

There would similarly seem to be some potential applicability of the pervasiveness rationale to the social media context. As noted previously, in the late 1990s the Supreme Court rejected efforts by Congress to apply the pervasiveness rationale to the Internet. However, much has changed in terms of how people go online, given the demise of the dial-up interface, the prevalence of always-connected mobile access, and the "push" dynamic that distinguishes social media platforms from the web as a whole. Given these characteristics, it would seem that social media platforms have become as uniquely pervasive as television or radio. When we consider that a user can suddenly, unexpectedly, and involuntarily encounter something as disturbing as a live-streamed murder or suicide in one's news feed in very much the same way that one can unexpectedly be exposed to foul language on the radio, it does seem that a compelling case for pervasiveness could be made.

The reasonably ancillary rationale may have relevance in the social media context as well. Social media platforms operate in an ancillary relationship to other regulated media, given the extent to which they increasingly serve as the means by which content from regulated sectors reaches audiences. If your social media news feed contains video from your local broadcast stations, for example, it is operating in a way that parallels how cable became an increasingly important means of accessing those stations as cable diffused throughout the 1970s and 1980s. Cable was deemed reasonably ancillary to broadcast because it evolved into an important distribution platform for broadcast programming. As social media platforms have evolved into a mechanism through which traditional media distribute their content, a similar ancillary relationship has developed.

IMPLICATIONS

To date, policy makers have not applied any government-articulated and -implemented notions of the public interest from previous generations of electronic media to social media platforms and organizations. The danger here is that as these platforms continue to grow, evolve, and possibly become an increasingly dominant part of the media ecosystem, the values, principles, and objectives that motivate regulation will apply to an ever-shrinking proportion of that ecosystem. In the past, when a new communications technology arrived, established regulatory models were, to some extent, transferred to that new technology. For instance, while television represented, in many ways, a fairly substantial departure from radio, the fact that television also relied on the broadcast spectrum meant that policy makers transferred the entire regulatory framework that had been developed for radio to television. Something similar happened (though to a lesser degree) when cable television was introduced.

In this case, as noted previously, the rationale of cable as "ancillary" to broadcast television meant that policy makers were able to transfer much—though not all—of the broadcast television/radio regulatory framework to cable.

The situation we are facing today has yet to offer any of this continuity. If the reasons (i.e., motivations) for government regulation of media apply in this context, but the rationales upon which regulations are imposed do not, then we are faced with a fundamental disconnect between the need for, and the ability to implement, media regulation and policy. More concretely, if the structure and performance of these new media platforms/institutions evolve in ways that run counter to the regulatory objectives that have governed the structure and performance of established media, but no technological rationale for addressing these problems exists, then we have a scenario in which government is powerless to solve compelling communications policy problems.

The Merger of AT&T and Time Warner

To illustrate the nature and consequences of this disconnect, it is worth considering a recently approved media merger.[76] In October 2016, telecommunications giant AT&T, the leading provider of wireless, broadband, and pay TV services in the United States, announced plans to acquire Time Warner, at the time the third largest media conglomerate in the world. Time Warner owned a major movie and television studio, and was also one of the largest owners of cable networks in the United States, with holdings that included such popular networks as HBO, CNN, TNT, and TBS.

There is certainly a long history of such media megamergers in the United States, especially as media ownership regulations have been steadily relaxed over the past forty years.[77] What is unique about this particular media merger, however, is that it took place without review and approval by the Federal Communications Commission, which oversees many of the industry sectors in which these two firms operate and has the responsibility for conducting a public-interest-focused analysis of proposed media mergers.

In the United States, proposed media mergers undergo an assessment by the Justice Department or the Federal Trade Commission to determine the likely effects of the proposed merger on competition in the marketplace. In addition, proposed media mergers undergo a separate public-interest review by the Federal Communications Commission.[78] This separate review takes into consideration not only the economic effects of the proposed merger, but also any relevant noneconomic considerations, such as its likely social or political impact. This is where established policy concerns such as diversity of sources and viewpoints, localism, and media users' ability to access information come into play. It is in this review that a robust notion of the public interest is supposed to be brought to bear, in which the impact of the proposed merger is considered not only in terms of the economic marketplace, but also in terms of the marketplace of ideas.

However, the case of the AT&T–Time Warner merger highlighted an important loophole in this system. To understand this loophole, it is important to recognize that the FCC's authority to engage in this public-interest standard of review is derived from the agency's authority to approve the transfer of broadcast licenses.[79] Because the FCC oversees the allocation and renewal of broadcast licenses (which are a scarce public resource), the agency must approve any transfers that arise when one firm acquires another. If no broadcast licenses are changing hands in a proposed media merger, then no FCC-led public-interest review takes place.

The AT&T–Time Warner merger presented just such a scenario. Despite being one of the world's largest media conglomerates, at the time the merger was proposed, Time Warner owned only one broadcast television station.[80] This situation led some analysts to speculate that if the company were to sell off that station, then the FCC would have no authority to impose a public-interest standard of review on the proposed merger, and the merger would only be subject to analysis of its effects on competition.[81] As predicted, Time Warner sold its one television station, relieving itself of its only terrestrial broadcast license;[82] and the FCC chairman Ajit Pai subsequently stated that, without the presence of such a license, the commission lacked the legal authority to review the merger.[83]

This scenario helps to highlight the growing disconnect between the public interest as a regulatory standard in the media sector and the very nature of the media sector toward which this standard is intended to be applied, as the media environment becomes increasingly digitized and broadcasting becomes a less central component of the ecosystem as a whole. The fact that a merger as large, wide-ranging, and impactful as that of AT&T and Time Warner can completely circumvent the public-interest standard of merger review on the basis of the absence of broadcast licenses raises questions about the adequacy of the regulatory rationales on which the public-interest standard of review is based. As this example illustrates, we have a regulatory system that is built upon—and justified by—the characteristics of an increasingly irrelevant communications technology.

The implications of this scenario for our discussion of social media and the public interest should be clear. The public-interest standard has no relevance for social media platforms, which are now arguably the most powerful intermediaries in the production, distribution, and consumption of news and information. A potential merger between Facebook and Twitter, for example, should trigger a degree of regulatory scrutiny that goes beyond economic effects of the proposed merger and considers the social and political implications. And this issue extends beyond the context of media mergers. More broadly, the fact that the public-interest standard has no regulatory foothold in either the structure or behavior of social media platforms means that we have a growing disconnect between regulatory motivations and rationales that needs to be addressed. This situation reinforces the dynamic described in the introduction to this book, in which companies that fundamentally are media companies are treated as if they are not.

PUBLIC-INTEREST OBLIGATIONS FOR SOCIAL MEDIA?

It is worth considering some of the contexts in which these unregulated social media platforms engage in activities that reflect regulatory concerns that have traditionally characterized electronic media.

These instances have become frequent enough that they have begun to raise questions about whether this regulatory status quo is appropriate. Media scholars Mike Ananny and Tarleton Gillespie label these instances "public shocks," which they describe as "public moments that interrupt the functioning and governance of these ostensibly private platforms, by suddenly highlighting a platform's infrastructural qualities and call it to account for its public implications. These shocks sometimes give rise to a cycle of public indignation and regulatory pushback that produces critical—but often unsatisfying and insufficient—exceptions made by the platform."[84]

The list of such "public shocks" is rapidly accumulating, and includes such high-profile instances as Facebook's conducting of "emotional contagion" research on users of its platform; the dramatic discrepancy across Facebook and Twitter in the reporting of the violence taking place in Ferguson, Missouri; the live-streaming on Facebook of the police shooting of Philando Castile; revelations that Facebook's advertising interface could be used to target anti-Semitic audiences; accusations of the suppression of conservative news stories on Facebook; the subsequent indications that fake news ran rampant across platforms such as Facebook, Twitter, and YouTube, and that these platforms passively facilitated the dissemination of fake news; the apparent role of foreign agents in using these platforms to disseminate both fake news and targeted political advertisements in their efforts to influence the outcome of the 2016 U.S. presidential election; and the revelations about the mishandling of user data by Facebook and Cambridge Analytica.[85] These "public shocks" have produced moments of attention to the issue of the governance of social media platforms, and produced responses by these platforms. The public shocks have also accumulated to such an extent that policy makers have begun to examine whether existing governance mechanisms are adequate and/or in need of substantive revision (as reflected in the many congressional hearings that took place in 2017, 2018, and 2019.)

Not all of these "public shocks" necessarily merit regulatory intervention. Nor would they all have been prevented had these digital media platforms operated under a public-interest regulatory framework reflective of other electronic media. In the aggregate, however, they do raise questions about if and how the notion of the public interest is being—or should be—applied within the context of social media. Drilling down into some of these occurrences illustrates specific disconnects between existing regulatory and legal structures directed at legacy electronic media and the operation and evolving function of these digital media platforms.

Consider, for instance, the live-streaming on Facebook of violent acts such as murders and suicides. This has happened on a number of occasions. Violent expressions of hate speech have also become prominent on social media platforms. Facebook has internal guidelines and procedures for policing its platform for such content and preventing its dissemination—despite the fact, it should be noted, that they are under no legal obligation (at least in the United States) to do so. Indeed, Facebook's own content filtering extends well beyond violence and hate speech, addressing other areas such as nudity and explicit sex.[86] From this standpoint, speakers on Facebook operate under a content regulatory model (applied by Facebook) that is more akin to the regulatory model that the FCC applies to broadcasting (with its various intrusions on speakers' free speech rights in the name of protecting children and other vulnerable groups from harmful or adult content).

However, the exact nature of this oversight and its associated procedures has been quite opaque, and when aspects of the process have been made public, the implications have been troubling. It was revealed, for instance, that Facebook's content-moderation guidelines contained a number of aspects that can be construed as "favor[ing] elites and governments over grassroots activists and racial minorities."[87] For instance:

> One document trains content reviewers on how to apply the company's global hate speech algorithm. The slide identifies three groups: female drivers, black children and white men. It asks: Which group is protected from hate speech? The correct answer: white men.
>
> The reason is that Facebook deletes curses, slurs, calls for violence and several other types of attacks only when they are directed at "protected categories"—based on race, sex, gender identity, religious affiliation, national origin, ethnicity, sexual orientation and serious disability/

disease. It gives users broader latitude when they write about "subsets" of protected categories. White men are considered a group because both traits are protected, while female drivers and black children, like radicalized Muslims, are subsets, because one of their characteristics is not protected.[88]

These instances raise questions about whether the self-governance framework for potentially harmful and offensive content on social media is adequate. Outside of the United States, we have begun to see moves toward more direct government oversight, with Germany, for instance, passing legislation that imposes fines on social media platforms that fail to take down posts that meet the government's standards of hate speech within a specified period of time.[89]

These actions by social media platforms to police their content—and their apparent shortcomings and biases in doing so—highlight what could be seen as a disconnect between established regulatory motivations and existing regulatory authority. Clearly, there is a perceived need to impose the kind of adult/harmful content restrictions that have characterized legacy electronic media in this newer media context, as evidenced by the fact that these platforms are voluntarily taking on this responsibility, though perhaps in ways that sometimes run counter to the public interest. Unless we see efforts to apply a regulatory rationale such as pervasiveness to the Internet (or to social media in particular), we are again faced with a disconnect between compelling motivations for regulatory intervention and access to effective regulatory rationales. I am not arguing that a government-imposed regulatory framework is necessarily the most appropriate and viable solution to the problem of the dissemination of violence and hate speech via social media; rather, I am trying to illustrate that this is another situation in which *if* such action were deemed to be desirable, no established regulatory rationale exists for justifying taking such action.

It is also worth considering the potential disconnect between regulatory motivations and rationales in relation to what became perhaps the defining issue of the 2016 presidential election—the prominence and potential impact of fake news. Within traditional media contexts, there are some established (though limited) legal and regulatory frameworks in place intended to distinguish between true and false news and information, and at least discourage the production and dissemination of falsity. In social media, so far, there are none.

First, as was noted in chapter 3, in the United States, media outlets are subject to libel laws that prohibit the knowing and malicious publication of false information that is damaging to an individual's reputation. These laws operate across all media technologies and in no way vary in their applicability in accordance with the characteristics of individual media. But, as chapter 3 also noted, false information that does not adversely affect individual reputations (e.g., Holocaust denial) does not fall within the prohibitions associated with U.S. libel laws.

However, some general restrictions on falsity have found their way into U.S. broadcast regulation. Specifically, FCC regulations prohibit broadcast licensees from knowingly broadcasting false information concerning a crime or catastrophe, if the licensee knows beforehand that "broadcasting the information will cause substantial 'public harm.'"[90] This public harm must be immediate and cause direct and actual damage to the property, health, or safety of the general public, or divert law enforcement or public health and safety authorities from their duties.[91] From the standpoint of contemporary debates about disinformation, these restrictions would apply only to a miniscule proportion of what might be considered identifiable fake news.

However, since the late 1960s, the FCC has also maintained a more general policy that it will "investigate a station for news distortion if it receives documented evidence of such rigging or slanting, such as testimony or other documentation, from individuals with direct personal knowledge that a licensee or its management engaged in the intentional falsification of the news."[92] According to the commission, "of particular concern would be evidence of the direction to employees from station management to falsify the news. However, absent such a compelling showing, the Commission will not intervene."[93] Indeed, news distortion investigations have been rare (especially since the deregulatory trend that began in the 1980s), and have seldom led to any significant repercussions for broadcast licensees.[94]

These limitations in the scope and actions directed at falsity in the news reflect the First Amendment tradition that has both implicitly and explicitly protected the production, dissemination, and consumption of fake news across an array of subject areas—unlike, for instance, the prohibition found in Canadian broadcast regulation.[95] The Canadian Radio-Television and Telecommunications Commission (CRTC, Canada's version of the FCC) has a blanket prohibition against the broadcasting of false or misleading news, though the CRTC has never taken actions against a station for violating this rule.[96]

Of course, as discussed and widely acknowledged, it is the digital media realm, rather than broadcasting, that has become the primary breeding ground for fake news. Unfortunately, even the limited public-interest protections described earlier do not apply to increasingly important sources of news and information such as search engines and social media platforms. This brings us back to section 230 of the Telecommunications Act of 1996, which was developed primarily to grant immunity from various forms of legal liability to online content providers for content produced or disseminated on the platform by third parties. Thus, aggregators and curators such as search engines, social media platforms, and video-hosting sites are immune from legal liabilities that might arise from their curation or dissemination of obscenity, hate speech, or libelous/false content that is produced by third parties. This immunity applies even if the platform operators actively engage in various forms of editorial discretion, such as content filtering, curation, and suppression based on internal standards and economic considerations.

Essentially, these digital media platforms possess the editorial authority of a publisher while simultaneously possessing the immunity from liability more akin to a common carrier. Critics of section 230 describe it as "a law that specifically mandates special treatment for Internet service providers and platforms that no other communications medium has,"[97] suggesting that once again technological characteristics are playing a determinative role in the construction of legal and regulatory frameworks—but, in this case, a legal and regulatory framework that is utterly disconnected from the public interest.

Implications

In this chapter, I have made the case that the public-interest principle has been systematically diminished and marginalized within the context of social media governance. These processes of diminishment and marginalization have been a function of the much narrower, techno-centric orientations of these technology firms that have taken on the functionality—though not the responsibility—of media organizations. It has also been a function of the technological particularism that has guided the construction of regulatory rationales. However, the problems and concerns being generated by the operation of social media platforms fit squarely within traditional notions of the public interest in media governance.

All of this leads to the question of what happens if the rationales for media regulation, which reflect specific technological contexts out of which they were generated, fail to apply to new technological contexts in which the motivations may be equally compelling. If the accompanying rationales do not translate to these newer technological contexts, then we are ultimately left with a decision to make: what matters more, the motivations for media regulation or the rationales? This question becomes particularly acute when we consider that the regulatory rationales discussed earlier are, for the most part, inapplicable to increasingly dominant and influential social media and search engine platforms, which play an increasingly influential role in the dissemination, consumption, and financial health of the media organizations that utilize the technologies and *do* fall within these regulatory rationales. In this way, the regulated and the unregulated sectors of the media ecosystem are increasingly intertwined—not unlike, it should be noted, the relationship that served as the catalyst for the "reasonably ancillary" rationale discussed earlier.

In 2011, the Federal Communications Commission conducted an extensive and ambitious proceeding dedicated to the complex topic of whether community information needs were being met in the digital age.[98] After producing a massive report on the topic, which illustrated the many threats to informed communities, despite (and, to some extent, because of) the diffusion of digital media, the commission proposed only modest exercises of existing regulatory authority, such as requiring broadcasters to make their public inspection file available online, and called for other institutions, such as foundations, to step in and help solve the problem.[99] The underlying message of these proposals was clear: the regulatory rationales that delineate the scope of the FCC's regulatory authority allowed the agency to, at best, nibble around the edges of a substantial communications policy problem—a problem that strikes at the heart of the effective functioning of the democratic process. In many ways, the outcome of this proceeding is a microcosm of the issue presented in this chapter—that a much-needed, more robust public-interest framework for social media governance has yet to emerge from either the relevant institutions or policy makers.

My discussion of the public-interest principle's traditional role in media governance is a reminder of how the norms of public service and a commitment to enhancing the democratic process have long been ingrained, and explicitly articulated, in the governance frameworks for traditional news media. However, many would argue that public-interest norms have long been inadequately represented in media governance, as decades of deregulation, along with increased commercialization and sensationalism, have led to a media ecosystem that has come to prioritize commercial imperatives over public service. This is a central theme of an extensive and compelling body of journalism and policy criticism.[100] It is difficult to dispute this perspective.

However, it is also important to remember that times of dramatic technological change—specifically, times when core infrastructures of communication have undergone transition—have provided opportunities to revisit, revise, and perhaps even rehabilitate the public-interest frameworks that apply to our media ecosystem. We can look back, for instance, to the late 1990s, when the Unites States was in the midst of the transition to digital television. This transition involved migrating television broadcast signals from analog to digital transmission systems, including new production and transmission equipment for television producers, stations, and networks well as new reception equipment (new televisions and/or set-top boxes) for many consumers.

An important, but somewhat forgotten, aspect of this transition was the associated efforts by policy makers to revisit the public-interest regulatory framework that governed television, in an effort to identify and address inadequacies and correct mistakes embedded in the regulatory framework that had become institutionalized over the previous seventy years. Toward these ends, in March of 1997, the Clinton administration established the Advisory Committee on the Public Interest Obligations of Digital Television Broadcasters.[101] The committee, a mix of industry executives, academics, and public-interest advocates, was charged with the task of "determining how the principles of public trusteeship that have governed broadcast television for more than 70 years should be applied in the new television environment."[102] The committee was essentially tasked with rethinking what the public interest could—and should—mean in the digital age, with the technological transition providing the impetus for this reconsideration.

After a series of reportedly contentious meetings, as well as consultations with outside experts and members of the public, the committee submitted a report to the White House.[103] The report suggested a number of modest modifications to the established public-interest framework. By far its most radical and controversial recommendation was the proposal that all political candidates receive five minutes of free television time each night in the thirty days leading up to an election.[104] The report also led to an FCC proceeding that was initially to include the free-air-time proposal but, under pressure from Congress, ultimately did not (incumbents generally oppose any proposal that could potentially level the playing field with their challengers).[105] Thus, while the digital television transition ultimately did not produce a dramatic reconfiguration of the public-interest framework that applies to television, it illustrates how a period of dramatic technological change can trigger a reexamination of the normative foundations of media governance.

One could argue that we are seeing something similar today within the journalism field. The disruption to well-established journalistic practices and business models brought about by technological change has triggered profound reexaminations of journalistic norms and the nature of the relationship between news organizations and their audiences.[106]

News organizations are rethinking, for instance, their traditional, some-what paternalistic relationship with their audience (see chapter 2).[107] Under this model, journalists and editors maintained more or less exclusive authority to determine what was important for news audiences. Today, that relational dynamic is being reconsidered, as news organizations explore more collaborative and directly engaged relationships with their audiences, in an effort to find a more viable model for sustainability in the digital age.[108] The place of the public in journalism's efforts to best serve the public interest is thus being reexamined, and this reexamination has been triggered in large part by the damaging and disruptive effects of social media and search engines as means of distributing and consuming news.

Media historian Robert McChesney has described such periods of technological change as key components of what he terms *critical junctures*: periods of time when the opportunities for dramatic change in the media system are at their greatest.[109] It is worth noting that other conditions McChesney identifies as contributing to such critical junctures include public discrediting of media content and major political crisis.[110] Based on these criteria, McChesney points to the Progressive Era (late 1890s to early 1900s) and the late 1960s/early 1970s as other critical junctures in American media history.

In light of how the rise of social media in the news ecosystem (technological change) has coincided with the increasing prominence of fake news (discrediting of media content), perhaps unprecedented levels of political polarization, and the election in 2016 of a president who seems to deviate from the norms of the office in a number of ways that appear dangerous to democracy (political crisis), it seems reasonable to suggest that we are in the midst of such a critical juncture right now, and that it should compel a reexamination of our system of media governance. This is the focus of the next chapter.

CHAPTER 6

Reviving the Public Interest

P erhaps the most troubling aspect of the wide range of concerns that continue to emerge around the operation and use of social media platforms is the sense that, given the scale and scope at which these platforms operate, these problems may ultimately be unsolvable. As Siva Vaidhyanathan, author of *Antisocial Media: How Facebook Disconnects Us and Undermines Democracy*, grimly put it in an interview with the *Atlantic*, "There is no reform. . . . So we are screwed."[1] While he may ultimately be right, this chapter begins from the premise that it is too soon to throw in the towel. Thus, in this chapter I will review ongoing efforts and initiatives, and outline some general and some more specific media-governance proposals that are intended to bring a stronger public-interest orientation to the operation of social media platforms and that hopefully would at least have a positive effect.

Platform Self-Governance

First, it is important to have a sense of the types of actions that the platforms have taken so far. The criticisms and controversies surrounding Facebook, Twitter, YouTube, and other social media platforms that have continued to mount in the wake of the 2016 election have certainly prompted a stronger public-interest orientation on the part of these companies. These platforms appear to be moving in the direction of "understand[ing] themselves as a new kind of media company, with obligations to protect the global public good."[2] These responses have included a variety of efforts to reduce the dissemination and consumption of disinformation, counteract the tendency toward filter bubbles, and better protect user data.

Some of these efforts have focused on undermining the ad-revenue support that fake news sites can receive from social media platforms. On this front, we have seen platforms such as Google and Facebook ban known fake-news-disseminating publishers from their ad networks; with Google extending their criteria for exclusion to sites that impersonate legitimate news sites.[3]

However, research has shown that fake news sites have migrated to other ad networks that are less stringent, and that advertisements designed to look like news stories are the most common type of ad format being utilized by these sites.[4] Sites have also focused their efforts on blurring the line between satire and misinformation in order to meet the criteria for inclusion outlined by many ad networks.[5]

Another approach has been to better inform users about the sources and content available to them. For instance, Google, Facebook, and Twitter have all begun displaying "trust indicators"—standardized disclosures developed by a nonpartisan consortium of news organizations—in an effort to better inform platform users about individual outlets and thus make it easier for them to identify reliable, high-quality content.[6] News sources that meet the established criteria for trustworthiness essentially get to display a badge saying so; the goal is that these badges will become an indicator of quality for news consumers. YouTube has offered workshops to young people on how to identify fake news and avoid filter bubbles.[7] It has also begun offering what YouTube executives call "information cues," by displaying links to fact-based content (primarily Wikipedia entries) alongside conspiracy-theory videos.[8] Twitter has employed a policy of user notification, notifying more than half a million users who followed, retweeted, or liked tweets disseminated by more than 50,000 automated accounts found to be linked to the Russian government, to inform them that they were exposed to Russian misinformation during the 2016 election period.[9] Initiatives such as these address the growing need for "tools of truth recognition" that operate "independent of the market in order for the market to be optimal."[10]

However, such efforts to affect behavior by providing more information do not always work as planned. In the wake of the 2016 election, Facebook partnered with third-party fact-checkers to label individual stories as "disputed" in a user's news feed if two separate fact-checking organizations independently rated the story as false. Users would not only see the disputed label accompanying a fact-checked story in their news feed, but would also receive a pop-up notification of the story's disputed status before being able to share the story. They would also receive a notification if any story they shared was subsequently fact-checked as false. It is also important to emphasize that this system relied (at least in in part) on users' reporting individual stories as disputed to trigger the fact-checking process.

After a year, however, Facebook abandoned this labeling approach for a variety of reasons.[11] Perhaps most importantly, the labeling by fact-checkers did not appear to be curbing the consumption or sharing of disinformation. In fact, in some instances the labeling was having the opposite effect. As Facebook researchers noted, "disputed flags could sometimes backfire."[12] According to one independent assessment, in some instances conservative news consumers became more proactive in their efforts to share "disputed" stories, in an effort to combat what they perceived as Facebook's efforts to muffle conservative viewpoints.[13]

This reaction reflects long-standing problems related to content labeling in media, in which ratings systems sometimes facilitate behaviors that are contradictory to the system's intent. For instance, the V-chip policy that Congress developed for U.S. television regulation was found to have what researchers labeled a "forbidden fruit effect." In this case, boys in particular often used the program-rating information to more effectively locate adult content.[14] As a result, their consumption of such content actually increased, because most parents were not bothering to utilize the V-chip's program blocking feature.[15]

In response to their evaluation of the problems with the "disputed" tag program, Facebook went in a different direction. The company reconfigured its Related Articles system, which was intended to make users aware of additional stories on a topic that had appeared in their news feed. In its new configuration, the platform placed links to articles on the same topic from other publishers (including third-party fact-checkers) below articles in a user's news feed identified by fact-checkers as fake. Users who shared a news story subsequently labeled as false by a fact-checker, or who were about to share such a story, continued to receive notifications of the story's disputed status. Users could continue to report stories as "false news" in order to trigger the fact-checking process.[16] The goal is to diversify the sources of information a user consults, thereby breaking down filter bubbles and undermining the consumption and dissemination of fake news.[17]

A key question that emerged in the wake of the 2016 election was how to make algorithms better curators of news. That is, are there ways in which protections against filter bubbles, disinformation, and generally low-quality content can be incorporated into algorithmic design? Essentially, how can these algorithms better serve the public interest? Toward this end, Twitter has been working to improve its automated tools for identifying and suspending accounts identified with malicious actors and bots.[18] YouTube has adjusted its search algorithm to prioritize "authoritative" sources in its search results.[19] As previously noted, Facebook has integrated the results of third-party fact-checks into its News Feed algorithm, in an effort to reduce the distribution of stories identified as false,[20] and began shrinking the size of links to content that fact-checkers have verified as false.[21] News stories identified as false are generally not removed (only downranked in news feeds)[22] unless they are judged to meet certain criteria, such as potentially leading to violence or containing false information regarding voting.[23] As was discussed in chapter 5, Facebook has also begun adjusting its algorithm to prioritize more "trustworthy" sources. Whereas the mechanisms behind the YouTube algorithm adjustment to prioritize authoritative sources remain unclear,[24] Facebook has described an approach based on a survey of a sample of Facebook users.

The lead-up to the 2018 midterm elections saw social media platforms becoming increasingly aggressive in identifying and shutting down "inauthentic" accounts. In the first quarter of 2018, Facebook shut down 583 million fake accounts,[25] many of which were focused on disseminating fake news and disinformation related to the 2018 election.[26] Twitter similarly deleted tens of millions of fake accounts, including many engaged in coordinated dissemination of election-related disinformation;[27] it deleted more than nine million accounts a week, on average, in the weeks approaching the 2018 election.[28]

The scale at which this policing is being conducted is staggering, and is well beyond what human screeners could accomplish without automated tools. These and other efforts will persist, in a process of trial and error, in what has been described as a never-ending game of "whack-a-mole" between these platforms and those actors trying to use them to undermine an informed citizenry.[29]

A number of app developers have also entered the fray, creating news apps and browser extensions designed to "burst" filter bubbles and diversify users' social media news consumption. These apps track users' news-consumption behaviors, evaluate where the news consumption is oriented in terms of the left-to-right political continuum, and, through story recommendations, seek to "nudge" users' news consumption in whatever direction takes them outside of their ideological comfort zone.[30] Such apps, however, require news consumers to take the affirmative steps of recognizing a partisan bias in their news consumption and deciding to do something to counteract it.

These efforts reflect the perspective put forth by former FCC chairman Tom Wheeler: "Algorithms got us into this situation. Algorithms must get us out."[31] However, if there is one lesson to be learned from the evolution of our algorithmic news ecosystem, it is that complete reliance on algorithmic systems would be a mistake. As Facebook's chief AI scientist, Yann LeCunn, has stated, "AI is part of the answer, but only part."[32] This is why the social media platforms have also dramatically increased their staffs devoted to identifying disinformation.[33] For instance, between 2017 and 2018 Google sought to add ten thousand content-screening staff to evaluate content on YouTube.[34] In addition, there are third-party providers such as NewsGuard, which offers a browser plug-in that rates more than 4,500 online news sources based on their trustworthiness, as determined by a team of journalists that evaluates each site.[35]

In the long run, the most important and effective actions that social media platforms take to address their shortcomings as news purveyors may be those actions that diminish their significance as news distributors.[36] Any initiatives that, either intentionally or unintentionally, at least partially "put the horse back in the barn" may represent an improvement over the status quo. Any path back to a more *pull* than *push* and less algorithmically mediated and hypertargeted relationship between news consumers and news producers represents a step in the right direction. The key caveat here is that this process must not be one in which the presence of—and reliance on—legitimate news organizations in social media declines while the prevalence and reach of purveyors of disinformation on social media persists or grows.

There have been some high-profile ways in which social media platforms have retreated a bit from the provision of news. Facebook, for instance, has eliminated its Trending feature,[37] and has adjusted its News Feed algorithm to slightly diminish the overall quantity of news in its News Feed.[38] Facebook's Trending feature became a political hot potato in the wake of accusations that editors for the feature suppressed conservative-leaning news stories. The announcement of the feature's closure, however, was accompanied by an announcement that the company was developing a number of "future news experiences,"[39] suggesting that Facebook's long-term goal may not be to extract itself in any meaningful way from its position as a news intermediary.

One trend that may be partially a function of efforts by social media platforms to recalibrate their operation in the news ecosystem is that, for the first time in the past decade, reliance on social media for news appears to be declining. According to the 2018 *Digital News Report* from Oxford University's Reuters Institute for Journalism, in a study of thirty-seven countries, growth in the use of social media to access news had leveled off or reversed.[40] In the United States, for instance, reported reliance on Facebook as a news source dropped nearly ten percentage points from 2017 to 2018.[41] Data from the online audience measurement firm Chartbeat indicates that from January 2017 to July 2018, Facebook's role in driving traffic to news sites declined by roughly 40 percent. These declines were more than offset by increases in direct access and search engine referrals.[42]

Of course, the horse is never going completely back into the barn. Even as social media usage for news declines, these declines are being replaced, to some extent, by a reliance on social messaging apps like WhatsApp (owned by Facebook). WhatsApp already has a fake news problem that has been described as "epidemic."[43] And, as the Reuters Institute study illustrated, social media platforms serve as a point of origin for much of the news sharing that takes place on social messaging apps.[44] Thus, an additional layer of complexity and interconnectivity is folded into to the always-evolving digital news ecosystem, and yet another category of tech company may need to start thinking like—and being treated like—a media company.

IN PURSUIT OF ALGORITHMIC DIVERSITY

Underlying many of the efforts described here is the principle of diversity, and an embracing of the marketplace-of-ideas perspective that exposure to diverse sources and content facilitates better-informed decision-making. The diversity principle has a long tradition in media governance.[45] Thus, as it begins to emerge as a more prominent principle of social media governance, it is worth looking at how it has been defined and put into practice within the traditional media realm.

There are three fundamental diversity components: source, content, and exposure. Source diversity refers to the distinguishing characteristics of the sources of news and information. This can include ownership or structural characteristics of media outlets, or even the demographic diversity of the personnel within outlets. Content diversity can take a variety of forms, including the kinds of story topics/types or political viewpoints. Greater diversity of sources has long been presumed to lead to a greater diversity of content. So, for instance, the FCC has regulated broadcast-station ownership in ways that were intended to increase the number of female and minority owners, under the presumption that these owners would bring different perspectives that would be reflected in the type of programming that they offered. The empirical support for this kind of presumed relationship, however, has not always been clear.[46]

Exposure diversity refers to the extent to which an individual is exposed to a diversity of sources or content. Under this logic, the more choices available to media users, the more they will take advantage of that choice. From a media-governance standpoint, historically, a much greater emphasis has been placed on source and content diversity than on exposure diversity.[47] Policy makers have focused their efforts on trying to enhance the diversity of sources and content available to media consumers in the hope that this might lead to greater diversity of exposure. This approach reflects the fact that regulating exposure diversity directly potentially represents an unacceptable intrusion upon individual freedoms and is politically fraught.[48] Thus, policy makers have pursued source and content diversity as a means of facilitating exposure diversity, through mechanisms such as ownership regulations and content regulations such as the Fairness Doctrine.

The irony here is that the unintended consequences of diversifying sources and content is that, at the individual level, exposure diversity may very well diminish.[49] A substantial body of research across both old and new media contexts has shown that media consumers have a tendency to respond to greater diversity of content offerings by consuming even more of their preferred content types.[50] This is the essence of the filter-bubble phenomenon—lots of people constructing their own distinct versions of the *Daily Me*, with lots of homogeneous content and sources that reinforce their established preferences and worldviews.

The dynamics of social media, however, provide an opportunity for these platforms to be proactive with regard to exposure diversity, in ways that traditional media could not. The combination of push and personalization that characterizes social media as a platform for the delivery of news means that social media platforms know more about what needs to be done to diversify a user's media exposure and have the capacity, through algorithmic personalization, to "nudge"[51] users in more diverse directions. That is, the extensive data that platforms have about their users' news consumption facilitates the identification of gaps that might need to be filled from a source and/or content diversity standpoint. This kind of information was largely unavailable to previous generations of content providers. This ability to identify diversity needs, so to speak, is now coupled with the ability to deliver that content directly to a user's news feed.

Of course, algorithmically diversifying a user's news feed runs completely counter to what we might call the personalization principle, which has been so central in the history of social media. While there has been a fair bit of research into incorporating diversity principles into algorithmic design, applications of this approach in the realms of content-recommendation systems and news-feed curation have been quite scarce.[52] Personalization to this point has largely meant providing users with content similar to what they (or their social network) have already consumed, given that more of this type of content generally leads to greater audience engagement. What personalization has not meant is providing users with content that is markedly different from what they have already consumed. This approach still represents a form of personalization, in that the process of algorithmic curation reflects a set of decisions made in response to a user's exhibited preferences. In a diversity-enhancing approach to personalization, however, algorithms would process and act on this information in a very different way.

Would such an approach be a kind of algorithmic paternalism? Absolutely. But then again, social media platforms have been engaging in some degree of algorithmic paternalism ever since they began filtering obscenity and hate speech and abandoned reverse-chronological news feeds in favor of algorithmically curated feeds. To the extent that every algorithmic criterion represents a choice made by coders that is intended to structure and influence our own decision-making, it becomes difficult to disentangle the notion of paternalism from the very idea of algorithmic curation. From this standpoint, algorithmic paternalism grounded in public-interest principles such as diversity, rather than personalization oriented around serving demonstrated preferences, can be seen as a more socially responsible approach to this core functionality.[53] Our understanding of the effects of social media on the digital news ecosystem has shown us that we need to act upon opportunities to algorithmically reassert journalism's role in providing us with what we need rather than what we want.

Needless to say, this is far from a straightforward task. Let's assume that, from a public-interest standpoint, diversifying a social media user's exposure is fundamentally more beneficial to democracy than catering to, and facilitating, a narrow media diet. If so, then the next question becomes how to do this well.[54] On this front, one thing platforms need to resist is what media scholar Sandra Braman has described as the "fetishization" of diversity—the tendency to value diversity in whatever form it might be measured, and to fail to take into consideration any limits to its value.[55]

Translating this concern to the context of news and journalism on social media highlights a couple of points. First, the process of facilitating diversity of exposure must not become fixated on the dichotomy of facilitating exposure to both liberal and conservative perspectives. Such an approach can lead to the creation of false equivalencies—situations in which two opposing perspectives are given equivalent status even when objective evaluation would overwhelmingly recognize that one perspective has greater validity than the other (think, for instance, of the cigarettes and cancer examples discussed in chapter 3's overview of the Fairness Doctrine). Social media must not fall into the Fairness Doctrine trap, or the trap that some critics of American journalism say the mainstream news media fell into in their efforts to provide "balanced" coverage of the candidates in the 2016 presidential campaign.[56] Objectivity and balance are not the same thing, though these two concepts often get conflated in discussions of the practice of journalism.

Fixating on the liberal-conservative continuum in any algorithmic mechanisms for enhancing exposure diversity in relation to journalism represents a fundamental mischaracterization of the functions of journalism. A fundamental dimension of journalism is to provide factual information to facilitate informed decision-making.[57] As media policy advocate Mark Cooper has stated, "the core concept of [journalism's] monitorial role involves the journalist serving as a neutral watchdog, rather than a partisan participant, holding social, economic, and political actors to account by presenting facts rather than advocating positions and offering opinions."[58] Today, however, a growing chorus of critics contend that the romanticized notion of the objective journalist may have been more of an ideal type than a reality, and that the pretense of objective journalism should be abandoned.[59] Certainly, the contemporary journalism landscape is one in which traditional, more objective forms of journalism seem to be getting displaced by more overtly partisan approaches. However, unless we are ready to give up on the notion of objective facts,[60] we need to maintain a recognition that conveying factual information in order to facilitate informed decision-making is a vital element in the functioning of journalism in a democracy, and that this functionality does not mesh well with partisan journalism. Ultimately, to paraphrase Winston Churchill,[61] objectivity may be the worst form of journalism, except for all the others.

For this reason, the curation of a diverse range of sources and content options must incorporate other diversity-relevant criteria beyond ideological orientation. These might include ownership and personnel characteristics, business models (e.g., commercial/noncommercial), and story type. To boil the notion of diversity down to the liberal-conservative continuum runs counter to the very idea of diversity.

Any efforts to effectively operationalize diversity must not be independent of curation based on criteria related to trustworthiness and credibility. The curation of hyperpartisan news sites from both ends of the political spectrum should not represent the essence of algorithmically facilitated exposure diversity. Under such an approach, the consumption of a "balanced" diet of hyperpartisan right- and left-wing news sources does not really lead to the ideal of an informed citizen, given that such news sources are likely to be lacking in the relevant factual information (see chapter 3). Thus, efforts to diversify exposure should happen in tandem with efforts to prioritize journalistic authority, credibility, and, yes, objectivity.

RELEGITIMIZING JOURNALISM

This point raises a related—though certainly controversial—direction that these platforms could pursue in their efforts to rehabilitate their position in the news ecosystem. These platforms are in a unique position to confer journalistic authority on deserving news organizations. The idea of social media platforms engaging in any kind of accreditation process for news organizations has been described as a journalistic "third rail."[62] However, as Campbell Brown, Facebook's head of news partnerships, has stated, "fake news may be pushing us into a world where we have to verify news organizations through quality signals or other means."[63] As has been discussed, over the past few years, social media platforms have been doing much more in this regard, in terms of evaluating the credibility of individual sources and diminishing the prominence of their content if they fail to meet certain standards. Increasingly, noncredible sources are removed outright.[64] Continued efforts in this direction could create a much more privileged status for legitimate journalism within the social media ecosystem.

Of course, many would object to social media platforms' engaging in this kind of more aggressive, evaluative assertion of their gatekeeping power. Indeed, the better approach might be if the journalism industry would move toward a model of self-accreditation, the results of which could dictate the gatekeeping decisions of social media platforms. Nonaccredited news sources would be ineligible for distribution on social media. Legal scholars Anna Gonzalez and David Schulz have put forth such a proposal, which would focus on a few fixed accreditation standards, such as (a) being a "generator of original content [that ascribes to] universal principles that define the goals and ethical practices of good journalism"; (b) "commitment to a generally reliable discipline of verification"; and (c) articulating and publishing "standard practices, which must advance the universal general principles and be considered reasonably rigorous by similarly situated news outlets."[65]

The news industry in the United States has never had any broadly encompassing accreditation system, a position that has proven increasingly damaging as media technology has evolved. There has been perhaps nothing more damaging to the institution of journalism than the way that the Internet, social media, and user-generated content gave rise to the mantra that now "everyone is a journalist."[66] This democratization of the practice of journalism was valorized in a way that fundamentally undermined the value of professional journalists. The devaluation of journalistic authority can be seen as playing a central role in the far-too-undifferentiated way in which news has been presented, shared, and consumed on social media. Even the term *news feed* as applied to one's social media feed fundamentally undermines any reasonably stringent notion of what constitutes news.

Over the past decade, it has become clear that the Internet and social media have not made everyone a journalist any more than they have made everyone a lawyer, or everyone a neurosurgeon. The pendulum needs to swing the other way, with the reestablishment and recognition of clear lines of distinction separating legitimate news and journalists from the vast oceans of content that might contain some superficial characteristics of journalism. The various technological changes that have, to this point, largely served to undermine journalistic authority need to be used now to rebuild it—to identify legitimate, professional journalism and elevate it to a privileged status within the operation of social media platforms.

Fortunately, this is already starting to happen. For instance, the journalistic subfield of fact-checking has adopted a rigorous accreditation process, along with accompanying accreditation criteria.[67] The International Fact-Checking Network, hosted by the Poynter Institute for Journalism, issues the accreditation and oversees the accreditation process, conducted by an external panel. This panel assesses a fact-checking organization according to criteria laid out in the Network's Code of Principles.[68] These criteria include nonpartisanship and fairness, transparency of funding and organization, and transparency of sources and methodology.[69] Facebook utilizes such accreditation when deciding whether to include a fact-checking organization in the network of fact-checkers that it relies upon to identify fake news stories.[70] It may be time to broaden the scope of this model.

Such a model would certainly diminish the quantity of news that circulates on social media and probably the consumption of news through social media as well. If that is a by-product of this proposed initiative, that is fine too. Once again, the underlying assumption here is that any actions directed at reconfiguring the dynamics of socially mediated news that also (intentionally or unintentionally) discourage reliance on social media for news represent a multipronged solution to the problem. Improving the performance of social media platforms as purveyors of news and diminishing the importance of social media platforms as purveyors of news are both reasonable paths forward.

IMPLICATIONS

Many of the ongoing and proposed efforts described so far move social media platforms further away from pure personalization tools and closer to news media in the traditional sense. The exercise of greater editorial authority raises legitimate concerns, however, about concentration of gatekeeping power in the hands of relatively few platforms.

Any proposals that involve social media platforms more aggressively and subjectively utilizing their gatekeeping position and systems of algorithmic curation to provide the most "authoritative," "trustworthy," or "diverse" content raises the specter of further empowering already powerful social media bottlenecks. The irony in this scenario is the extent to which it reflects a transition back toward the limited number of powerful gatekeepers that characterized the prefragmentation mass media era, but in a technological context in which many of the barriers to entry characteristic of that era are no longer present. The mass media era was accompanied by critiques about concentration of ownership and the accompanying systemic homogeneity of viewpoints.[71] In the era of three dominant broadcast networks, Walter Cronkite's authoritative sign-off, "And that's the way it is," was seen by many critics at the time as reflecting an unacceptable level of cultural hegemony, in which the "mainstream" media could easily stifle and exclude alternative viewpoints.[72] These critiques gave rise to concerns about the production and influence of propaganda that are similar to the concerns that underlie the fake-news and filter-bubble scenarios we face now.[73] Given the extent to which different technological contexts seem to lead to surprisingly similar outcomes, one is tempted to conclude that a media ecosystem comprised of a fairly limited number of powerful gatekeepers is an inevitability, borne of larger institutional and economic forces, as well as innate audience behavior tendencies.[74]

Fortunately, from a journalistic standpoint, it is also the case that the mass media era of few, powerful gatekeepers facilitated a stronger public-service ethos than has been present since technological change facilitated increased fragmentation and competition, and an associated need for news organizations to prioritize audience and revenue maximization over public service.[75] We do not want to fall into the trap of overly romanticizing the past, but it is worth remembering that the news divisions of those three dominant broadcast networks ran deficits of millions of dollars a year, secure that their losses would be subsidized by the tremendous profits of the entertainment divisions.[76] Of course, within some media sectors (e.g., broadcasting), this public-service ethos could be attributed, at least in part, to a government-imposed public- interest regulatory framework. But before exploring this direction in relation to social media, it is worth considering self-regulatory approaches.

WHAT SOCIAL MEDIA CAN LEARN
FROM AUDIENCE MEASUREMENT

Any proposal involving a more proactive role for platforms in the curation of news faces the inevitable—and legitimate—concern about whether this kind of authority and judgment should be wielded by a select few platforms, whose personnel tend to have inadequate interest, background, or training in making these types of decisions. What we have at this point is perhaps best described as *platform unilateralism*, in which individual platforms, each with tremendous global reach and impact, individually and independently make governance decisions with wide-ranging implications for journalism, an informed citizenry, and democracy. Here is where the notion of multistakeholder governance can potentially come into play. Algorithmic design in the public interest should involve a wider range of stakeholders.[77] We have seen some movement in this direction. In November 2018, Mark Zuckerberg announced plans to create an independent body that would hear appeals about the platform's content-moderation decisions.[78]

Self-regulation has a long tradition in the media sector, with the motion picture, music, television, and videogame industries all adopting self-imposed and -designed content ratings systems to restrict children's access to adult content. These systems all arose in response to threats of direct government regulation.[79] These threats typically took the form of congressional hearings or inquiries—classic instances of what is often called "regulation by raised eyebrow."[80]

The issues of concern here are far more complex and multifaceted than concerns about children being exposed to adult content (though this is also a problem that confronts social media platforms).[81] There is, however, another media-related self-regulatory context that may better reflect the nature of the concerns surrounding social media, and thus may provide some useful guidance: the audience-measurement industry.

Whether for television, radio, online, or print, increasingly interconnected audience-measurement systems provide content providers and advertisers with data on who is consuming what, and on the various demographic (and in some cases behavioral and psychographic) characteristics of these audiences. The dynamics of audience measurement are similar to those of social media in a number of ways.

Audience measurement suffers from the same absence of robust competition that characterizes the social media sector. In audience measurement, the Nielsen Company has established itself in a dominant position, as the leading provider of television, radio, and online audience measurement in the United States and in many other nations around the world.[82] Even in countries where Nielsen is not dominant, the audience-measurement industry has exhibited a very strong tendency toward monopoly. Some analysts have contended that audience measurement is a natural monopoly[83]—an argument that has been made within the context of social media platforms as well (see chapter 4).[84]

The similarities do not end there. The actions of audience-measurement firms can, like those of social media platforms, have significant social repercussions. If an audience-measurement system underrepresents a certain demographic group in its methodology, the amount of content produced for that group's needs/interests may diminish, or the outlets serving that group may suffer economically. For instance, there have been cases in which a shift in radio or television audience-measurement methodologies have led to sudden and dramatic declines in Hispanic or African American audiences. In this way, issues of accuracy, fairness, and media diversity are tied up in the dynamics of audience measurement.[85] Therefore, there is a prominent public-interest dimension to audience ratings and the work of audience-measurement firms.

Both audience-measurement systems and social media platforms are susceptible to manipulation by third parties. In audience measurement, ratings systems need to insulate themselves from various forms of rating distortion. The integrity of television and radio audience ratings can be affected, for instance, if members of the measurement sample are affiliated with, or known to, any of the media outlets being measured; and are thus subject to influence or manipulation. Radio and television programmers have also been known to try to "hype" ratings during measurement periods with actions such as contests or sweepstakes intended to temporarily boost audience sizes beyond their normal levels.[86] In online audience measurement, bots are a common tool for creating inflated audience estimates and thus must be policed vigilantly.[87]

These scenarios are not unlike those facing social media platforms, which face constant efforts by third parties seeking to "game" their news-feed algorithms in order to achieve higher placement and wider distribution of their content for economic or political gain.[88] An entire industry has arisen around "optimizing" content for social media curation algorithms. At the same time, platforms are constantly adjusting their algorithms in ways to diminish the prominence of clickbait and other forms of low-quality content that often are produced with an eye toward exploiting what is known about the algorithms' ranking criteria and how these criteria affect the performance of various types of content.[89]

It is also worth noting the somewhat ambiguous First Amendment status of both the ratings data produced by audience-measurement firms and the algorithms produced by social media firms. In both cases, there remains room for debate as to whether ratings data and algorithms represent forms of speech that are deserving of full First Amendment protection. The uncertainty in both cases derives from the broader (and still contentious) question of whether data represent a form of speech eligible for First Amendment protection.[90] Data are the primary output of audience-measurement systems. And in the case of social media algorithms, data are the key input that gener-ates their content-curation outputs. Thus, the two contexts represent somewhat different instances of the intersection of data and speech, and the First Amendment uncertainty that can arise.[91] This issue is of particular relevance to discussions of possible government regula-tion in these spheres, given the extent to which the First Amendment provides substantial protections against government intervention and increases the likelihood of a self-regulatory model taking hold in speech-related contexts.

Finally, measurement firms and social media platforms share an interest in keeping the details of their methodology or algorithms pro-prietary. This is to prevent manipulation, as well as for competitive reasons. Therefore, it is not surprising that audience-measurement sys-tems, like social media algorithms, have frequently been characterized as "black boxes."[92]

So far, at least in the United States, despite the lack of competition, we have not seen direct government regulation of the audience-measurement industry. What we have seen instead is a form of self-regulation, instituted through the establishment of an organization known as the Media Rating Council (MRC). The Media Rating Council was created in the 1960s (when it was initially called the Broadcast Rating Council). In keeping with the other self-regulatory structures in the media sector, the impetus for the Media Rating Council came from a series of congressional hear-ings investigating the accuracy and reliability of television and radio audi-ence-measurement systems.[93] The MRC's membership represents a cross section of the media industries and associated stakeholders, including media companies in television, radio, print, and online media, as well as advertising agencies, advertisers, and media buyers.[94]

The MRC has two primary responsibilities: setting standards and accreditation. In the standard-setting realm, the MRC establishes and maintains minimum standards pertaining to the quality and the integ-rity of the process of audience measurement. Under this heading, the MRC outlines minimum methodological standards related to issues such as sample recruitment, training of personnel, and data processing. The MRC also establishes and maintains standards with regard to disclosure and which methodological details must be made available to the customers of an audience-measurement service. Included in this requirement is that all measurement services must disclose "all omissions, errors, and biases known to the ratings service which may exert a significant effect on the findings shown in the report."[95] Measurement firms must disclose substantial amounts of methodological detail related to sampling procedures and weighting of data. They must also disclose whether any of the services they offer have not been accredited by the MRC.

The accreditation process is the second key aspect of the MRC's role. The MRC conducts confidential audits of audience-measurement systems to certify that they are meeting minimum standards of methodological rigor and accuracy. While the audit decision is made public, key methodological details of the audience-measurement service remain confidential. Leaks of audit details have been incredibly rare. As with audience-measurement systems, we need to recognize the practical limits of mandated or voluntary transparency in relation to the operation of social media algorithms.[96]

In establishing and applying standards of accuracy, reliability, and rigor to the increasingly complex process of audience measurement, the MRC offers a potentially useful template for self-regulation for social media. In some ways, given the spate of congressional hearings focusing on issues such as the role of social media platforms in the dissemination of fake news in connection with the 2016 election, their data-gathering and data-sharing practices, and claims of suppression of conservative viewpoints, one could argue that media history tells us that some sort of self-regulatory initiative is inevitable. Then again, one recurring theme of this book has been the extent to which social media companies do not see themselves as media companies, and perhaps they will not respond to congressional raised eyebrows in the same way that traditional media companies have in the past.

However, one could imagine the establishment of a self-regulatory body that addresses issues similar to those addressed by the MRC, with a similar multistakeholder construction. This hypothetical Social Media Council could establish standards regarding the gathering and sharing of user data. It could create disclosure standards for the algorithmic details that need to be made publicly available (similar to the MRC's disclosure requirements). Likewise, this council could set the standards for a public-interest component of news-curation algorithms. In connection with these standards, it could establish MRC-like auditing teams with the relevant expertise to determine whether news-curation algorithms meet these minimum standards, and be similarly capable of maintaining the necessary confidentiality of the audit details. And, just as significant methodological changes in audience-measurement systems require reaccreditation from the MRC, a process could be established in which significant algorithmic changes would require assessment and accreditation.

In what would appear to be an initial step in this direction, in September 2018, social media companies such as Facebook, Google, and Twitter, along with advertisers, developed and submitted to the European Commission a voluntary Code of Practice on Disinformation. According to the European Commission, this Code of Practice represents the "first time worldwide that industry agrees, on a voluntary basis, to self-regulatory standards to fight disinformation."[97] The code includes pledges by the signatories to significantly improve the scrutiny of ad placements, increase transparency of political advertisements, develop more rigorous policies related to the misuse of bots, develop tools to prioritize authentic and authoritative information, and help users identify disinformation and find diverse perspectives. Though an encouraging step, the code has been criticized for lacking meaningful commitments, measurable objectives, and compliance or enforcement tools.[98]

This last criticism highlights a key characteristic of the MRC, which is that it has no enforceable authority. Participation by audience-measurement services is voluntary. Measurement firms are free to bring new services to the market without MRC accreditation if they so choose. The embracing of MRC accreditation as an important indicator of data quality by the market as a whole is intended to discourage such actions, and for the most part it does.

However, not all stakeholders have been convinced that this voluntary-compliance model provides adequate oversight. Consequently, in 2005, at the urging of some television broadcasters, Senator Conrad Burns of Montana introduced the Fairness, Accuracy, Inclusiveness, and Responsibility in Ratings Act, which sought to confer greater regulatory authority upon the MRC, making MRC accreditation mandatory for any television audience measurement services on the market. Any methodological or technological changes to existing measurement systems would also be subject to mandatory MRC accreditation.[99] Thus, Congress would essentially confer upon the MRC a degree of oversight authority that it lacked. Under this model of "regulated self-regulation,"[100] the self-regulatory apparatus remains, but the heightened authority emanates from congressional decree.

Some industry stakeholders supported the proposed legislation.[101] Many other industry stakeholders, however, were opposed to conferring this greater authority upon the MRC.[102] Even the MRC itself opposed any legislation granting it greater authority, citing antitrust and liability concerns.[103]

Within the context of social media, could we similarly assume that the presence or absence of some sort of Social Media Council "stamp of approval" would sufficiently affect the behaviors of platform users, content providers, and advertisers to compel participation in the accreditation process by these platforms? Perhaps. If not, this process would need to overlap into the policy-making realm to a greater extent than has been the case so far in audience measurement.

IMPLICATIONS

Would the establishment of this type of self-regulatory apparatus be burdensome to algorithmic media platforms? Absolutely. However, one of the most important lessons of the past few years has been that the ability of platforms to unilaterally construct and adjust the criteria that increasingly determine the flow of news and information represents not only an unhealthy concentration of gatekeeping authority, but a process that tends to operate in a way that is largely divorced from the news values that connect with the information needs of citizens in a democracy.

Would the establishment of this type of self-regulatory apparatus potentially discourage platforms from engaging in the distribution of news? Possibly. However, the disintermediation of the relationship between news organizations and news consumers likely has positive dimensions that outweigh the negatives. While it is unrealistic to assume that social media platforms will cease to operate as news intermediaries, if efforts to improve their performance also have the effect of diminishing their centrality in the news ecosystem, facilitating more direct relationships between news outlets and news consumers, then this is a comparatively desirable outcome.

Policy Evolution

We turn now to the other key dimension of media governance, policy making, and ongoing efforts and proposals in this area. Policy makers and researchers, both within the United States and abroad, have begun to consider—and in some cases implement—a variety of regulatory interventions in the realm of social media.[104] In the United States, a 2018 white paper from Virginia Senator Mark Warner laid out a range of possible interventions. These include requiring that platforms label bots and authenticate the origin of accounts or posts, codifying platforms' "information fiduciary" responsibilities, revising section 230 of the Communications Decency Act to increase platform liability in areas such as defamation and public disclosure of private facts,[105] and adopting some form of auditing mechanism for algorithmic decision-making systems.[106]

At this point, few of these proposals have taken the form of proposed legislation or regulatory agency action. One area of activity has been in the realm of political advertising. For instance, in December 2017, the Federal Election Commission issued a ruling that disclosure requirements regarding political-ad sponsors must extend to Facebook.[107] The FEC is mulling a further extension of disclosure requirements to all online political advertising.[108] Obviously, a regulatory requirement that applies only to a single social media platform would seem to be of limited effectiveness, essentially inviting bad actors to focus their efforts on other platforms. Congress has similarly focused on political advertising, with bills intended to bring greater transparency to political-ad sponsorship making their way through both the House and the Senate.[109]

The data-sharing improprieties at the heart of the Cambridge Analytica scandal have produced a more aggressive response than have revelations about fake news and disinformation. The Federal Trade Commission quickly opened an investigation of Facebook, focused on whether the company's mishandling of user data violated the terms of a 2011 consent orderthat required the company to obtain user permissions for certain changes in privacy settings.[110] In addition, a bipartisan group of thirty-seven state attorneys general sent a letter to Facebook seeking details about the data breach and threatening to take action if it were determined that Facebook failed to adequately protect users' personal information.[111] The Cambridge Analytica scandal also led to the introduction of the bipartisan Social Media Privacy Protection and Consumer Rights Act of 2018,[112] as well as the Democrat-sponsored Customer Online Notification for Stopping Edge-provider Network Transgressions (CONSENT) Act.[113] These bills are clearly inspired by the European General Data Protection Regulation, which went into effect in May 2018.[114] If passed, the Social Media Privacy Protection and Consumer Rights Act would require greater transparency from social media companies regarding the types of user data collected and how such data are shared. It also grants users much more control over their data, giving them the right to opt out of data collection and to demand deletion of their data.[115] The CONSENT Act would require "edge providers" such as social media platforms to obtain "opt in" from users before using, sharing, or selling their personal information, and to provide levels of transparency similar to those described in the Social Media Privacy Protection and Consumer Rights Act.[116] The fact that the Cambridge Analytica scandal was followed in late 2018 by further revelations that Facebook continued to share access to user data with other large tech companies such as Apple, Amazon, Microsoft, and Netflix has provided further incentive for regulatory interventions related to how social media platforms gather and monetize user data.

The bulk of the U.S. legal and regulatory response to the various social media–related issues confronting policy makers could thus end up focusing on the protection of user data. U.S. policy makers have a long history of prioritizing the economic dimensions of media policy over the political dimensions,[117] and thus the audience as consumer over the audience as citizen.[118] The reorientation of social media policy concerns around the protection of user data, couched in the language of consumer protections, reflects this tendency.

Certainly, a focus on consumer data protection represents a clearer path for policy interventions. It is somewhat less fraught with conflicting partisan self-interest (given the somewhat indirect relationship between privacy and the news and information that affect citizen voting behaviors), and less entangled in thorny First Amendment issues. However, a focus on consumer privacy is, at best, an indirect approach to dealing with issues such as fake news. I say indirect because limitations on the gathering and usage of consumer data certainly have the potential to undermine the precision with which fake news or deceptive political advertising can target users. If fake news purveyors or deceptive advertisers could not target their desired audience as effectively, this would likely reduce their reach or impact, and might even discourage, to some extent, the use of social media platforms for these purposes. However, the consumer data protections being proposed are most likely not, in themselves, sufficient for solving these problems. They address one piece of a larger puzzle.

The consumer data protections that are in place in Europe are being accompanied by various degrees of policy intervention directed at fake news and disinformation. The European Union established a High Level Group to advise on policy initiatives to combat the spread of fake news and disinformation online.[119] Importantly, this initiative was directed not only at possible legal and regulatory responses to the production and dissemination of fake news, but also at identifying means of enhancing quality journalism, developing self-regulatory responses, and improving digital media literacy. This group's fairly broad recommendations include enhancing transparency in online news, promoting media and information literacy, developing tools for empowering users and journalists to tackle disinformation, and safeguarding the diversity and sustainability of the European news media ecosystem.[120]

Britain has announced plans to establish a dedicated "national security communications unit" that will be "tasked with combating disinformation by state actors and others"[121] and is considering a range of additional interventions, including using content standards established for television and radio broadcasters relating to accuracy and impartiality as a basis for setting standards for online content, along wtih government-conducted audits of social media platforms' algorithms.[122] This is a relatively rare instance, so far, of a regulatory framework for traditional media informing social media regulation.

In France, President Emmanuel Macron has been particularly aggressive in seeking to combat fake news on social media platforms. In early 2018, he introduced legislation directed at preventing the dissemination of fake news during election campaign periods. This would be achieved through mandated transparency for social media platforms, requiring them to reveal who is paying for sponsored content. Spending caps on social media advertising are also part of the proposed plan. In addition, judges would have the authority to order takedowns of false content and block access to websites where such content appears.[123] While this legislation did not pass the Senate, a bill that allows a candidate or political party to seek a court injunction preventing the publication of "false information" during the three months leading up to a national election was passed in November 2018.[124] France has also taken the unprecedented step of "embedding" a team of regulators within Facebook to observe how the company addresses hate speech. Of particular relevance here is that this action is taking place with Facebook's cooperation.[125]

Some of the most aggressive actions taken so far are in Germany, where, in January 2018, the Netzwerkdurchsetzungsgesetz (NetzDG) law took effect. This law requires social media platforms with more than two million users to remove fake news, hate speech, and other illegal material within twenty-four hours of notification, or receive fines of up to fifty million Euros.[126] The platforms are required to process and evaluate submitted complaints and to make the determination as to whether individual posts merit deletion. Not surprisingly, this law has come under criticism for leading to deletions of legitimate speech.[127] However, justice ministers for the German states have asked for the law to be tightened, and loopholes to be eliminated,[128] which suggests that the law is moving in the direction of becoming more expansive rather than straining under intensive backlash. In many ways, this law is a canary in the coal mine for democracies around the world.

RETHINKING LEGAL AND REGULATORY FRAMEWORKS

As the previous chapters have shown, neither the legal nor the regulatory frameworks that have traditionally been applied to the media sector in the United States appear to adequately reflect or encompass the nature of social media platforms, and thus are in need of reinterpretation or revision. This situation helps to explain the degree of inaction that has characterized policymaking in the United States thus far. In the sections that follow, I offer some ideas for how our legal and regulatory frameworks can be adapted to a changing media landscape.

I make these suggestions fully recognizing that the current political climate in the United States makes this perhaps the most dangerous time in generations (at least since the Nixon administration) to suggest any kind of more rigorous regulatory framework for any part of the media sector, given the level of hostility that the current administration has shown toward the press. At the same time, it seems within the bounds of reasoned optimism to consider the current situation something of an historical anomaly. The following discussion operates from this longer-term perspective.

RETHINKING THE FIRST AMENDMENT

Legal doctrines and regulatory frameworks represent fundamental components of media governance. Within the context of U.S. media regulation, the First Amendment has traditionally served as the fundamental legal constraint on regulatory models and interventions. Thus, any consideration of the overall regulatory framework for social media should begin with a consideration of the legal parameters within which such a framework operates.

The key issue here is whether there are any alterations that can—or should—be made to how the First Amendment functions within the context of social media governance. Legal scholar Tim Wu recently explored the provocative question "Is the First Amendment obsolete?"[129] As Wu illustrates, the First Amendment originated when opportunities to speak and reach an audience were relatively limited. Now, as Wu notes, technological changes have meant that "speakers are more like moths—their supply is apparently endless. The massive decline in barriers to publishing makes information abundant, especially when speakers congregate on brightly lit matters of public controversy. The low costs of speaking have, paradoxically, made it easier to weaponize speech."[130] Along similar lines, technology scholar Zeynep Tufekci has made the case that "many more of the most noble old ideas about free speech simply don't compute in the age of social media."[131]

The key implications of these arguments is that the technological conditions underlying our speech environment have changed so profoundly that the First Amendment, as a fundamental institution of media governance, may be undermining as much as enhancing the democratic process. Within the realm of social media, the First Amendment facilitates a speech environment that is now capable of doing perhaps unprecedented harms to the democratic process, while restricting regulatory interventions that could potentially curb those harms.

Fortunately, the natural end point of this perspective is not that the First Amendment is genuinely obsolete. Rather, the problem may be that certain aspects of First Amendment theory remain underdeveloped, or underutilized. As Tim Wu puts it, "the First Amendment should be adapted to contemporary speech conditions."[132] There are some specific ways that this could happen.

The Diminishment of the Counterspeech Doctrine

As I discussed in chapter 3, the assumption of the efficacy of counterspeech should wield less influence in any applications of the First Amendment to cases involving social media. It seems appropriate that, for First Amendment cases related to news on social media, the counter-speech doctrine should receive the same kind of more circumspect and limited application that has been advocated for in speech contexts such as hate speech and adopted by the courts in contexts such as libel. The Supreme Court's recognition that "false statements of fact" are partic-ularly resistant to counterspeech[133] needs to extend beyond the context of individual reputation that provided the basis for that decision. First Amendment jurisprudence needs to recognize that, despite the appar-ent free flow of news and information from diverse and antagonistic sources that the Internet has been seen to epitomize, the dissemination and consumption of news in the increasingly social-mediated online environment merits inclusion among those speech contexts in which reliance on counterspeech is increasingly ineffectual and potentially damaging to democracy.

As legal scholar Frederick Schauer points out, the troubling irony is that First Amendment theory has seldom grappled with the issue of truth versus falsity—or, in today's vernacular, facts versus "alternative facts."[134] As Schauer convincingly demonstrates, "nearly all of the components that have made up our free speech tradition . . . in the cases and in the literature, and in the political events that inspired free speech controver-sies, have had very little to say about the relationship between freedom of speech and questions of demonstrable fact. Implicit in much of that tradition may have been the belief that the power of the marketplace of ideas to select for truth was as applicable to factual as to religious, ideo-logical, political, and social truth, but rarely is the topic mentioned."[135] Continuing in this vein, Schauer distressingly notes, "although factual truth is important, surprisingly little of the free speech tradition is addressed directly to the question of the relationship between a regime of freedom of speech and the goal of increasing public knowledge of facts or decreasing public belief in false factual propositions."[136] As a result, the First Amendment has essentially facilitated the type of speech that, ironically, undermines the very democratic process that the First Amendment is intended to serve and strengthen.

Historically, different categories of speech have received different levels of First Amendment protection based on their relevance and value to the democratic process.[137] For instance, commercial speech receives less First Amendment protection (and more rigorous restrictions against falsity) than political speech, which represents the pinnacle of speech protection because of its centrality to the democratic process.[138] The irony here is that fake news is a type of speech that is most directly and irrefutably damaging to the integrity of the democratic process, yet because it resides within the large and undifferentiated protective bubble of political speech (where journalism generally resides), it receives (as long as it is not libelous) the highest level of First Amendment protection.

Going forward, the distinction between the factual and the subjective dimensions of journalism needs to be better integrated into First Amendment jurisprudence, as part of the larger project of establishing a more robust First Amendment tradition directed at carving out a more distinct space where falsity (at least in relation to news) resides within the free speech landscape.

Embracing the Collectivist First Amendment

The fallout from the 2016 election has also helped to remind us that there have long been two somewhat competing interpretations of the First Amendment: the *individualist* and the *collectivist* interpretations.[139] It is worth briefly reviewing these two approaches before making the case that an interpretive shift is in order.

The more dominant First Amendment approach has been the individualist interpretation,[140] which prioritizes preserving and enhancing the free speech rights of the individual citizen (or media outlet). This emphasis on individual autonomy emanates from the fact that constitutional rights are traditionally perceived as protecting the individual from government intrusion.[141] Within this interpretive framework, free speech rights are typically conceived of as a "negative liberty"[142]—that is, in terms of freedom from external interference in doing what one wants.

The collectivist interpretation of the First Amendment focuses on creating a speech environment that supports the community-based objectives associated with the First Amendment, such as stability, collective decision-making, and, most important, the effective functioning of the democratic process.[143] The First Amendment thus functions as the means to ends that explicitly prioritize the welfare of the collective citizenry over the welfare of the individual speaker. Reflecting this assignment of value, a central guiding principle of the collectivist approach is that "what is essential is not that everyone shall speak, but that everything worth saying shall be said."[144]

From an application standpoint, the key point of departure of the collectivist interpretation from the individualist interpretation is that the collectivists reject the absolutist interpretation of the First Amendment's command that Congress make no law abridging freedom of speech or of the press. From the collectivist perspective, the phrasing of the First Amendment clearly grants Congress the authority to make laws that *enhance* the free speech environment. Indeed, many proponents of the collectivist interpretation of the First Amendment advocate the imposition of government regulations in order to correct perceived inadequacies in the current system of communicating information to citizens.[145] Under this perspective, while the state "remains a threat to free expression, [it] also needs to serve as a necessary counterweight to developing technologies of private control and surveillance."[146]

The point here, and the natural extension of the arguments of scholars such as Wu and Tufekci, is that technological change may finally be compelling the embracing of the collectivist approach to the First Amendment over the individualist approach. This should be seen not as a diminishment of the First Amendment, but rather as an adjustment in emphasis—an adjustment that many collectivist proponents have compellingly argued is in fact the more democracy-reflective and -enhancing interpretation of the First Amendment.

Arguments for a shift to a more collectivist interpretation of the First Amendment are far from new. They have a long history.[147] The key point here, however, is that the news production, distribution, and consumption dynamics that characterize social media may represent the most compelling case yet for this interpretive shift to finally take place.

To apply this collectivist perspective to the context of social media, if there are prominent aspects of the algorithmic marketplace of ideas that are fundamentally (to use Tufekci's term) "democracy poisoning" rather than democracy enhancing (e.g., fake news that leads to misinformed voting behaviors), then the collectivist approach offers what is in actuality a First Amendment–friendly (rather than hostile) path toward regulatory interventions.

An individualist-oriented First Amendment functions primarily as a constraint on policy makers' actions. In contrast, a collectivist-oriented First Amendment functions more as a distinct policy objective, rather than as a boundary line to be respected in the pursuit of other policy objectives. The nature and function of social media platforms may represent the necessity that triggers the prioritization of the collectivist interpretation of the First Amendment over the individualist.

RECONCILING REGULATORY MOTIVATIONS AND RATIONALES

One important ramification of a more collectivist approach to the First Amendment is how it can facilitate a reconfiguration of our public-interest regulatory framework for media in a way that allows it to extend to social media platforms. As discussed in the previous chapter, the media regulatory framework in the United States is characterized by the distinction between motivations and rationales. The regulatory rationales are technologically derived justifications for regulations that would otherwise represent infringements on the First Amendment rights of media outlets. The motivations are the actual problems or concerns (fake news, adult content, lack of diversity, etc.) that attract regulatory attention. This framework reflects a fundamentally individualist approach to the First Amendment, in that regulatory action to address speech-related problems represents a de facto intrusion on individual speech rights unless some mitigating technological anomaly is present.

Given this situation, the key questions become (1) is there an alternative approach to regulatory rationales other than the reactive "technological particularism"[148] that has characterized the U.S. regulatory apparatus? and (2) what would be some implications of such an approach? The purpose in asking these questions is to consider if and how a more robust public-interest-oriented regulatory framework might be applied to social media. Exploring this possibility seems particularly relevant in light of the fact that perhaps the most applicable general rationale for intervention—that social media represent a monopolistic or oligopolistic situation—is vulnerable to the argument that the barriers to entry for new online competitors remain low.[149] If Google has yet to be treated as a regulated monopoly in search, then Facebook's being treated as a regulated monopoly in social seems unlikely as well.

Considering the first question, the reality is that regulatory motivations typically beget regulatory rationales. For instance, as discussed in chapter 5, concerns about the political influence of broadcasting led to the scarcity rationale. These rationales are typically derived from the contemporary characteristics of a media technology or service, and are thus inherently vulnerable to the inevitable evolution that affects all media technologies.[150] If regulatory motivations and rationales were more tightly intertwined, this would not be a problem, because the technological changes undermining an established regulatory rationale would simultaneously be addressing and alleviating the motivations. So, for instance, the argument that the scarcity of the broadcast spectrum is much less a factor today than it was fifty years ago might bear directly on the FCC's motivations to regulate on behalf of diversity of sources/content (because more content providers are now able to reach audiences, through so many additional technologies and services). However, the relative presence or absence of scarcity has no strong bearing on, say, the FCC's motivations to protect children from harmful content (though certainly other rationales such as the pervasiveness and public-resource rationales do).

Is there a way, then, that regulatory rationales can emerge from somewhere other than the contemporary technological characteristics of specific media and be better intertwined with core regulatory motivations?[151] Can regulatory motivations and rationales essentially converge? One possibility might be for the public-interest concept to serve such a unifying role. To some extent, the public interest already serves as something of a bridge concept. It operates as a broad, general motivation for regulatory oversight and intervention, as the mandate

that guides the FCC; and through its history, the public-interest principle has been populated with various, more specific policy objectives
(diversity, localism, etc.).[152]

The public interest can also be seen as a rationale, in that in many industry sectors, the question of regulatory intervention hinges on a determination as to whether an industry, technology, or service is "affected with
a public interest." This notion of an industry being affected with a public
interest has a long history that developed primarily within the context
of debates over the right of the government to set prices in monopolistic
situations.[153] This descriptor has typically served as a rationale for various forms of government oversight and intervention. The terminology
has most often been applied to "essential services" such as utilities.[154]
However, this terminology has not been limited exclusively to utilities
regulation, nor has it been limited to the regulation of pricing.[155] Legal
scholar Frank Pasquale has argued for its application to search engines.[156]

As the affected-with-a-public-interest concept became refined over
time, one particular category of business seems particularly relevant to
the context at hand: "businesses which though not public at their incep-
tion may be said to have risen to be such."[157] This description would seem
to effectively characterize social media platforms and the evolutionary
trajectory that they have followed.[158]

IMPLICATIONS

This merging of the public-interest principle as regulatory motivation and rationale is premised on the ongoing convergence of media
technologies and services; the multiplatform nature of how content is
produced, distributed, and consumed; and the inherent interconnectedness and interdependence of the contemporary media ecosystem.
Indeed, if we think about media from an ecosystem perspective,[159] the
inherent interconnectedness and interdependence of all of the components means that an action (by a regulator, or a regulated or unregulated
industry stakeholder) that affects one component of the ecosystem is
likely to have ripple effects on others. Regulatory rationales that isolate

individual components of this ecosystem ignore this interconnectedness and independence in a way that is fundamentally incompatible with the very concept of an ecosystem. For these reasons, making technological characteristics no longer the starting place for establishing regulatory rationales makes the most sense going forward.

This approach would require that explicit, general criteria be articulated for whether media technologies or services are "affected with a public interest." It would thus involve taking the public-interest concept beyond the fairly vague regulatory principle for which it has been criticized and infusing it with specific criteria (reflecting core regulatory motivations) that could then be applied to specific media technologies and services.

For instance, particularly in light of contemporary concerns, a fundamental public-interest criterion is the nature and extent of the role that a technology or service plays in the democratic process. Arguments for protecting and enhancing the democratic process as a regulatory rationale are well established,[160] even if they have not been consistently embraced by policy makers and the courts. If a platform meets certain criteria associated with centrality to—or impact on—the democratic process, then this could trigger those aspects of the public-interest regulatory framework associated with preserving and enhancing the democratic process.

Inherent in this approach would be an assessment of the nature and magnitude of the role and impact that a platform has within the broader news ecosystem—something that could be reevaluated at regular intervals or as conditions warrant. Such an approach could also be sensitive to how a technology or service evolves over time. For instance, Facebook, in its original incarnation as a platform for staying in touch with friends and family members, would not merit classification as infused with the public interest. However, the contemporary version of Facebook, in its role as a central distributor of, and means of accessing, journalism, and as an increasingly prominent mechanism for political advertising and political communication, certainly would.

This example raises an important question: Can we imagine a scenario in which a set of public-interest regulatory rationales/motivations are developed that apply to some social media platforms but not others on the basis of criteria such as functionality and usage? Or should such criteria apply uniformly across media categories such that one entity could, in effect, trigger the application of the public-interest regulatory framework to all entities in that category? Germany is utilizing a user-base trigger of two million users for its regulation of hate speech and fake news on social media.[161] We might also consider an approach based on the proportion of a platform's posts or participants that fit basic criteria for journalism and/or political communication. Or self-reported usage behaviors might serve as the basis, not unlike how the Federal Communications Commission utilized survey data on the extent to which individuals relied on different media for news in order to assess the level of media diversity present in individual communities.[162]

This discussion of a more robust public-interest regulatory framework has focused exclusively on social media. This relatively narrow focus raises another question: Can we imagine a scenario in which a strong public-interest regulatory framework is applied to social media in particular, but not to the Internet as a whole? In considering this question, it is worth revisiting a classic analysis, by legal scholar and Columbia University President Lee Bollinger, of the different regulatory models applied to print media and broadcast media in the United States.[163] As Bollinger points out (and as discussed in chapter 5), the technologically derived rationales for broadcast regulation do not hold up particularly well under scrutiny.

However, according to Bollinger, while the specific logic of treating broadcasting differently than print is faulty, the ultimate outcome not only is desirable, but also makes compelling sense when an alternative rationale is brought to bear. Specifically, according to Bollinger, given that (as discussed earlier) there are both speech-enhancing and speech-impeding aspects to media regulation,[164] it makes practical sense to apply a more proactive regulatory model to one component of the media system and a more laissez-faire approach to the other. As Bollinger argues, in light of the double-edged character of media regulation, the most logical response is a "partial regulatory scheme," in which different regulatory approaches are applied to different media sectors, media users are able to reap the benefits of both models, and these different models operate as a type of checks-and-balances system upon each other.[165]

As the Internet essentially subsumes all other forms of media (including print), the suggestion here is that this rationale for a "partial regulatory scheme" might apply similarly online, with the broader Internet operating in a relatively unregulated matter, but with social media platforms operating under greater regulatory oversight. This partial regulatory scheme highlights the fact that, regardless of what types of regulatory interventions are considered for social media, the broader Internet still operates as a largely unregulated space.[166] Content or sources that might be deemed inappropriate for social media platforms are still likely to be accessible online. Thus, this content is not suppressed, but it is denied the tremendous amplification and targeting opportunities afforded by social media—opportunities that perhaps should be more judiciously allocated in the name of democracy. In this way, Bollinger's case for a partial system of regulation can resurface today and help guide the path forward.

■ ■ ■

The public-interest regulatory model as it has existed in the United States has persisted despite—rather than because of—the logical foundation upon which it has been justified. If we accept this premise, and agree with the need to not completely abdicate government oversight of the media sector, then we should recognize the logic in developing a more unified, less technologically particularistic approach to rationalizing regulatory interventions. The evolving role, functions, and effects of social media may represent the much-needed incentive for doing so. In the end, the goal here has not been to suggest specific regulatory obligations to be imposed on social media platforms, but rather to suggest a revised regulatory framework that would facilitate such actions if they were deemed necessary.

Conclusion

This book has provided a media-centric perspective on platforms that have traditionally been resistant to being thought of as media. Although there is certainly much that distinguishes social media platforms from the media technologies and platforms that preceded them, the fact that there are also many similarities, and that these platforms have become inextricably intertwined with other media, means that it is important that we consider the governance of these platforms in light of established norms, principles, and regulatory models associated with traditional media.

The book has also provided historical context, in terms of how—and why—our media ecosystem evolved into its present state, with social media platforms so quickly ascending to a position of such prominence. Here, I have focused on how social media provided solutions to problems that the Internet had created for content producers/distributors, advertisers, and users.

It has also illustrated how this evolution has affected core principles of media governance, such as the First Amendment, the marketplace of ideas, and the public interest. Here, my goal was to illustrate the ways in which the intersection of social media and journalism has been undermining these core principles.

Finally, this book has sketched out some broad contours of regulatory and self-regulatory frameworks that would better integrate these platforms into established norms and structures of media governance. Here, my focus was primarily on regulatory/self-regulatory models and rationales and secondarily on specific actions and interventions. The logic here was that we need to address these foundational issues in order to have stable, coherent, and defensible bases for any such actions or interventions. One of the goals here has been to provoke, and contribute to, deliberations on that front.

As I stated in the acknowledgments at the beginning of the book, I have tried to take aim at a rapidly moving target. Throughout the research process, events have threatened to overtake the analysis and arguments. However, as rapidly as technologies, market conditions, and user behaviors can change, institutions and policies tend to change much more slowly. So it is likely that many of the core issues and concerns will remain unresolved at the time this book is published, and for some time beyond.

The other challenge in addressing this topic is that there is much we still do not know about the intersection of social media, journalism, and the democratic process that could—and should—inform social media governance.[1] Indeed, this is a topic that is producing a consistent stream of relevant studies. Certainly, we know at this point that social media platforms have had a disruptive effect on the news and information ecosystem. Recent research tells us that disinformation disguised as journalism remains prominent on these platforms, despite a variety of preventive efforts, and that social media platforms have contributed to increased political polarization.[2] Some research, however, has also shown that disinformation appears to be diminishing on some platforms (Facebook), but increasing on others (Twitter).[3] Given that Facebook has been more aggressive in policing fake news than Twitter, this pattern illustrates how the problem will evolve in response to the evolutionary dynamics and governance structures and policies within the various components of the platform ecosystem. Disinformation will follow the paths of least resistance, as long as these paths lead to a large enough audience to justify the effort.

The core question of whether the democratic process has been fundamentally damaged remains open to debate. As discussed in chapter 4, experts in political communication can, at best, offer informed speculation when it comes, for example, to the question of whether Russian intervention affected the outcome of the 2016 election.[4] Some have argued that the reach and impact of socially mediated disinformation and politically polarized filter bubbles on users, and thus on the democratic process, has been minimal.[5] In addition, as discussed in chapter 2, recent data suggest that reliance on social media for accessing news is in decline. From this perspective, regulatory interventions may represent premature overreactions to a problem of uncertain magnitude and/or diminishing significance. It is possible that the magnitude of the effect may turn out to be less than we fear, or that we have already seen the peak of social media's potential for impact, with the usage pendulum perhaps now swinging the other way.

However, we also have to be aware of the unique policy context at issue here. Consider some other policy areas, such as health policy, economic policy, or environmental policy. In these areas, if we wait for clear and irrefutable evidence of a problem requiring intervention, the means of crafting policy solutions remain unaffected, although reacting late to the problem can make the problem more difficult—or even impossible—to solve. In contrast, if we are talking, as we have been in this book, about a problem related to the effective functioning of the democratic process, then the very nature of the problem undermines the means for developing and adopting solutions. A broken democracy is, by definition, debilitated in terms of effectively formulating and implementing the policy solutions necessary to fix itself. That is, by the time we have incontrovertible proof that social media are being used in ways that fundamentally undermine the democratic process, the undermining of that process will have simultaneously undermined one of the key mechanisms—the policy-making process—for solving the problem.

This is why being more proactive and anticipatory seems both justifiable and advisable in this context. The nature of the concerns being raised by the intersection of social media and journalism are uniquely resistant to being addressed in a post hoc manner. The dangers of not being proactive are simply too great.

At the same time, political polarization and partisanship have come to affect the workings of our government to an extent that many of us have not seen in our lifetimes. From this standpoint, greater government intervention in our media ecosystem can be seen to represent as compelling a threat to an informed citizenry and the integrity of the democratic process as government inaction. In some ways, it seems that the most appropriate analogy for our current situation might be cancer treatment. For those suffering from cancer, the treatment can often produce different, but equally damaging, health problems. The irony here, of course, is that this polarization and partisanship are in part a product of the way in which our media ecosystem has evolved, with fragmentation leading to greater incentives to cater to and stoke partisanship. This relationship leads us back once again to the intertwining of the problem's causes and its potential solutions.

However, as we struggle to untangle this Gordian knot, it is worth remembering that social media platforms are not synonymous with the Internet, and certainly are not synonymous with journalism. The point here is that any governmental or self-regulatory efforts to address the problematic distribution, curation, and consumption dynamics associated with social media need not intrude upon the broader digital media ecosystem, which, pre–social media, generated fewer of the problems we are confronting today. When social media platforms have briefly gone down, people immediately reverted to their old habits of accessing the news directly.[6] We can never expect, as the saying goes, to put the horse back in the barn as it relates to the intersection of social media and journalism. However, as I have emphasized at various points in the book, if efforts by government, platforms, or self-regulatory bodies to more aggressively regulate how these platforms operate as distributors and curators of journalism have the additional consequence of discouraging the use of these platforms as a means of producing, disseminating, and consuming news, then our democracy will likely be the better for it.

Notes

Introduction

1. Steve Annear, "Mark Zuckerberg Couldn't Stop Mentioning Harvard Dorm During Facebook Testimony," *Boston Globe*, April 11, 2018, https://www.bostonglobe.com /metro/2018/04/11/mark-zuckerberg-couldn-stop-mentioning-his-harvard-dorm -room-during-facebook-testimony/slW4rCXyIdyctzEuB93J4L/story.html.

2. Andre Picard, "The History of Twitter, 140 Characters at a Time," *Globe and Mail*, March 28, 2018, https://www.theglobeandmail.com/technology/digital-culture/the -history-of-twitter-140-characters-at-a-time/article573416/.

3. See, for example, Joshua Braun and Tarleton Gillespie, "Hosting the Public Discourse, Hosting the Public," *Journalism Practice* 5, no. 4 (2011): 383–398; Rebecca MacKinnon, *Consent of the Networked: The Worldwide Struggle for Internet Freedom* (New York: Basic Books, 2013); Zeynep Tufekci, *Twitter and Tear Gas: The Power and Fragility of Networked Protest* (New Haven, CT: Yale University Press, 2017); Zeynep Tufekci, "YouTube, the Great Radicalizer," *New York Times*, March 10, 2018, https://www.nytimes.com/2018/03/10 /opinion/sunday/youtube-politics-radical.html.

4. Edison even referred to the device as the "musical telephone." See "Loud-Speaking Telephone," *Thomas A. Edison Papers*, Rutgers School of Arts and Sciences, October 28, 2016, http://edison.rutgers.edu/loud.htm.

5. This purpose is reflected in radio's originally being referred to as the wireless telegraph. See Tom Standage, *Writing on the Wall: Social Media—the First 2,000 Years* (New York: Bloomsbury, 2013), 191.

6. As with radio, cable's original label, community antenna television (CATV), reflected its narrower original purpose.

7. As reflected in its original moniker, Advanced Research Projects Agency Network (ARPANET). See Standage, *Writing on the Wall*, 215–216.

8. See John Carey and Martin C. J. Elton, *When Media Are New: Understanding the Dynamics of New Media Adoption and Use* (Ann Arbor: University of Michigan Press, 2010).

9. See Carey and Elton, *When Media Are New*.

10. As Geert Lovink has noted in his critique of social media, "mathematicians did not foresee the (mis)use of computers for media purposes. Why listen to records on a computer? If you want to see a film, visit the cinema"; Geert Lovink, *Networks Without a Cause: A Critique of Social Media* (Malden, MA: Polity), 148.

11. Gwyneth Jackaway, *Media at War: Radio's Challenge to the Newspapers, 1924–1939* (Westport, CT: Praeger, 1995).

12. See Carey and Elton, *When Media Are New*.

13. See Michael Zarkin, *The FCC and the Politics of Cable TV Regulation, 1952–1980* (Amherst, NY: Cambria Press, 2010).

14. Matt McGee, "Facebook Cuts Into Google's Lead as Top Traffic Driver to Online News Sites," *Marketing Land*, February 28, 2014, https://marketingland.com/facebook -cuts-googles-lead-top-traffic-driver-online-news-sites-report-75578.

15. Pares.ly, "External Referrals in the Parse.ly Network," May 2018, https://www.parse.ly /resources/data-studies/referrer-dashboard/.

16. Elisa Shearer and Jeffrey Gottfried, "News Use Across Social Media Platforms 2017," *Pew Research Center*, September 7, 2017, http://www.journalism.org/2017/09/07/news -use-across-social-media-platforms-2017/.

17. Shearer and Gottfried, "News Use Across Social Media Platforms 2017."

18. Shearer and Gottfried, "News Use Across Social Media Platforms 2017."

19. Emily Bell, "Facebook Is Eating the World," *Columbia Journalism Review*, March 7, 2016, https://www.cjr.org/analysis/facebook_and_media.php.

20. Joanna M. Burkhardt, "History of Fake News," *Library Technology Reports* 53, no. 8 (2017): 5–10.

21. Mark Zuckerberg, Testimony Before the United States Senate Committee on the Judiciary and the United States Senate Committee on Commerce, Science, and Transportation (April 10, 2018), 1, https://www.judiciary.senate.gov/imo/media/doc/04-10-18%20 Zuckerberg%20Testimony.pdf.

22. Bell, "Facebook Is Eating the World."

23. The most recent iteration of this tension emerged from Mark Zuckerberg's April 2018 testimony before Congress, during which certain members of Congress seemed unsure of how to classify Facebook; see Mary Louise Kelly, "Media or Tech Company? Facebook's Profile Is Blurry," *NPR*, April 11, 2018, https://www.npr.org/2018/04/11/601560213/media -or-tech-company-facebooks-profile-is-blurry.

24. Thanks to Robyn Caplan for her valuable contributions to this section.

25. William Uricchio, "The Algorithmic Turn: Photosynth, Augmented Reality and the Changing Implications of the Image," *Visual Studies* 26, no. 1 (2011): 25–35.

26. See, for example, Axel Bruns, *Gatewatching and News Curation: Journalism, Social Media, and the Public Sphere* (New York: Peter Lang, 2018); Frank Pasquale, *The Black*

Box Society: The Secret Algorithms That Control Money and Information (Cambridge, MA: Harvard University Press, 2015).

27. Tarleton Gillespie, "The Relevance of Algorithms," in *Media Technologies: Essays on Communication, Materiality, and Society*, ed. Tarleton Gillespie, Pablo J. Boczkowski, and Kristen A. Foot (Cambridge, MA: MIT Press, 2014), 167.

28. Pasquale, *The Black Box Society*; Christopher Steiner, *Automate This: How Algorithms Took Over Our Markets, Our Jobs, and the World* (New York: Penguin, 2012).

29. Jerome Cukier, "Why Is Uber Considered a Technology Company and a Lot of People Place It Among Tech Giants Like Google, Facebook, etc?" *Quora*, March 1, 2016, https://www.quora.com/Why-is-Uber-considered-a-technology-company-and-a-lot-of-people-place-it-among-tech-giants-like-Google-Facebook-etc.

30. Michael Carney, "As Uber Fights to Maintain Its Technology Company Classification in India, the Rest of the World Watches," *Pando*, February 20, 2015, https://pando.com/2015/02/20/as-uber-fights-to-maintain-its-technology-company-classification-in-india-the-rest-of-the-world-watches/.

31. Philip M. Napoli and Robyn Caplan, "Why Media Companies Insist They're Not Media Companies, Why They're Wrong, and Why It Matters," *First Monday* 22, no. 5 (2017), http://firstmonday.org/ojs/index.php/fm/article/view/7051.

32. Mark Peterson, "Can Ford Turn Itself Into a Tech Company?" *New York Times Magazine*, November 9, 2019, https://www.nytimes.com/interactive/2017/11/09/magazine/tech-design-autonomous-future-cars-detroit-ford.html.

33. See, for example, Miguel Helft, "Is Google a Media Company?" *New York Times*, August 10, 2008, http://www.nytimes.com/2008/08/11/technology/11google.html; Bill Mickey, "Are You a Technology Company or a Media Company?" *Folio*, October 29, 2013, http://www.foliomag.com/are-you-technology-company-or-media-company/.

34. Choire Sicha, "Inside Gawker Media's First Company-Wide Meeting," *Awl*, September 8, 2011, https://theawl.com/inside-gawker-medias-first-company-wide-meeting-8abf673bf61#.umax6qp27; Nick Tjaardstra, "Vox Media: Tech Company First, Publisher Second," *World News Publishing Focus*, April 20, 2015, http://blog.wan-ifra.org/2015/04/20/vox-media-tech-company-first-publisher-second.

35. Quoted in Danny Sullivan, "Schmidt: Google Still a Tech Company Despite the Billboards," *Search Engine Watch*, June 12, 2006, https://searchenginewatch.com/sew/news/2058565/schmidt-google-still-a-tech-company-despite-the-billboards.

36. Quoted in Seth Fiegerman, "Dear Facebook, You're a Media Company Now. Start Acting Like One," *Mashable*, June 15, 2016, http://mashable.com/2016/05/15/facebook-media-company/#4xjvChg3NaqP.

37. Kelly Fiveash, "'We're a Tech Company Not a Media Company,' Says Facebook Founder," *Ars Technica*, August 20, 2016, https://arstechnica.com/tech-policy/2016/08/germany-facebook-edit-hateful-posts-zuckerberg-says-not-media-empire/.

38. Jeff John Roberts, "Why Facebook Won't Admit It's a Media Company," *Fortune*, November 14, 2016, http://fortune.com/2016/11/14/facebook-zuckerberg-media/.

39. Quoted in Nick Bilton, "Is Twitter a Media Company or Technology Company?" *New York Times*, July 25, 2012, http://bits.blogs.nytimes.com/2012/07/25/is-twitter-a-media-or-technology-company/.

40. Quoted in Andy Langer, "Is Steve Jobs the God of Music?" *Esquire*, July 2003, http://www.esquire.com/news-politics/a11177/steve-jobs-esquire-interview-0703/.

41. See, for example, Robert Picard, *The Economics and Financing of Media Companies*, 2nd ed. (New York: Fordham University Press, 2011).

42. The term "pure public good" refers to how economists think about media products as "public goods"—goods that are "nonexcludable" and "nondepletable." Think, for instance, of a motion picture or a television program that, once produced, can be shown and reshown for years after, without incurring any additional production costs. A "pure public good" is a media product that does not even need to be embedded in a physical object (such as a disk or paper) in order to be distributed and consumed. For a discussion of public goods and pure public goods, see Philip M. Napoli, *Audience Evolution: New Technologies and the Transformation of Media Audiences* (New York: Columbia University Press, 2011).

43. Josh Constine, "Zuckerberg Implies Facebook Is a Media Company, Just 'Not a Traditional Media Company,'" *TechCrunch*, December 21, 2016, https://techcrunch.com/2016/12/21/fbonc.

44. Michael Curtin, Jennifer Holt, and Kevin Sanson, *Distribution Revolution: Conversations About the Digital Future of Film and Television* (Berkeley, CA: University of California Press, 2014).

45. Quoted in Joshua Benton, "Elizabeth Spiers on BuzzFeed and Other 'Tech' Companies: "'You're Still a Media Company,'" *Nieman Lab*, August 11, 2014, http://www.niemanlab.org/2014/08/elizabeth-spiers-on-buzzfeed-and-other-tech-companies-youre-still-a-media-company/.

46. Philip M. Napoli, "Requiem for the Long Tail: Towards a Political Economy of Content Aggregation and Fragmentation," *International Journal of Media & Cultural Politics* 12, no. 3 (2016): 343–356.

47. Conor Dougherty and Emily Steel, "YouTube Introduces YouTube Red, a Subscription Service," *New York Times*, October 21, 2015, https://www.nytimes.com/2015/10/22/technology/youtube-introduces-youtube-red-a-subscription-service.html; DarrellEtherington, "Facebook Exploring Creation of Its Own Content," *TechCrunch*, December 14, 2016, https://techcrunch.com/2016/12/14/facebook-exploring-creation-of-its-own-original-video-content/; Sarah Perez and Jonathan Shieber, "YouTube Unveils YouTube TV, Its Live TV Streaming Service," *Tech Crunch*, February 27, 2017, https://techcrunch.com/2017/02/28/youtube-launches-youtube-tv-its-live-tv-streaming-service/.

48. Quoted in Staci D. Kramer, "Google Is Still a Tech Company. Really," *Gigaom*, June 12, 2006, https://gigaom.com/2006/06/12/google-is-still-a-tech-company-really/.

49. John Koetsier, "Exclusive: Cheezburger Will Take Page Out of Reddit's Playbook, Allow Users to Create Own Subsites," *VentureBeat*, August 22, 2012, http://venturebeat.com/2012/08/22/exclusive-cheezburger-will-take-page-out-of-reddits-playbook-allow-users-to-create-own-subsites/.

50. Scott Woolley, *The Network: The Battle for the Airwaves and the Birth of the Communications Age* (New York: Ecco, 2016).

51. Mark Deuze, *Media Work* (Cambridge, UK: Polity Press), 73.

52. See, for example, Daniel Trielli, Sean Mussenden, Jennifer Stark, and Nicholas Diakopoulos, "Googling Politics: How the Google Issue Guide on Candidates Is Biased," *Slate*, June 7, 2016, http://www.slate.com/articles/technology/future_tense/2016/06/how_the_google_issue_guide_on_candidates_is_biased.html.

53. See, for example, Fiveash, "'We're a Tech Company Not a Media Company'"; Mike Isaac, "Facebook, Nodding to Its Role in Media, Starts a Journalism Project," *New York Times*, January 11, 2017, https://www.nytimes.com/2017/01/11/technology/facebook-journalism-project.html?_r=0.

54. Tarleton Gillespie, "The Politics of 'Platforms,'" *New Media & Society* 12, no. 3 (2010): 347–364.

55. Fiveash, "'We're a Tech Company Not a Media Company.'"

56. Anthony M. Nadler, *Making the News Popular: Mobilizing U.S. News Audiences* (Urbana: University of Illinois Press, 2016).

57. Napoli, *Audience Evolution*, 26.

58. See Philip M. Napoli, "Automated Media: An Institutional Theory Perspective on Algorithmic Media Production and Consumption," *Communication Theory* 24 (2014), 340–360.

59. Michael A. DeVito, "From Editors to Algorithms: A Values-Based Approach to Understanding Story Selection in the Facebook News Feed," *Digital Journalism* 5, no. 6 (2017): 753–773.

60. See, for example, Tarleton Gillespie, "Algorithmically Recognizable: Santorum's Google Problem and Google's Santorum Problem," *Information, Communication & Society* 20, no. 1 (2017): 63–80; Rob Kitchin, "Thinking Critically About and Researching Algorithms," *Information, Communication & Society* 20, no. 1 (2017): 14–29; Sofiya Noble, *Algorithms of Oppression: How Search Engines Reinforce Racism* (New York: NYU Press, 2018).

61. Tarleton Gillespie, *Custodians of the Internet: Platforms, Content Moderation, and the Hidden Decisions That Shape Social Media* (New Haven, CT: Yale University Press, 2018).

62. See, for example, David Pierson and Paresh Dave, "If Facebook Promotes Propaganda, Can It Be a Neutral News Platform?" *Los Angeles Times*, May 31, 2016, http://www.latimes.com/business/la-fi-tn-eu-tech-20160531-snap-story.html.

63. Marc Scott and Mike Isaac, "Facebook Restores Iconic Vietnam War Photo It Censored for Nudity," *New York Times*, September 10, 2016, http://www.nytimes.com/2016/09/10/technology/facebook-vietnam-war-photo-nudity.html.

64. Scott and Isaac, "Facebook Restores Iconic Vietnam War Photo."

65. Fiegerman, "Dear Facebook, You're a Media Company Now."

66. Sam Levin, "Is Facebook a Publisher? In Public It Says No, but in Court It Says Yes," *Guardian*, July 3, 2018, https://www.theguardian.com/technology/2018/jul/02/facebook-mark-zuckerberg-platform-publisher-lawsuit.

67. Matthew Ingram, "Facebook's Biggest Problem Is That It's a Media Company," *Gigaom*, May 16, 2012, https://gigaom.com/2012/05/16/facebooks-biggest-problem-is-that-its-a-media-company/; Michael Wolff, "Facebook: A Tale of Two Media Models," *Guardian*,

May 15, 2012, https://www.theguardian.com/commentisfree/cifamerica/2012/may/15/facebook-tale-two-media-models.

68. Suman Bhattacharyya, "Digital Ads to Overtake Traditional Ads in U.S. Local Markets by 2018," *Advertising Age*, October 26, 2016, http://adage.com/article/cmo-strategy/local-ads-digital-2018-bia-kelsey/306468/.

69. Gillespie, "The Politics of 'Platforms,' " 348.

70. Bernard D. Nossiter, "The FCC's Big Giveaway Show," *Nation*, October 26, 1985, 402.

71. Justin Fox, "Why It's Good to Be a 'Technology Company,' " *Harvard Business Review*, August 13, 2014, https://hbr.org/2014/08/why-its-good-to-be-a-technology-company/.

72. See, for example, Paul Bond, "Fresh Facebook Draws Attention," *Hollywood Reporter*, September 28, 2007, http://www.hollywoodreporter.com/news/fresh-facebook-draws-attention-151237; Roberts, "Why Facebook Won't Admit It's a Media Company."

73. Brian Morrissey, "BuzzFeed's Dao Nguyen: 'We Don't Think of Ourselves as an Island,' " *Digiday*, May 6, 2016, http://digiday.com/publishers/buzzfeed-dao-nguyen-digiday-podcast/.

74. Quoted in Benton, "Elizabeth Spiers on BuzzFeed and Other 'Tech' Companies."

75. Michael Nunez, "Want to Know What Facebook Really Thinks of Journalists? Here's What Happened When It Hired Some," *Gizmodo*, May 3, 2016, https://gizmodo.com/want-to-know-what-facebook-really-thinks-of-journalists-1773916117.

76. See Philip M. Napoli, *Foundations of Communications Policy: Principles and Process in the Regulation of Electronic Media* (Cresskill, NJ: Hampton Press, 2001).

77. Philip M. Napoli, "Issues in Media Management and the Public Interest," in *Handbook of Media Management and Economics*, ed. A. B. Albarran, S. C. Olmsted, and M. O. Wirth (Mahwah, NJ: Erlbaum, 2005), 275–295.

78. Mark Fowler and Daniel Brenner, "A Marketplace Approach to Broadcast Regulation," *Texas Law Review* 60 (1982): 207–257, 207.

79. Some of the more utopian perspectives on the democratization of the media can be found in Yochai Benkler, *The Wealth of Networks: How Social Production Transforms Markets and Freedom* (New Haven, CT: Yale University Press, 2006); and Clay Shirky, *Here Comes Everybody: The Power of Organizing Without Organizations* (New York: Penguin, 2008).

80. Prior to beginning work on this book, I was told by one scholar whose work I greatly admire and respect that the public interest "is an old media term" and thus of little relevance to contemporary conversations about the governance of digital media. This book is, in many ways, a response to that perspective.

81. Manuel Puppis, "Media Governance: A New Concept for the Analysis of Media Policy and Regulation," *Communication, Culture & Critique* 2 (2010): 134–149.

82. Puppis, "Media Governance."

83. For more detailed discussions of the media governance concept, see Avshalom Ginosar, "Media Governance: A Conceptual Framework or Merely a Buzzword?" *Communication Theory* 23 (2013): 356–374; Uwe Hasebrink, "The Role of the Audience Within Media Governance: The Neglected Dimension of Media Literacy, *Media Studies* 3, no. 6 (2012): 58–73; Natali Helberger, "From Eyeball to Creator—Toying with Audience Empowerment

in the Audiovisual Media Services Directive, *Entertainment Law Review* 6 (2008): 128–137; Ganaele Langlois, "Participatory Culture and the New Governance of Communication: The Paradox of Participatory Media," *Television & New Media* 14 (2012): 91–105; David Nolan and Tim Marjoribanks, "'Public Editors' and Media Governance at the *Guardian* and the *New York Times*," *Journalism Practice* 5, no. 1 (2011): 3–17.

84. Lawrence Lessig, *Code: And Other Laws of Cyperspace* (New York: Basic Books, 1999), 3.

85. Napoli, "Automated Media."

1. The Taming of the Web and the Rise of Algorithmic News

1. The Web 1.0 terminology refers to the Web of the 1990s, which is also often referred to as the "read-only" Web because users' activities were primarily limited to reading websites that were posted online and connected via hyperlinks.

2. Today, of course, these categories of stakeholders are far from mutually exclusive. Audiences serve as content providers and are thus also affected as such via the conditions described in this chapter.

3. This is merely an observation, not a normative position. It is not necessarily the case that Web 2.0 is inherently better than Web 1.0. Rather, the point here is that the characteristics of Web 2.0 are more compatible with a number of established institutional and individual norms and practices.

4. For a more detailed discussion of media and audience fragmentation, see Philip M. Napoli, *Audience Evolution: New Technologies and the Transformation of Media Audiences* (New York: Columbia University Press, 2011).

5. See discussion of the democratization of the media in the introduction to this book.

6. The search-engine market of the late 1990s and early 2000s is filled with long-forgotten competitors such as Lycos, InfoSeek, WebCrawler, and Excite—all of which arrived on the scene well before Google.

7. Philip Bump, "From Lycos to Ask Jeeves to Facebook: Tracking the Twenty Most Popular Web Sites Every Year Since 1996," *Washington Post*, December 15, 2014, https://www.washingtonpost.com/news/the-intersect/wp/2014/12/15/from-lycos-to-ask-jeeves-to-facebook-tracking-the-20-most-popular-web-sites-every-year-since-1996/?utm_term=.adcc41e1a7a0.

8. The TV Guide Channel began to phase out offering its scrolling program listings back in 2009 and diversified into providing original programming. See Michael Learmonth, "TV Guide Channel to Ditch the Scroll," *Advertising Age*, April 1, 2009, http://adage.com/article/media/tv-guide-channel-ditch-program-guide-scroll/135721/.

9. For an overview of television channel repertoire research, see James G. Webster and Patricia F. Phalen, *The Mass Audience: Rediscovering the Dominant Model* (Mahwah, NJ: Erlbaum, 1997).

10. See Philip M. Napoli, *Audience Economics: Media Institutions and the Audience Marketplace* (New York: Columbia University Press, 2003).

11. See Napoli, *Audience Economics.*

12. For more detailed discussion, see Napoli, *Audience Economics.*

13. In *Audience Evolution,* I refer to this as the "dark matter" of audience attention—audience attention that we know is there but that cannot be captured by our available measurement systems.

14. Philip M. Napoli, Paul J. Lavrakas, and Mario Callegaro, "Internet and Mobile Audience Ratings Panels," in *Online Panel Research: A Data Quality Perspective,* ed. Mario Callegaro et al. (West Sussex, UK: Wiley, 2014), 387–407.

15. For a more detailed discussion of ad networks, see Robert W. Gehl, *Reverse Engineering Social Media* (Philadelphia: Temple University Press, 2014), 103–105.

16. By 2020, it is estimated that more than 86 percent of all digital display ads will be purchased through automated channels (see Laura Fisher, "US Programmatic Ad Spending Forecast for 2018," *eMarketer,* April 5, 2018, https://www.emarketer.com/content/us-programmatic-ad-spending-forecast-2018. For more details on the rise of ad tech platforms, see Joshua A. Braun and Jessica L. Eklund, "Fake News, Real Money: Ad Tech Platforms, Profit-Driven Hoaxes, and the Business of Journalism," *Digital Journalism* (in press).

17. See Napoli, *Audience Evolution,* for a more detailed discussion.

18. See, for example, Thomas H. Davenport and John C. Beck, *The Attention Economy: Understanding the New Currency of Business* (Cambridge, MA: Harvard Business Review Press, 2001); Michael H. Goldhaber, "The Attention Economy and the Net," *First Monday* 2, no. 4 (1997), http://journals.uic.edu/ojs/index.php/fm/article/view/519; Richard A. Lanham, *The Economics of Attention: Style and Substance in the Age of Information* (Chicago: University of Chicago Press, 2006).

19. See, for example, Matthew Crain, "Financial Markets and Online Advertising Demand: Reevaluating the Dotcom Investment Bubble," paper presented at the 2013 Association of Internet Researchers Conference, Denver, CO.

20. Matthew Hindman, *The Internet Trap: How the Digital Economy Builds Monopolies and Undermines Democracy* (Princeton, NJ: Princeton University Press, 2018).

21. Chris Anderson, "The Long Tail," *Wired,* October 1, 2004, https://www.wired.com/2004/10/tail/; Chris Anderson, *The Long Tail: Why the Future of Business Is Selling Less of More* (New York: Hyperion, 2006).

22. Philip M. Napoli, "Requiem for the Long Tail: Towards a Political Economy of Content Aggregation and Fragmentation," *International Journal of Media & Cultural Politics* 12, no. 3 (2016): 343–356.

23. Anderson, *The Long Tail.*

24. Napoli, "Requiem for the Long Tail."

25. See, for example, Yochai Benkler, *The Wealth of Networks: How Social Production Transforms Markets and Freedom* (New Haven, CT: Yale University Press, 2006); Rebecca MacKinnon, *Consent of the Networked: The Worldwide Struggle for Internet Freedom* (New York: Basic Books, 2013).

26. Recall the discussion in the introduction to this book.

27. See https://www.facebook.com/zuck/posts/10103739373053221.

28. Rafe Needleman, "Twitter Still Has No Business Model, and That's OK," *CNET,* May 26, 2009, https://www.cnet.com/news/twitter-still-has-no-business-model-and-thats-ok/.

29. "Like other social networking sites, notably YouTube and Facebook, Twitter relied on the strategy of building an audience of users first and finding revenue streams later." José Van Dijck, *The Culture of Connectivity: A Critical History of Social Media* (Oxford: Oxford University Press, 2013), 80.

30. Jacob Silverman, *Terms of Service: Social Media and the Price of Constant Connection* (New York: HarperCollins, 2015), 112.

31. Tarleton Gillespie, *Custodians of the Internet: Platforms, Content Moderation, and the Hidden Decisions That Shape Social Media* (New Haven, CT: Yale University Press, 2018).

32. Communications Decency Act of 1996, Pub. L. No. 104–104 (Tit. V), 110 Stat. 133 (Feb. 8, 1996).

33. Telecommunications Act of 1996, Pub. L. No. 104–104, 110 Stat. 56 (Feb. 8, 1996).

34. Communications Decency Act of 1996, Pub. L. No. 104–104 (Tit. V), 110 Stat. 133 (Feb. 8, 1996).

35. Communications Decency Act of 1996, Pub. L. No. 104–104 (Tit. V), 110 Stat. 133 (Feb. 8, 1996).

36. William Uricchio, "The Algorithmic Turn: Photosynth, Augmented Reality and the Changing Implications of the Image," *Visual Studies* 26, no. 1 (2011): 25–35.

37. "Facebook Newsfeed Algorithm History," *Wallaroo Media*, January 30, 2018, https://wallaroomedia.com/facebook-newsfeed-algorithm-change-history/#eight.

38. "Facebook Newsfeed Algorithm History."

39. Matt McGee, "EdgeRank Is Dead: Facebook's News Feed Algorithm Now Has Close to 100K Weight Factors," *Marketing Land*, August 16, 2013, https://marketingland.com/edgerank-is-dead-facebooks-news-feed-algorithm-now-has-close-to-100k-weight-factors-55908.

40. Kia Kokalitcheva, "Twitter's New Algorithmic Filtering Is Here and Optional," *Fortune*, February 10, 2016, http://fortune.com/2016/02/10/twitter-filtering-optional/; Will Oremus, "Twitter's New Order," *Slate*, March, 5, 2017, http://www.slate.com/articles/technology/cover_story/2017/03/twitter_s_timeline_algorithm_and_its_effect_on_us_explained.html.

41. Josh Constine, "Instagram Is Switching Its Feed from Chronological to Best Posts First," *TechCrunch*, March 15, 2016, https://techcrunch.com/2016/03/15/filteredgram/.

42. Casey Newton, "How YouTube Perfected the Feed," *Verge*, August 30, 2017, https://www.theverge.com/2017/8/30/16222850/youtube-google-brain-algorithm-video-recommendation-personalized-feed.

43. Newton, "How YouTube Perfected the Feed."

44. Matthew Ingram, "Here's What's Wrong with Algorithmic Filtering on Twitter," *Fortune*, February 8, 2016, http://fortune.com/2016/02/08/twitter-algorithm/. For an analysis of this resistance, see Michael A. DeVito, Darren Gergle, and Jeremy Birnholtz, "'Algorithms Ruin Everything': #RIPTwitter, Folk Theories, and Resistance to Algorithmic Change in Social Media," *Proceedings of the Conference on Human Factors in Computing Systems* (New York: ACM, 2017), 3163–3174.

45. Lauren J. Young, "Five Big Questions About Instagram's Controversial Algorithm," *Inverse Innovation*, March 18, 2016, https://www.inverse.com/article/13022-5-big-questions-about-instagram-s-controversial-algorithm.

46. "See the Moments You Care About First," *Instagram*, March 15, 2016, http://blog
.instagram.com/post/141107034797/160315-news; Kia Kokalitcheva, "Why Filtering in
Social Media Is Becoming Inevitable," *Fortune*, March 28, 2016, http://fortune.com
/2016/03/28/instagram-filtering-complaining/.

47. Victor Luckerson, "Here's Why Facebook Won't Put Your News Feed in Chronological
Order," *Time*, July 9, 2015, http://time.com/3951337/facebook-chronological-order/.

48. Newton, "How YouTube Perfected the Feed." Newton chronicles the evolution of
YouTube's recommendation system and the role that artificial intelligence has played in
improving this system, noting that "getting users to spend more time watching videos
[is] YouTube's primary aim." For an account of earlier efforts by YouTube to increase
audience engagement, see Casey Newton, "YouTube's Effort to Get People to Watch
Longer," *SF Gate*, July 28, 2011, http://www.sfgate.com/business/article/YouTube-s-effort
-to-get-people-to-watch-longer-2352967.php. For an analysis of the political ramifications of the engagement imperative, see Wael Ghonim, "Transparency: What's
Gone Wrong with Social Media and What Can We Do About It?" Shorenstein Center
Working Paper, March 2018, https://shorensteincenter.org/wp-content/uploads/2018/03
/Transparency-Social-Media-Wael-Ghonim.pdf?x78124.

49. Oremus, "Twitter's New Order."

50. Oremus, "Twitter's New Order."

51. Ingram, "Here's What's Wrong with Algorithmic Filtering on Twitter."

52. Stephen Luntz, "New Study Suggests We're Approaching The 'Big Crunch,'" *IFL
Science*, March 24, 2015, http://www.iflscience.com/physics/big-crunch-back-possible-end
-universe/.

53. Wendy Boswell, "The Top Ten Most Popular Sites of 2018," *Lifewire*, January 2, 2018,
https://www.lifewire.com/most-popular-sites-3483140.

54. Napoli, *Audience Evolution*.

55. Frankie Rose, "The Fast-Forward, On-Demand, Network-Smashing Future of Television,"
Wired, October 1, 2003, https://www.wired.com/2003/10/tv-3/.

56. TiVo was not always accurate in this regard, as evidenced by the early 2000s news
media and popular culture meme, "My TiVo Thinks I'm Gay." See, for example,
Jeffrey Zaslow, "If TiVo Thinks You Are Gay, Here's How to Set It Straight," *Wall Street
Journal*, November 26, 2002, https://www.wsj.com/articles/SB1038261936872356908.
See also Jonathan Coh, "My TiVo Thinks I'm Gay: Algorithmic Culture and Its
Discontents," *Television & New Media* 17, no. 8 (2006), http://journals.sagepub.com
/doi/abs/10.1177/1527476416644978.

57. See, for example, Sue Halpern, "Cambridge Analytica and the Perils of Psychographics,"
New Yorker, March 30, 2018, https://www.newyorker.com/news/news-desk/cambridge
-analytica-and-the-perils-of-psychographics.

58. See, for example, Vincent Flood, "Is Facebook a Friend, Foe or Frenemy to Publishers? #NVF16," *Video Ad News*, November 2, 2016, https://videoadnews.com/2016/11/02
/is-facebook-a-friend-foe-or-frenemy-to-publishers-nvf16/; Lucia Moses, "Publishers on Their Facebook Relationship: It's Complicated," *Digiday*, September 20, 2016,
https://digiday.com/media/publishers-facebook-still-frenemy/; Paul Armstrong, "How

Media Companies Can Fight Frenemies Facebook, Twitter, Apple and Google," *Forbes*, January 4, 2016, https://www.forbes.com/sites/paularmstrongtech/2016/01/04/how-media-companies-can-fight-frenemies-facebook-twitter-apple-and-google/#3f0c7ad44afb.

59. "Facebook Gets Strong Majority of World's Social Ad Spending," *eMarkerter*, July 25, 2016, https://www.emarketer.com/Article/Facebook-Gets-Strong-Majority-of-Worlds-Social-Ad-Spending/1014252.

60. "Contrary to general impressions, most U.S. newspapers were not slow in adopting Internet technologies for news delivery." See H. Iris Chyi, *Trial and Error: U.S. Newspapers' Digital Struggles Toward Inferiority* (Pamplona, Spain: University of Navarra Press, 2013), 9. For an early critical take on newspapers' rush to be online, see Jon Katz, "Online or Not, Newspapers Suck," *Wired*, September 1, 1994, https://www.wired.com/1994/09/news-suck/.

61. The widespread decision to make content available online for free has been described as journalism's "original sin." See John Huey, Martin Nisenholtz, Paul Sagan, and John Geddes, "Riptide: An Oral History of the Epic Collision Between Journalism and Technology, from 1980 to the Present," Shorenstein Center on Media, Politics & Public Policy, 2013, https://www.digitalriptide.org/introduction/.

62. Jack Shafer, "What If the Newspaper Industry Made a Colossal Mistake?" *Politico Magazine*, October 17, 2016, http://www.politico.com/magazine/story/2016/10/newspapers-digital-first-214363.

63. Hsiang Iris Chyi, "Reality Check: Multiplatform Newspaper Readership in the United States, 2007–2015," *Journalism Practice* 11, no. 7 (2007): 798–819.

64. For an empirical study motivated by this question, see Alice Ju, Sun Ho Jeong, and Hsiang Iris Chyi, "Will Social Media Save Newspapers?" *Journalism Practice 8*, no. 1 (2014), 1–17.

65. W. Russell Neuman, *The Future of the Mass Audience* (New York: Cambridge University Press, 1991).

66. See, for example, Kelly Liyakasa, "NBC Universal's Evolving Media Empire Hinges on a Marriage of Data and Premium Content," *Ad Exchanger*, November 3, 2014, https://adexchanger.com/digital-tv/nbcuniversals-evolving-media-empire-hinges-on-a-marriage-of-data-and-premium-content/.

67. Napoli, *Audience Economics*, 18.

68. See, for example, Nicholas Negroponte, *Being Digital* (New York: Vintage, 1995). For a more recent articulation and applications, see Stefan Geiß, Melanie Leidecker, and Thomas Roessing "The Interplay Between Media-for-Monitoring and Media-for-Searching: How News Media Trigger Searches and Edits in *Wikipedia*," *New Media & Society* 18, no. 11 (2016), 2740–2759; James G. Webster, 2014, *The Marketplace of Attention: How Audiences Take Shape in a Digital Age* (Cambridge, MA: MIT Press).

69. Negroponte, *Being Digital*, 84.

70. Garett Sloane, "'Lean Back': Facebook Looks to Woo Viewers and Brands with TV-Like Content," *AdAge*, June 20, 2017, http://adage.com/article/digital/lean-back-facebook-viewers-comfortable/309488/.

71. "Push media are generally associated with linear delivery systems that exploit 'passive' audience members by serving up a diet of whatever the media order. Pull media are often associated with nonlinear media in which 'active' audience members pick and choose whatever they have a taste for." Webster, *The Marketplace of Attention*, 67.

72. See, for example, Geiß, Leidecker, and Roessing, "The Interplay Between Media-for-Monitoring and Media-for-Searching."

73. "Percentage of All Web Pages Served to Mobile Phones from 2009 to 2018," *Statista*, 2018, https://www.statista.com/statistics/241462/global-mobile-phone-website-traffic -share/.

74. Philip M. Napoli and Jonathan A. Obar, "The Mobile Conversion, Internet Regression, and the 'Re-Passification' of the Media Audience," in *Produsing Theory 2.0: The Intersection of Audiences and Production in a Digital World*, Volume 2, ed. Rebecca Ann Lind (New York: Peter Lang, 2015), 125–140.

75. Rob Walker, "Are Smartphones and Tablets Turning Us Into Sissies?" *Yahoo! News*, March 4, 2013, http://news.yahoo.com/are-smartphones-and-tablets-turning-us-into -sissies--175359859.html.

76. Harmeet Sawhney, "Innovation at the Edge: The Impact of Mobile Technologies on the Character of the Internet," in *Mobile Technologies: From Telecommunications to Media*, ed. Gerard Goggin and Larissa Hjorth (New York: Routledge: 2009), 105–117, 106.

77. Napoli and Obar, "The Mobile Conversion."

78. Napoli and Obar, "The Mobile Conversion."

79. It is difficult to imagine a time when having a personal web page was deemed a virtual necessity. In a time of LinkedIn, Facebook, Twitter, and Instagram, such an idea seems both quaint and mildly ridiculous.

80. Michael Arrington, "Facebook Users Revolt, Facebook Replies," *TechCrunch*, September 6, 2006, https://techcrunch.com/2006/09/06/facebook-users-revolt-facebook-replies/.

81. Samantha Murphy, "The Evolution of Facebook News Feed," *Mashable*, March 12, 2013, https://mashable.com/2013/03/12/facebook-news-feed-evolution/#uUdauGOgMPq5.

82. Eric Eldon, "Myspace to Introduce Web-Wide Ads, a News Feed, and Private Profiles," *VentureBeat*, November 26, 2007, https://venturebeat.com/2007/11/26/myspace -to-introduce-web-wide-ads-a-news-feed-and-split-profiles/.

83. Arrington, "Facebook Users Revolt."

84. Webster, *The Marketplace of Attention*, 67.

85. Alfred Hermida, "Twittering the News," *Journalism Practice* 4, no. 3 (2010), 297–308.

86. Brian Stelter, "Finding Political News Online, the Young Pass It On," *New York Times*, March 27, 2008, http://www.nytimes.com/2008/03/27/us/politics/27voters.html.

87. Joshua Benton, " 'If the News Is That Important, It'll Find Me.' But What Determines If It's Important?" *NiemanLab*, February 20, 2014, http://www.niemanlab.org/2014/02 /if-the-news-is-that-important-itll-find-me-but-what-determines-if-its-important/. Benton notes, "I can't tell you how many conferences, how many symposia, how many gatherings of worthies I've been at where some version of that line has been tossed around." Indeed, the phrase generates more than 3,700 results in a Google search, and an additional 12,300 if the word "that" is removed. See also Gina Masullo Chen,

"Readers Expect News to Find Them," *NiemanLab*, October 7, 2009, http://www.niemanlab.org/2009/10/readers-expect-news-to-find-them/.

88.   Stelter, "Finding Political News Online."

89.   Elisa Shearer and Jeffrey Gottfried, "News Use Across Social Media Platforms 2017," *Pew Research Center*, September 7, 2017, http://www.journalism.org/2017/09/07/news-use-across-social-media-platforms-2017/.

90.   See Pablo J. Boczkowski, Eugenia Mitchelstein, and Mora Matassi, "'News Comes Across When I'm in a Moment of Leisure': Understanding the Practices of Incidental News Consumption on Social Media," *New Media & Society* 20, no. 10: 3523–3539.

91.   Sonia Livingstone, "The Changing Nature of Audiences: From the Mass Audience to the Interactive Media User," in *Blackwell Companion to Media Studies*, ed. Angharad Valdivia (Oxford, UK: Blackwell, 2003), 337–359, 338.

92.   See "AOL's Walled Garden," *Wall Street Journal*, September 4, 2000, https://www.wsj.com/articles/SB968104011203980910.

93.   Ann Kellan, "AOL Time Warner Merger Could Net Consumers More and Less," *CNN*, January 11, 2001, http://www.cnn.com/2001/TECH/computing/01/11/aol.tw.merger/index.html.

94.   At the time of the merger, Time Warner was the largest copyright holder in the world, an indicator of the massive content library that could potentially be exploited and repurposed online in various forms of exclusive access for AOL subscribers.

95.   See Rita Gunther McGrath, "Lessons for Entrepreneurs from the World's Worst Merger," *Inc.*, January 22, 2015, https://www.inc.com/rita-gunther-mcgrath/lessons-for-entrepreneurs-from-the-world-s-worst-merger.html.

96.   This point is made quite frequently in the media and tech sector trade press. See, for example, "Snap Inc.: One More Walled Garden, but Endless Opportunities for Brands," *AdWeek*, November 18, 2016, http://www.adweek.com/digital/chandler-sopko-adaptly-guest-postosnap-inc-walled-garden/; Dorian Benkoil, "Advertisers, Publishers Look for Ways to Counter Facebook and Google," *Media Shift*, September 27, 2016, http://mediashift.org/2016/09/advertisers-publishers-look-ways-counter-facebook-google/; Saqib Shah, "Walled Garden: Instagram Blocking Profile Links to Snapchat and Telegram," *Digital Trends*, March 3, 2016, https://www.digitaltrends.com/photography/instagram-blocks-snapchat-telegram-links/.

97.   Shalini Nagarajan, "Twitter Partners with Bloomberg for Streaming TV News: WSJ," *Reuters*, April 30, 2017, http://www.reuters.com/article/us-twitter-bloomberg/twitter-partners-with-bloomberg-for-streaming-tv-news-wsj-idUSKBN17X10P; Jonathan Chew,"Here Are the NFL Games That Will Be Streamed Live on Twitter," *Fortune*, April 15, 2016, http://fortune.com/2016/04/15/nfl-twitter-games/. Twitter later lost the streaming rights to NFL games to Amazon. Alec Nathan, "Amazon to Live-Stream NFL Thursday Night Football Games, Replacing Twitter," April 4, 2017, http://bleacherreport.com/articles/2701845-amazon-to-livestream-nfl-thursday-night-football-games-replacing-twitter.

98.   Brian Stelter, "CNN and Other Media Brands Come to Snapchat," *CNN*, January 27, 2015, http://money.cnn.com/2015/01/27/media/snapchat-discover-media-deals/index.html.

99. Michael Reckhow, "Introducing Instant Articles," *Facebook Media*, https://media .fb.com/2015/05/12/instantarticles/.

100. Reckhow, "Introducing Instant Articles."

101. According to many accounts, publishers have been disappointed with the Instant Articles program, with major publishers such as the *New York Times* quickly dropping out. See Lucia Moses, "Facebook Faces Increased Publisher Resistance to Instant Articles," *Digiday*, April 11, 2017, https://digiday.com/media/facebook-faces-increased -publisher-resistance-instant-articles/.

102. "Instant Articles: Frequently Asked Questions," Facebook, https://developers.facebook .com/docs/instant-articles/faq/.

103. Ansha Yu and Sami Tas, "Taking Into Account Time Spent on Stories," *Facebook Newsroom*, June 12, 2015, https://newsroom.fb.com/news/2015/06/news-feed-fyi-taking -into-account-time-spent-on-stories/.

104. Will Oremus, "Who Controls Your Facebook Feed," *Slate*, January 3, 2016, http://www .slate.com/articles/technology/cover_story/2016/01/how_facebook_s_news_feed _algorithm_works.html.

105. Yu and Tas, "Taking Into Account Time Spent on Stories."

106. See, for example, Daeho Lee and Dong-Hee Shin, "The Effects of Network Neutrality on the Incentive to Discriminate, Invest, and Innovate: A Literature Review" *info* 18, no. 3 (2016), 42–57; Aaron Sankin, "The Six Worst Net Neutrality Violations in History," *Daily Dot*, May 21, 2015, https://www.dailydot.com/layer8/net-neutrality-violations-history/.

107. Federal Communications Commission, *Restoring Internet Freedom*, January 4, 2018, https://transition.fcc.gov/Daily_Releases/Daily_Business/2018/db0104/FCC-17-166A1 .pdf.

2. Algorithmic Gatekeeping and the Transformation of News Organizations

1. See, for example, Christopher Mims, "How Facebook's Master Algorithm Powers the Social Network," *Wall Street Journal*, October 22, 2017, https://www.wsj.com/articles /how-facebooks-master-algorithm-powers-the-social-network-1508673600. For an excellent take on the opaque nature of algorithms and their increasing influence in various sectors of society and the economy (including media), see Frank Pasqual, *The Black Box Society: The Secret Algorithms That Control Money and Information* (Cambridge, MA: Harvard University Press, 2015).

2. For a critique of the application of the black-box concept to algorithmic media, see Taina Bucher, "Neither Black Nor Box: Ways of Knowing Algorithms," ed. Sebastian Kubitschko and Anne Kaun (Cham, Switzerland: Palgrave Macmillan, 2016), 81–98.

3. For a discussion of some of the challenges, see Nicholas Diakopoulos, "Algorithmic Accountability," *Digital Journalism* 3, no. 3 (2014): 398–415.

4. A recent analysis by Matthew Weber and Allie Kosterich of the underlying code and algorithms of open-source news apps illustrates some of the ways in which black boxes

can be made much less opaque. See Matthew S. Weber and Allie Kosterich, "Coding the News," *Digital Journalism* 6, no. 3 (2017): 310–329.

5. For an overview, see Maxwell McCombs, *Setting the Agenda: Mass Media and Public Opinion*, 2nd ed. (Malden, MA: Polity Press, 2014).

6. See, for example, Sharon Meraz, "Is There an Elite Hold? Traditional Media to Social Media Agenda Setting Influence in Blog Networks," *Journal of Computer-Mediated Communication* 14, no. 3 (2009): 682–707.

7. David M. White, "The 'Gate Keeper': A Case Study in the Selection of News," *Journalism Quarterly* 27 (1950): 383–390.

8. For more background and context for the Mr. Gates study, see Stephen Reese and Jane Ballinger, "The Roots of a Sociology of News: Remembering Mr. Gates and Social Control in the Newsroom," *Journalism & Mass Communication Quarterly* 78, no. 4 (2001): 641–654.

9. White, "The 'Gate Keeper.' "

10. White, "The 'Gate Keeper.' "

11. See, for example, Paul Snider, " 'Mr. Gates' Revisited: A 1966 Version of the 1949 Case Study," *Journalism Quarterly* 44, no. 3 (1967): 419–427; Glen Bleske, "Ms. Gates Takes Over," *Newspaper Research Journal* 12, no. 4 (1991): 88–97; Pamela Shoemaker, Martin Eicholz, Eunyi Kim, and Brenda Wrigley, "Individual and Routine Forces in Gatekeeping," *Journal & Mass Communication Quarterly* 78, no. 2 (2001): 233–246.

12. Paul M. Hirsch, "Occupational, Organizational, and Institutional Models in Mass Media Research," in *Strategies for Communication Research*, ed. Paul M. Hirsch, Peter V. Miller, and F. Gerald Kline (Thousand Oaks, CA: Sage, 1977), 13–42.

13. For a more detailed discussion, see Pamela J. Shoemaker and Stephen D. Reese, *Mediating the Message in the Twenty-First Century: A Media Sociology Perspective* (New York: Routledge, 2014).

14. Johan Galtung and Mari Ruge, "The Structure of Foreign News: The Presentation of the Congo, Cuba and Cyprus Crises in Four Norwegian Newspapers," *Journal of International Peace Research* 1 (1965): 64–91.

15. Tony Harcup and Deirdre O'Neil, "What Is News?" *Journalism Studies* 18, no. 12 (2017): 1470–1488.

16. For detailed explorations—and critiques—of the audience-as-citizen-versus-consumer dichotomy, see Sonia Livingstone, Peter Lunt, and Laura Miller, "Citizens, Consumers and the Citizen-Consumer: Articulating the Citizen Interest in Media and Communications Regulation," *Discourse & Communication* 1, no. 1 (2007): 63–89; Marc Raboy, Bram Dov Abramson, Serge Prouix, and Roxanne Welters, "Media Policy, Audiences, and Social Demand," *Television & News Media* 2, no. 2 (2001): 95–115; Nick Couldry, "The Productive 'Consumer' and the Dispersed 'Citizen,' " *International Journal of Cultural Studies* 7, no. 1 (2004): 21–32.

17. Jennifer Brandel, "Give the Audience What They Want or What They Need? There's an Even Better Question," *Medium*, May 25, 2016, https://medium.com/we-are-hearken /give-the-audience-what-they-want-or-what-they-need-theres-a-better-question -220a9479dc05.

18. There is a substantial literature on the economics of bundling, particularly as it relates to the bundling of media products such as news. See, for example, James T. Hamilton, *All the News That's Fit to Sell: How the Market Transforms Information Into News* (Princeton, NJ: Princeton University Press, 2004).

19. For a discussion of the historical role, function, and impact of letters to the editor, see Mike Ananny, "Networked Press Freedom and Social Media: Tracing Historical and Contemporary Forces in Press-Public Relations," *Journal of Computer-Mediated Communication* 19, no. 4 (2014): 938–956.

20. For a discussion of audience letters as feedback, see Philip M. Napoli, *Audience Evolution: New Technologies and the Transformation of Media Audiences* (New York: Columbia University Press, 2011).

21. John H. McManus, *Market-Driven Journalism: Let the Citizen Beware?* (Thousand Oaks, CA: Sage, 1994).

22. See, for example, Göran Bolin and Jonas Schqarz, "Heuristics of the Algorithm: Big Data, User Interpretation and Institutional Translation," *Big Data & Society* 2, no. 2 (2015): 1–12. For an overview of the increasing influence, and increasing sophistication, of audience analytics in news organizations, see Federica Cherubini and Rasmus Kleis Nielsen, "Editorial Analytics: How News Media Are Developing and Using Audience Data and Metrics," Report of the Reuters Institute for the Study of Journalism, 2016, http://www.digitalnewsreport.org/publications/2016/editorial-analytics -2016/; Franklin Foer, "When Silicon Valley Took Over Journalism," *Atlantic*, September 2017, https://www.theatlantic.com/magazine/archive/2017/09/when-silicon -valley-took-over-journalism/534195/.

23. See, for example, Herbert Gans, *Deciding What's News* (New York: Random House, 1979). For an overview of the research in this area, see Napoli, *Audience Evolution*.

24. See, for example Julian Wallace, "Modeling Contemporary Gatekeeping: The Rise of Individuals, Algorithms and Platforms in Digital News Dissemination," *Digital Journalism* 6, no. 3 (2018): 274–293.

25. Jane B. Singer, "User-Generated Visibility: Secondary Gatekeeping in a Shared Media Space," *New Media & Society* 16, no. 1 (2013): 55–73.

26. See, for example, Caitlin Dewey, "Forget Click-Bait. We're Living in the World of Share-Bait Now," *Washington Post*, August 27, 2014, https://www.washingtonpost.com/news /the-intersect/wp/2014/08/27/forget-click-bait-were-living-in-the-world-of-share -bait-now/. See legal scholar Jon M. Garon's discussion of the increasing importance of the "curatorial audience." Jon M. Garon, "Wiki Authorship, Social Media, and the Curatorial Audience," *Harvard Journal of Sports & Entertainment Law* 1, no. 1 (2010): 96–143.

27. Maksym Gabielkov, Arthi Ramachandran, Augustin Chaintreau, and Arnaud Legout, "Social Clicks: What and Who Gets Read on Twitter?" *ACM Sigmetrics*, June 2016, https://hal.inria.fr/hal-01281190/document.

28. See, for example, Peter Bro and Filip Wallberg, "Gatekeeping in a Digital Era," *Journalism Practice* 9, no. 1 (2014): 92–105.

29. For a discussion, see Stefaan Verhulst, "Mediation, Mediators, and New Intermediaries: Implications for the Design of New Communications Policies," in *Media Diversity*

and Localism: Meaning and Metrics, ed. Philip M. Napoli (Mahwah, NJ: Erlbaum, 2007), 113–138.

30. See, for example, Carolin Lin, "Changing Network-Affiliate Relations Amidst a Competitive Video Marketplace," *Journal of Media Economics* 7, no. 1 (1994): 1–12.

31. The recent repeal of net neutrality regulations in the United States of course raises the possibility that this generalization will no longer hold true. But so far no major reconfigurations of the common carrier–like orientation of Internet provision have taken place.

32. See Robert W. Crandall and Harold Furchtgott-Roth, *Cable TV: Regulation or Competition* (Washington, DC: Brookings Institution Press, 1996); Michael Zarkin, *The FCC and the Politics of Cable TV Regulation, 1952–1980* (Amherst, NY: Cambria Press).

33. For more details on the must-carry rules and their objectives, see Philip M. Napoli, "Retransmission Consent and Broadcaster Commitment to Localism," *CommLaw Conspectus* 20 (2012): 345–362.

34. Napoli, "Retransmission Consent."

35. The FCC stated as recently as 2012, "The Commission has long held, and the Supreme Court has agreed, that cable subscribers' use of an 'A/B switch' to access over-the-air signals is not a legitimate replacement for access to those signals on the cable system itself." See Federal Communications Commission, "Carriage of Digital Television Signals: Amendment of Part 76 of the Commission's Rules, Fourth Further Notice of Proposed Rulemaking and Declaratory Order," February 10, 2012, http://transition.fcc .gov/Daily_Releases/Daily_Business/2012/db0210/FCC-12-18A1.doc. For a detailed discussion of the A/B switch issue, see the Supreme Court's decision upholding the FCC's must-carry rules, Turner Broadcasting System v. Federal Communications Commission, 520 U.S. 180 (1997).

36. See, for example, Will Oremus, "Who Controls Your Facebook Feed," *Slate*, January 3, 2016, http://www.slate.com/articles/technology/cover_story/2016/01/how_facebook_s _news_feed_algorithm_works.single.html; Alfred Lua, "Decoding the Facebook Algorithm: A Fully Up-to-Date List of the Algorithm Factors and Changes," *Buffer Social*, October 18, 2017, https://blog.bufferapp.com/facebook-news-feed-algorithm.

37. Kelley Cotter, Janghee Cho, and Emilee Rader, "Explaining the News Feed Algorithm: An Analysis of the 'News Feed FYI'" Blog," *Proceedings of the 2017 CHI Conference* (New York: ACM, 2017), 1553–1560.

38. Cotter, Cho, and Rader, "Explaining the News Feed Algorithm."

39. Michael A. DeVito, "A Values-Based Approach to Understanding Story Selection in the Facebook News Feed," *Digital Journalism* 5, no. 6 (2017): 753–773.

40. DeVito, "A Values-Based Approach."

41. DeVito, "A Values-Based Approach."

42. Mike Ananny and Kate Crawford, "A Liminal Press: Situating News App Designers Within a Field of Networked News Production," *Digital Journalism* 3, no. 2 (2014): 192–208.

43. Ananny and Crawford, "A Liminal Press," 200.

44. Frank Michael Russell, "The New Gatekeepers," *Journalism Studies* (in press), DOI: 10.1080/1461670X.2017.1412806. According to Russell, while the interview subjects

"maintained that algorithms are needed to sift through information to bring forward relevant content for users," it remained "uncertain what considerations Silicon Valley uses to govern access to information" (8).

45. Russell, "The New Gatekeepers."

46. Anders Olof Larsson, "I Shared the News Today, Oh Boy," *Journalism Studies* 19, no. 1 (2016): 43–61.

47. Zeynep Tufekci, "Algorithmic Harms Beyond Facebook and Google: Emergent Challenges of Computational Agency," *Journal on Telecommunications & High Technology Law* 13 (2015): 203–217.

48. The social media platforms analyzed were Pinterest, Google+, Delicious, Facebook, Twitter, and Stumble-Upon.

49. Mark T. Bastos, "Shares, Pins, and Tweets: News Readers from Daily Papers to Social Media," *Journalism Studies* 16, no. 3 (2015): 305–325.

50. Amy Mitchell, Elisa Shearer, Jeffery Gottfried, and Michael Barthel, "The Modern News Consumer," *Pew Research Center*, July 7, 2016, http://www.journalism.org/2016/07/07 /social-engagement/.

51. Michael Nunez, "Former Facebook Workers: We Routinely Suppressed Conservative News," *Gizmodo*, May 9, 2016, https://gizmodo.com/former-facebook-workers-we -routinely-suppressed-conser-1775461006.

52. Michael Nunez, "Senate GOP launches Inquiry Into Facebook's News Curation," *Gizmodo*, May 10, 2016, https://gizmodo.com/senate-gop-launches-inquiry-into-facebook -s-news-curati-1775767018.

53. Michael Nunez, "Facebook's Fight Against Fake News Was Undercut by Fear of Conservative Backlash," *Gizmodo*, November 14, 2016, *https://gizmodo.com/facebooks -fight-against-fake-news-was-undercut-by-fear-1788808204.*

54. Michael Nunez, "Facebook Removes Human Curators from Trending Module," *Gizmodo*, August 26, 2016, https://gizmodo.com/facebook-removes-human-curators -from-trending-topic-mod-1785818153; Sam Thielman, "Facebook Fires Trending Team, and Algorithm Without Humans Goes Crazy," *Guardian*, August 29, 2016, https://www.theguardian.com/technology/2016/aug/29/facebook-fires-trending- topics-team-algorithm; Olivia Solon, "In Firing Human Editors, Facebook Has Lost the Fight Against Fake News," *Guardian*, August 29, 2016, https://www.theguardian .com/technology/2016/aug/29/facebook-trending-news-editors-fake-news-stories.

55. Todd Spangler, "Mark Zuckerberg: Facebook Will Hire 3,000 Staffers to Review Violent Content, Hate Speech," *Variety*, May 3, 2017, http://variety.com/2017/digital/news /mark-zuckerberg-facebook-violent-hate-speech-hiring-1202407969/; Josh Constine, "Facebook Will Hire 1,000 and Make Ads Visible to Fight Election Interference," *TechCrunch*, October 2, 2017, https://techcrunch.com/2017/10/02/facebook-will-hire -1000-and-make-ads-visible-to-fight-election-interference/.

56. For a review, see Shoemaker and Reese, *Mediating the Message.*

57. See, for example, Kjerstin Thorson and Chris Wells, "Curated Flows: A Framework for Mapping Media Exposure in the Digital Age," *Communication Theory* 26, no. 3 (2016): 209–328; Stephen D. Reese and Pamela J. Shoemaker, "A Media Sociology for the

Networked Public Sphere: The Hierarchy of Influences Model," *Mass Communication and Society* 19, no. 4 (2016): 389–410. Taina Bucher has coined the term *technography* to reflect the greater technology focus that needs to be integrated into the ethnographic methods that have been employed in media sociology research; Bucher, "Neither Black Nor Box.

58. Tarleton Gillespie, "Algorithmically Recognizable: Santorum's Google Problem, and Google's Santorum Problem," *Information, Communication & Society* 20, no. 1 (2016): 63–80.

59. Facebook News Feed Algorithm History, https://wallaroomedia.com/facebook -newsfeed-algorithm-history/.

60. For a detailed discussion of this issue, see Laura Hazard Owen, "Did Facebook's Faulty Data Push News Publishers to Make Terrible Decisions on Video?" *Nieman Lab*, October 17, 2018, http://www.niemanlab.org/2018/10/did-facebooks-faulty-data-push -news-publishers-to-make-terrible-decisions-on-video/.

61. Nikki Usher, "What Impact Is SEO Having on Journalists? Reports from the Field," *Nieman Lab*, September 23, 2010, http://www.niemanlab.org/2010/09/what-impact -is-seo-having-on-journalists-reports-from-the-field/; Murray Dick, "Search Engine Optimisation in UK News Production," *Journalism Practice* 5, no. 4 (2011): 462–477.

62. See, for example, Daniel Roth, "The Answer Factory: Demand Media and the Fast, Dis- posable, and Profitable as Hell Media Model," *Wired*, October 19, 2009, https://www .wired.com/2009/10/ff_demandmedia/all/1/; Usher, "What Impact Is SEO Having on Journalists?"

63. See, for example, Dimitrios Giomelakis and Andreas Veglis, "Investigating Search Engine Optimization Factors in Media Websites," *Digital Journalism* 4, no. 3 (2016): 379–400.

64. Shan Wang, "The *New York Times* Built a Slack Bot to Help Decide Which Stories to Post to Social Media," *Nieman Lab*, August 15, 2015, http://www.niemanlab.org/2015/08 /the-new-york-times-built-a-slack-bot-to-help-decide-which-stories-to-post-to -social-media/.

65. Wang, "The *New York Times* Built a Slack Bot." See also John Ellet, "New AI-Based Tools Are Transforming Social Media Marketing," *Forbes*, July 27, 2017, https://www .forbes.com/sites/johnellett/2017/07/27/new-ai-based-tools-are-transforming-social -media-marketing/#459b0c8169a2.

66. Wang, "The *New York Times* Built a Slack Bot."

67. Wang, "The *New York Times* Built a Slack Bot."

68. Ahmed Al-Rawi, "A Comparative Study of Twitter News," *Journalism Practice* 11, no. 6 (2017): 705–720; Ahmed Al-Rawi, "News Values on Social Media: News Organizations' Facebook Use," *Journalism* 18, no. 7 (2016): 871–889. It should be emphasized, however, that the scope of this study was quite limited, focusing on the social media activity of four Arabic-language TV stations.

69. Peter Andringa, David Duquette, Deborah L. Dwyer, Philip M. Napoli, and Petra Ronald, "How Is Social Media Gatekeeping Different? A Multi-Platform Comparative Analysis of the *New York Times*," paper presented at the 2018 meeting of the Associa- tion of Internet Researchers, Montreal.

70. See, for example, Rasmus Kleis Nielsen and Sarah Anne Ganter, "Dealing with Digital Intermediaries: A Case Study of the Relations Between Publishers and Platforms," *New Media & Society* 20, no. 4 (2018): 1600–1617. See also Robyn Caplan and danah boyd, "Isomorphism through Algorithms: Institutional Dependencies in the Case of Facebook," *Big Data & Society* 5, no. 1 (2018): 1–12.

71. Media critic Jacob Silverman noted in relation to the online news site *BuzzFeed*, "BuzzFeed, like some other digital media organizations, believes that home pages don't matter much anymore—which is one reason why the home page of BuzzFeed.com is a mass of links, none of them communicating their relative importance." Jacob Silverman, *Terms of Service: Social Media and the Price of Constant Connection* (New York: HarperCollins, 2015), 117.

72. For a more detailed discussion, see Silverman, *Terms of Service*.

73. Silverman, *Terms of Service*; Jonathan Taplin, *Move Fast and Break Things: How Facebook, Google, and Amazon Cornered Culture and Undermined Democracy* (New York: Little, Brown, 2017).

74. Some critics have even contended that the dependence of contemporary news media on platforms such as Facebook and Google may affect how news organizations cover these platforms—what Efrat Nechushtai terms *infrastructural capture*. See Efrat Nechushtai, "Could Digital Platforms Capture the Media Through Infrastructure?" *Journalism* 19, no. 8 (2018): 1043–1058.

75. Adam Mosseri, "Building a Better News Feed for You," *Facebook Newsroom*, June 29, 2016, https://newsroom.fb.com/news/2016/06/building-a-better-news-feed-for-you/.

76. Varun Kacholia and Minwen Ji, "News Feed FYI: Helping You Find More News to Talk About," *Facebook Newsroom*, December 2, 2013, https://newsroom.fb.com/news/2013/12/news-feed-fyi-helping-you-find-more-news-to-talk-about/.

77. Jayson DeMers, "Has Facebook's Latest Algorithm Change Finally Doomed Publishers and Marketers for Good?" *Forbes*, July 6, 2016, https://www.forbes.com/sites/jaysondemers/2016/07/06/has-facebooks-latest-algorithm-change-finally-doomed-publishers-and-marketers-for-good/#6fae78466847.

78. Mark Zuckerberg, *Facebook*, January 11, 2018, https://www.facebook.com/zuck/posts/10104413015393571?pnref=story.

79. Zuckerberg, *Facebook*.

80. See, for example, Andrew Gruen, "Yes, Facebook Referral Traffic Crashed and Burned, but Not for These Nonprofit Publishers," *Nieman Lab*, October 26, 2018, http://www.niemanlab.org/2018/10/yes-facebook-referral-traffic-crashed-and-burned-but-not-for-these-nonprofit-publishers/; Lucia Moses, "As Promised, Facebook Traffic to News Publishers Declines Again, Post News-Feed Change," *Digiday*, February 19, 2018, https://digiday.com/media/promised-facebook-traffic-news-publishers-declines-post-news-free-change/.

81. Will Oremus, "The Great Facebook Crash," *Slate*, June 27, 2018, https://slate.com/technology/2018/06/facebooks-retreat-from-the-news-has-painful-for-publishers-including-slate.html.

82. See, for example, Nathan Robinson, "I Run a Small, Independent Magazine. I Worry Facebook Will Kill Us Off," *Guardian*, January 21, 2018, https://www.theguardian.com /commentisfree/2018/jan/21/small-independent-magazine-facebook; Alyssa Newcomb and Clair Atkinson, "Facebook's News Feed Changes Are Latest Blow to Publishers, Brands," *Euronews*, January 12, 2018, http://www.euronews.com/2018/01/12 /facebook-s-news-feed-changes-are-latest-blow-publishers-brands-n837196.

83. See, for example, Roy Greenslade, "Why Facebook Is Public Enemy Number One for Newspapers, and Journalism," *Guardian*, September 20, 2016, https://www.theguardian .com/media/greenslade/2016/sep/20/why-facebook-is-public-enemy-number -one-for-newspapers-and-journalism.

84. Shan Wang, Christine Schmidt, and Laura H. Owen, "Publishers Claim They're Taking Facebook's News Feed Changes in Stride. Is the 'Bloodletting' Still to Come?" *Nieman Lab*, January 19, 2018, http://www.niemanlab.org/2018/01/publishers-claim -theyre-taking-facebooks-news-feed-changes-in-stride-is-the-bloodletting-still-to -come/.

85. Wang, Christine, and Owen, "Publishers Claim They're Taking Facebook's News Feed Changes in Stride." For an elaboration of this perspective, see Joshua Topolsky, "Facebook Killing News Is the Best Thing That Ever Happened to News," *Future*, https:// theoutline.com/post/2936/facebook-news-feed-changes-are-actually-good-for -news?zd=1.

86. Nicholas Negroponte, *Being Digital* (New York: Knopf, 1995).

87. Eugene Kim, "Mark Zuckerberg Wants to Build the 'Perfect Personalized Newspaper' for Every Person in the World," *Business Insider*, November 6, 2014, http://www .businessinsider.com/mark-zuckerberg-wants-to-build-a-perfect-personalized -newspaper-2014-11.

88. For a discussion of mimicking and the broader process of media evolution, see Carlos A. Scolari, "Media Evolution: Emergence, Dominance, Survival, and Extinction in the Media Ecology," *International Journal of Communication* 7 (2013): 1418–1441.

89. Alexander Spangher, "Building the Next *New York Times* Recommendation Engine," *New York Times*, August 11, 2015, https://open.blogs.nytimes.com/2015/08/11/building -the-next-new-york-times-recommendation-engine/.

90. Spangher, "Building the Next *New York Times* Recommendation Engine."

91. For a more detailed discussion of collaborative topic modeling, see Chong Wang and David M. Blei, "Collaborative Topic Modeling for Recommending Scientific Articles," *Proceedings of the Seventeenth ACM SIGKDD International Conference on Knowledge Discovery and Data Mining* (New York: ACM, 2011), 448–456.

92. Spangher, "Building the Next *New York Times* Recommendation Engine."

93. Liz Spayd, "A 'Community' of One: The *Times* Gets Tailored," *New York Times*, March 18, 2017, https://www.nytimes.com/2017/03/18/public-editor/a-community-of-one -the-times-gets-tailored.html.

94. Ricardo Bilton, "All the News That's Fit for You: The *New York Times* Is Experimenting with Personalization to Find New Ways to Expose Readers to Stories,"

Nieman Lab, September 28, 2017, http://www.niemanlab.org/2017/09/all-the-news -thats-fit-for-you-the-new-york-times-is-experimenting-with-personalization-to-find -new-ways-to-expose-readers-to-stories/.

95. Bilton, "All the News That's Fit for You."

96. "Answering Your Questions About Our New Home Page," *New York Times*, October 1, 2018, https://www.nytimes.com/2018/10/01/reader-center/home-page-redesign.html.

97. Laura Hazard Owen, "With 'My WSJ,' the *Wall Street Journal* Makes a Personalized Content Feed Central to Its App," *Nieman Lab*, December 11, 2017, http://www.nieman-lab.org/2017/12/with-my-wsj-the-wall-street-journal-makes-a-personalized-content -feed-central-to-its-app/.

98. Ricardo Bilton, "The *Washington Post* Tests Personalized 'Pop-Up' Newsletters to Promote Its Big Stories," *Nieman Lab*, May 12, 2016, http://www.niemanlab.org/2016/05 /the-washington-post-tests-personalized-pop-up-newsletters-to-promote-its-big -stories/.

99. Serla Rusli, "How *Washington Post*'s Data-Driven Product Development Engages Audiences," *Reuters*, n.d., https://agency.reuters.com/en/insights/articles/articles-archive /how-washington-post-data-driven-product-development-engages-audiences.html.

100. Ryan Graff, "How the *Washington Post* Used Data and Natural Language Processing to Get People to Read More News," *Knight Lab*, June 3, 2015, https://knightlab.northwestern .edu/2015/06/03/how-the-washington-posts-clavis-tool-helps-to-make-news-personal/.

101. Bilton, "The *Washington Post* Tests Personalized 'Pop-Up' Newsletters."

102. Owen, "With 'My WSJ.' "

103. Shannon Liao, "BBC Will Use Machine Learning to Cater to What Audiences Want to Watch," *Verge*, October 19, 2017, https://www.theverge.com/2017/10/19/16503658/bbc -data-analytics-machine-learning-curation-tv.

104. See, for example, Charles Buzz, "Tronc Is the Absorption of Digital Media Into Legacy Media," *Motherboard*, June 24, 2016, https://motherboard.vice.com/en_us/article /bmv7y3/tronc-is-the-absorption-of-digital-media-into-legacy-media.

105. Perhaps not surprisingly, this video can no longer be found online. For details on tronc reverting back to Tribune, see Nick Statt, "tronc to Change Name Back to Tribune Publishing after Years of Ridicule," *The Verge*, June 18, 2018, https://www.theverge.com /2018/6/18/17476412/tronc-tribune-publishing-name-change-la-times-sale.

106. The John Oliver segment can be found at "Journalism: Last Week Tonight with John Oliver," *HBO*, August 7, 2016, https://www.youtube.com/watch?v=bq2_wSsDwkQ.

107. The original press release can be found at Kimbre Neidhart, "Tribune Publishing Announces Corporate Rebranding, Changes Name to tronc," Tribune Publishing News Release, June 2, 2016, http://investor.tronc.com/phoenix.zhtml?c=254385&p =irol-newsArticle&ID=2174771.

108. Erik Wemple, "Tribune Publishing, Now 'tronc,' Issues Worst Press Release in the History of Journalism," *Washington Post*, June 2, 2016, https://www.washingtonpost.com /blogs/erik-wemple/wp/2016/06/02/tribune-co-now-tronc-issues-worst-press -release-in-the-history-of-journalism/?utm_term=.98d8eea98b4c.

109. Kimbre Neidhart, "Tronc Begins Trading on Nasdaq, Joins Leading Tech Firms," Tribune Publishing News Release, June 20, 2016, http://investor.tronc.com/phoenix .zhtml?c=254385&p=irol-newsArticle&ID=2178684.

110. https://www.linkedin.com/jobs/view/data-scientist-machine-learning-at-the-new -york-times-1073768014/

111. Smaller, local news organizations, it should be emphasized, are largely continuing to operate without massive stores of data and algorithmic decision-making systems, given that they generally lack the resources to adopt and maintain these systems. As Cherubini and Nielsen note in their study of the use of analytics by news media, "many news organisations still have a very rudimentary approach to analytics. This is especially true for smaller legacy news organisations like local and regional newspapers and for some public service broadcasters." Federica Cherubini and Rasmus Kleis Nielsen, "Editorial Analytics: How News Media Are Developing and Using Audience Data and Metrics," Report of the Reuters Institute for the Study of Journalism, 2016, http://www .digitalnewsreport.org/publications/2016/editorial-analytics-2016/. The result is an emerging digital divide, of sorts, between small and large news organizations.

112. Greg Satell, "Tronc's Data Delusion," *Harvard Business Review*, June 23, 2016, https:// hbr.org/2016/06/troncs-data-delusion.

113. See, for example, Franklin Foer, "When Silicon Valley Took Over Journalism," *Atlantic*, September 2017, https://www.theatlantic.com/magazine/archive/2017/09/when-silicon -valley-took-over-journalism/534195/.

114. John West, "Humans Are Losing the Battle Against Kardashian-Loving Algorithms for the Soul of New Media," *Quartz*, April 19, 2016, https://qz.com/664591/humans-are -losing-the-battle-against-kardashian-loving-algorithms-for-the-soul-of-new-media/.

115. The integration of big data and algorithmic audience analytics essentially represents the most recent step in the long-running process of the rationalization of audience understanding that I discuss in my previous book. See Napoli, *Audience Evolution*.

116. Paul F. Lazarsfeld, Bernard Berelson, and Hazel Gaudet, *The People's Choice: How the Voter Makes Up His Mind in a Presidential Campaign* (New York: Duell Sloan and Pearce, 1944).

117. Elihu Katz and Paul F. Lazarsfeld, *Personal Influence: The Part Played by People in the Flow of Mass Communications* (New York: Free Press, 1955).

118. For an important early effort in this regard, in which the compression of the two-step flow into a single step was proposed, see W. Lance Bennett and Jarol B. Manheim, "The One-Step Flow of Communication," *Annals of the American Academy of Political and Social Science* 608, no. 1 (2006): 213–232.

119. For a discussion, see John N. Cappella, "Vectors Into the Future of Mass and Interpersonal Communication Research: Big Data, Social Media, and Computational Social Science," *Human Communication Research* 43, no. 4 (2017): 545–558.

120. See, for example, Sherry Turkle, *Alone Together: Why We Expect More from Technology and Less from Each Other* (New York: Basic Books, 2011).

121. See, for example, Nicholas M. Anspach, "The New Personal Influence: How Our Facebook Friends Influence the News We Read," *Political Communication* 34 (2017):

590–606; Klus Bruhn Jensen, "Three-Step Flow," *Journalism* 10, no. 3 (2009): 335–337; Gilad Lotan, Erhardt Graeff, Mike Ananny, Devin Gaffney, Ian Pearce, and Danah Boyd, "The Revolutions Were Tweeted: Information Flows During the 2011 Tunisian and Egyptian Revolutions," *International Journal of Communication* 5 (2011): 1375–1405; Shaomei Wu, Jake M. Hofman, Winter A. Mason, and Duncan J. Watts, "Who Says What to Whom on Twitter," *Proceedings of the Twentieth International Conference on World Wide Web Pages* (New York: ACM, 2011), 704–719.

122. For analyses of opinion leadership in the social media age, see Annika Bergstrom and Maria Jervelycke Belfrage, "News in Social Media," *Digital Journalism* 6, no. 5 (2018): 583–598; Jason Turcotte, Chance York, Jacob Irving, Rosanne Scholl, and Raymond Pingree, "News Recommendations from Social Media Opinion Leaders: Effects on Media Trust and Information Seeking," *Journal of Computer-Mediated Communication* 20, no. 5 (2015): 520–535; Matthew C. Nisbet and John E. Kotcher, "A Two-Step Flow of Influence?" *Science Communication* 30, no. 3 (2009): 328–354.

123. Josh Schwartz, "What Happens When Facebooks Goes Down? People Read the News," *Nieman Lab*, October 22, 2018, http://www.niemanlab.org/2018/10/what-happens -when-facebook-goes-down-people-read-the-news/.

124. Elisa Shearer and Katarina Eva Matsa, "News Use Across Social Media Platforms 2018," *Pew Research Center*, September 2018, http://www.journalism.org/2018/09/10 /news-use-across-social-media-platforms-2018/.

125. Nic Newman with Richard Fletcher, Antonis Kalogeropoulos, David A. L. Levy, and Rasmus Kleis Nielsen, *Reuters Institute Digital News Report 2018*, http://media.digi talnewsreport.org/wp-content/uploads/2018/06/digital-news-report-2018.pdf?x89475.

3. The First Amendment, Fake News, and Filter Bubbles

1. See Philip M. Napoli, *Foundations of Communications Policy: Principles and Process in the Regulation of Electronic Media* (Cresskill, NJ: Hampton Press, 2001).

2. See, for example, Lee Bollinger, *Images of a Free Press* (Chicago: University of Chicago Press, 1991).

3. See, for example, Mostafa M. El-Bermawy, "Your Filter Bubble Is Destroying Democracy," *Wired*, November 18, 2016, https://www.wired.com/2016/11/filter-bubble-destroying -democracy; Olivia Solon, "Facebook's Failure: Did Fake News and Polarized Politics Get Trump Elected?" *Guardian*, November 10, 2016, https://www.theguardian.com /technology/2016/nov/10/facebook-fake-news-election-conspiracy-theories; Jen Wee- don, William Nuland, and Alex Stamos, "Information Operations and Facebook," Facebook, April 27, 2017, https://fbnewsroomus.files.wordpress.com/2017/04/facebook -and-information-operations-v1.pdf; Alice Marwick and Rebecca Lewis, "Media Manipulation and Disinformation Online," Data & Society, May 2017, https://datasociety .net/pubs/oh/DataAndSociety_MediaManipulationAndDisinformationOnline.pdf.

4. See Clive Thompson, "Social Networks Must Face Up to Their Political Impact," *Wired*, January 5, 2017, https://www.wired.com/2017/01/social-networks-must-face

-political-impact/; Alex Kantrowitz, "How the 2016 Election Blew Up in Facebook's Face," *BuzzFeed*, November 21, 2016, https://www.buzzfeed.com/alexkantrowitz/2016 -election-blew-up-in-facebooks-face; Nathaniel Persily, "Can Democracy Survive the Internet?" *Journal of Democracy* 28, no. 2 (2017): 63–76; Joshua A. Tucker, Yannis Theocharis, Margaret E. Roerts, and Pablo Barbera, "From Liberation to Turmoil: Social Media and Democracy," *Journal of Democracy* 28, no. 4 (2017): 46–59.

5. See, for example, European Commission, *A Multi-Dimensional Approach to Disinformation: Report of the Independent High Level Group on Fake News and Online Disinformation* (Luxembourg: Publications Office of the European Union, 2018); House of Commons Digital, Culture, Media and Sport Committee, *Disinformation and "Fake News": Final Report* (February 14, 2019), https://publications.parliament.uk/pa /cm201719/cmselect/cmcumeds/1791/1791.pdf.

6. Katrina Hennhold, "Germany Acts to Tame Facebook, Learning from Its Own History of Hate," *New York Times*, March 19, 2018, https://www.nytimes.com/2018/05/19 /technology/facebook-deletion-center-germany.html.

7. See, for example, *Putin's Asymmetric Assault on Democracy in Russia and Europe: Implications for U.S. National Security*, Minority Staff Report Prepared for the Use of the Committee on Foreign Relations, U.S. Senate (Washington, DC: U.S. Government Printing Office, January 10, 2018); United States House of Representatives, Judiciary Committee, Hearing on Filtering Practices of Social Media, April 26, 2018, https://docs.house.gov /Committee/Calendar/ByEvent.aspx?EventID=108231; United States Senate, Select Committee on Intelligence, Hearing on Social Media Influence in the 2016 Elections, November 1, 2017, https://www.intelligence.senate.gov/hearings/open-hearing-social -media-influence-2016-us-elections; United States Senate, Committee on the Judiciary, Hearing on Cambridge Analytica and the Future of Data Privacy, May 16, 2018, https://www .judiciary.senate.gov/meetings/cambridge-analytica-and-the-future-of-data-privacy.

8. For overviews of the counterspeech doctrine, see David A. Locke, "Counterspeech as an Alternative to Prohibition: Proposed Federal Regulation of Tobacco Promotion in American Motorsport," *Indiana Law Review* 70 (1994): 217–253; Robert D. Richards and Clay Calvert, "Counterspeech 2000: A New Look at the Old Remedy for 'Bad' Speech," *BYU Law Review* 2000 (2000): 553–586.

9. 274 U.S. 327 (1927).

10. "The ultimate good desired is better reached by free trade in ideas—that the best test of truth is the power of the thought to get itself accepted in the competition of the market, and that truth is the only ground upon which their wishes safely can be carried out. That, at any rate, is the theory of our Constitution." Abrams v. United States, 250 U.S. 616, 630 (1919) (Holmes, J., dissenting). See also Alvin I. Goldman and James C. Cox, "Speech, Truth, and the Free Market for Ideas," *Legal Theory* 2 (1996): 1–32; Ronald Coase, "The Market for Goods and the Market for Ideas," *American Economic Review* 63 (1974): 384–391.

11. "Of course, semiautomatic firearms technology didn't exist in any meaningful sense in the era of the founding fathers. They had something much different in mind when they drafted the Second Amendment. The typical firearms of the day were muskets and

flintlock pistols. They could hold a single round at a time, and a skilled shooter could hope to get off three or possibly four rounds in a minute of firing. By all accounts they were not particularly accurate either." Christopher Ingraham, "What 'Arms' Looked Like When the Second Amendment Was Written," *Washington Post*, June 13, 2016, https://www.washingtonpost.com/news/wonk/wp/2016/06/13/the-men-who-wrote -the-2nd-amendment-would-never-recognize-an-ar-15/?utm_term=.d1aae1c1f927.

12. Ultimately, social media platforms may be the AR-15s of communication technologies, in that they operate in a way that is so far beyond what the framers of the Constitution could have imagined.

13. 274 U.S. 357 (1927) (Brandeis, J., concurring).

14. 274 U.S. 357 (1927) (Brandeis, J., concurring), 377.

15. See Daniel E. Ho and Frederick Schauer, "Testing the Marketplace of Ideas," *NYU Law Review* 90 (2015): 1160–1228.

16. See, generally, Napoli, *Foundations of Communications Policy*.

17. See, for example, Darren Bush, "'The Marketplace of Ideas': Is Judge Posner Chasing Don Quixote's Windmills?" *Arizona State Law Journal* 32 (2000): 1107–1147; Stanley Ingber, "The Marketplace of Ideas: A Legitimizing Myth," *Duke Law Journal* 1984 (1984): 1–91.

18. Abrams v. United States, 250 U.S. 616, 630 (Holmes, J., dissenting). The marketplace of ideas metaphor will be discussed in more detail in chapter 4.

19. See, generally, Alexander Meiklejohn, *Political Freedom: The Constitutional Powers of the People* (New York: Harper, 1960); Cass Sunstein, *Democracy and the Problem of Free Speech* (New York: Free Press, 1995).

20. James Surowiecki, *The Wisdom of Crowds* (New York: Anchor Books, 2004).

21. Yochai Benkler, *The Wealth of Networks: How Social Production Transforms Markets and Freedom* (New Haven, CT: Yale University Press, 2006).

22. "The best test of truth is the power of the thought to get itself accepted in the competition of the market." Abrams v. United States, 250 U.S. 616, 630 (1919) (Holmes, J., dissenting).

23. "The first of these assumptions [the "rational audience" assumption in First Amend-ment jurisprudence] is that audiences are capable of rationally assessing the truth, quality, and credibility of core speech." Lyrissa Barnett Lidsky, "Nobody's Fools: The Rational Audience as First Amendment Ideal," *University of Illinois Law Review* 2010 (2010): 799–850, 801.

24. "Thus, if consumers have no very strong preference for truth as compared with other goods or dimensions of goods, then there is no reason to expect that the bundle of intellectual goods provided and "traded" in a competitive market will have maximum truth content. If people valued falsehood, then perfect competition would provide falsehood in a Pareto-optimal way." Goldman and Cox, "Speech, Truth, and the Free Market for Ideas," 18.

25. See McConnell v. FEC, 540 U.S. 93, 258–259 (2003) (Scalia, J., concurring in part and dissenting in part).

26. See, for example, Bush, "'The Marketplace of Ideas'"; Ingber, "The Marketplace of Ideas."

27. Jared Schroeder, "Toward a Discursive Marketplace of Ideas: Reimagining the Marketplace Metaphor in the Era of Social Media, Fake News, and Artificial Intelligence," *First Amendment Studies* 52, no. 1/2 (2018): 38–60.

28. For a review, see Richards and Calvert, "Counterspeech 2000."

29. For a more detailed discussion of the Fairness Doctrine and its relationship to counterspeech, see Adam Welle, "Campaign Counterspeech: A New Strategy to Control Sham Issue Advocacy in the Wake of FEC v. Wisconsin Right to Life," *Wisconsin Law Review* 2008 (2008): 795–839.

30. See Report on Editorializing by Broadcast Licensees, 13 F.C.C. 1246 (1949).

31. See In re Complaint of Syracuse Peace Council, 2 F.C.C.R 5043, 5047 (1987).

32. See, for example, William E. Porter, *Assault on the Media: The Nixon Years* (Ann Arbor: University of Michigan Press, 1976).

33. For an overview of relevant regulations and court decisions, see Rickert v. State Pub. Disclosure Commission, 168 P.3d 826, 827 nn. 2–3 (Wash. 2007).

34. Reasons included the court's rejection of the notion that "the State possesses an independent right to determine truth and falsity in political debate" (827), as well as the fact that the statute did not require proof of the defamatory nature of the speech (828–829). Rickert v. State Pub. Disclosure Commission, 168 P.3d 826 (Wash. 2007).

35. Rickert v. State Pub. Disclosure Commission, 168 P.3d 826, 830–831 (Wash. 2007).

36. Rickert v. State Pub. Disclosure Commission, 168 P.3d 826, 831 (Wash. 2007).

37. Rickert v. State Pub. Disclosure Commission, 168 P.3d 826, 855 (Wash. 2007).

38. Rickert v. State Pub. Disclosure Commission, 168 P.3d 826, 855–856 (Wash. 2007).

39. 418 U.S. 323, 340–341 (1973).

40. See Frederick Schauer, "Facts and the First Amendment," *UCLA Law Review* 57 (2009–2010): 897–919, 912–914.

41. See Potter Stewart, "Or of the Press," *Hastings Law Journal* 26 (1974–1975): 631–637.

42. For an historical overview, see Anthony Lewis, *Make No Law: The Sullivan Case and the First Amendment* (New York: Vintage Books, 1991).

43. Hustler Magazine, Inc. v. Falwell, 485 U.S. 46, 52 (1988).

44. New York Times Co. v. Sullivan, 376 U.S. 254, 270 (1964).

45. See Schauer, "Facts and the First Amendment," 897. For a discussion of the First Amendment protections for Holocaust deniers, see Jonathan D. Varatt, "Deception and the First Amendment: A Central, Complex, and Somewhat Curious Relationship," *UCLA Law Review* 53 (2006): 1107–1141.

46. New York Times Co. v. Sullivan, 376 U.S. 254, 271 (1964).

47. New York Times Co. v. Sullivan, 376 U.S. 254, 272 (1964).

48. See Jamie Bartlett and Alex Krasodomski-Jones, "Counter-Speech on Facebook," Demos, September 2016, https://www.demos.co.uk/wp-content/uploads/2016/09/Counter-speech-on-facebook-report.pdf; Jamie Bartlett and Alex Krasodomski-Jones, "Counter-Speech: Examining Content That Challenges Extremism Online," Demos, October 2015, https://www.demos.co.uk/wp-content/uploads/2015/10/Counter-speech.pdf. It is worth noting that while these studies seek to document the prevalence of counterspeech on Facebook, they do not seek to determine its effectiveness.

49. Online Civil Courage Initiative, Facebook, https://www.facebook.com/pg/OnlineCivil Courage/about/.

50. Online Civil Courage Initiative.

51. @TweeSurfing, "Counter Speech on Social Media: The New Age Activism," Twitter, December 2, 2016, https://twitter.com/i/moments/804541593340366848. Twitter's VP of Public Policy, Government, & Philanthropy writes, "Twitter's open and real-time nature is a *powerful antidote to the spreading of all types of false information.* This is important because we cannot distinguish whether every single Tweet from every person is truthful or not. We, as a company, should not be the arbiter of truth. Journalists, experts and engaged citizens Tweet side-by-side correcting and challenging public discourse in seconds. *These vital interactions happen on Twitter every day* [original emphasis]." Colin Crowell, "Our Approach to Bots and Misinformation," June 14, 2017, https://blog.twitter.com/official/en_us/topics/company/2017/Our-Approach-Bots-Misinformation.html. For a study of the prevalence (but not the effectiveness) of counterspeech on Twitter, see Susan Benesch, Derek Ruths, Kelly P. Dillon, Haji Mohammad Saleem, and Lucas Wright, "Counterspeech on Twitter: A Field Study," Report for Public Safety Canada, 2016, https://dangerousspeech.org/counterspeech-on-twitter-a-field-study/.

52. Richard Salgado, Testimony Before the Senate Judiciary Subcommittee on Crime and Terrorism, Hearing on Extremist Content and Russian Information Online: Working with Tech to Find Solutions, November 1, 2017, 6, https://www.judiciary.senate.gov/imo/media/doc/10-31-17%20Salgado%20Testimony.pdf.

53. Salgado, Testimony.

54. See, for example, R. Kelly Garrett and Natalie Jomini Stroud, "Partisan Paths to Exposure Diversity: Differences in Pro- and Counterattitudinal News Consumption," *Journal of Communication* 64 (2014): 680–701; Michael A. Beam, "Automating the News: How Personalized News Recommender System Design Choices Impact News Reception," *Communication Research* 41 (2014): 1019–1041; D. J. Flynn, Brendan Nyhan, and Jason Reifler, "The Nature and Origins of Misperceptions: Understanding False and Unsupported Beliefs About Politics," *Political Psychology* 38 (2017): 127–150. See also Alessandro Bessi, Fabio Petroni, Michela Del Vicario, Fabiana Zollo, Aris Anagnostopoulos, Antonio Scala, and Guido Caldarelli, "Homophily and Polarization in the Age of Misinformation," *European Physical Journal Special Topics* 225 (2016): 2047–2059, which discusses research showing a correlation between polarized social networks and participation in the consumption and spread of false news and information.

55. Schauer, "Facts and the First Amendment," 898.

56. Lidsky, "Nobody's Fools." We will return to this theme in chapter 6.

57. Vincent Blasi, "Reading Holmes Through the Lens of Schauer: The Abrams Dissent," *Notre Dame Law Review* 72 (1997): 1343–1360.

58. Richard Delgado and David Yun, " 'The Speech We Hate': First Amendment Totalism, the ACLU, and the Principle of Dialogic Politics," *Arizona State Law Journal* 27 (1995): 1281–1300.

59. Owen Fiss, *The Irony of Free Speech* (Cambridge, MA: Harvard University Press, 1996), 25.

60. Mari Matsuda argues that minority groups have "diminished access to private remedies such as effective counterspeech." Mari J. Matsuda, Charles R. Lawrence III, Richard Delgado, and Kimberlè Williams Crenshaw, *Words That Wound: Critical Race Theory, Assaultive Speech, and the First Amendment* (Boulder, CO: Westview Press, 1993), 48.

61. Kevin Munger, "Tweetment Effects on the Tweeted: Experimentally Reducing Racist Harassment," *Political Behavior* 39, no. 3 (2017): 639–649.

62. See, for instance, Schauer, "Facts and the First Amendment," 899. Schauer's recognition of the apparent "increasing and unfortunate acceptance of factual falsity in public communication" does not address how the evolution of the media sector might be contributing to this increase.

63. Nebiha Syed, "Real Talk About Fake News: Towards a Better Theory for Platform Governance," *Yale Law Journal Forum* 127 (2017–2018): 337–357, 337–338.

64. See, for example, Margaret Sullivan, "The Term 'Fake News' Has Lost All Meaning. That's Just How Trump Wants It," *Washington Post*, April 4, 2018, https://www .washingtonpost.com/lifestyle/style/the-term-fake-news-has-lost-all-meaning-thats -just-how-trump-wants-it/2018/04/03/ce102ed4-375c-11e8-8fd2-49fe3c675a89_story .html?utm_term=.d04dec539de5

65. "In a typical free speech case, . . . use of verbal formulae or case matching to determine the category in which to place the speech in question works well enough. There is often precedent so factually similar that it really is controlling; or even in the absence of such truly controlling precedent, categorizing the speech in question one way rather than the other so clearly promotes the values underlying free speech doctrine that a judge can intuitively make the right choice." James Weinstein, "Speech Characterization and the Limits of First Amendment Formalism: Lessons from Nike v. Kasky," *Case Western Reserve Law Review* 54 (2004): 1091–1142, 1093.

66. For a similar discussion, see Lee McIntyre, *Post-Truth* (Cambridge, MA: MIT Press, 2018), chapter 4.

67. "As almost everyone knows, the economic foundation of the nation's newspapers, long supported by advertising, is collapsing, and newspapers themselves, which have been the country's chief source of independent reporting, are shrinking—literally. Fewer journalists are reporting less news in fewer pages, and the hegemony that near-monopoly metropolitan newspapers enjoyed during the last third of the twentieth century, even as their primary audience eroded, is ending. Commercial television news, which was long the chief rival of printed newspapers, has also been losing its audience, its advertising revenue, and its reporting resources." Leonard Downie, Jr., and Michael Schudson, "The Reconstruction of American Journalism," *Columbia Journalism Review*, November/December 2009, 1, http://archives.cjr.org/reconstruction /the_reconstruction_of_american.php.

"The effect of the current changes in the news ecosystem has already been a reduction in the quality of news in the United States." C. W. Anderson, Emily Bell, and Clay Shirky, "Post-Industrial Journalism: Adapting to the Present," Tow Center for Digital Journalism, 2014, 2, https://academiccommons.columbia.edu/doi/10.7916 /D8N01JS7.

68. Bureau of Labor Statistics, "Newspaper Publishers Lose Over Half Their Employment from January 2001 to September 2016," April 3, 2017, https://www.bls.gov/opub /ted/2017/mobile/newspaper-publishers-lose-over-half-their-employment-from -january-2001-to-september-2016.htm.

69. See, for example, Dan Gillmor, *We the Media: Grassroots Journalism by the People, for the People* (Sebastopol, CA: O'Reilly Media, 2004).

70. See Pew Research Center, *State of the News Media 2016*, June 2016, http://www.journalism .org/2016/06/15/state-of-the-news-media-2016/.

71. "The Future of Newspapers," *Independent*, November 13, 2006, http://www.independent .co.uk/news/media/the-future-of-newspapers-5331270.html.

72. For an excellent treatment of this issue, see Steven Rosenfeld and Ivy Olesen, "Vampire Web Pages Suck Content from Legitimate Progressive News Sites," *Alter-Net*, March 6, 2017, https://www.alternet.org/media/vampire-webpages-suck-content -legitimate-progressive-news-sites.

73. Even producers of fake news engage in rampant cannibalization of other fake news producers. "Most of the posts on these sites are aggregated, or completely plagiarized, from fringe and right-wing sites in the U.S." Craig Silverman and Lawrence Alexander, "How Teens in the Balkans Are Duping Trump Supporters with Fake News," *BuzzFeed*, November 3, 2016, https://www.buzzfeed.com/craigsilverman/how-macedonia-became -a-global-hub-for-pro-trump-misinfo?utm_term=.jgOP8e208#.mc5dvo9bv.

74. The term *echo chamber*, often used synonymously with *filter bubble*, may be a better fit for describing the circulation of parasitic journalism through social media.

75. See, for example, David Uberti, "The Real History of Fake News," *Columbia Journalism Review*, December 15, 2016, http://www.cjr.org/special_report/fake_news_history.php.

76. See Jacob Soll, "The Long and Brutal History of Fake News," *Politico*, December 18, 2016, http://www.politico.com/magazine/story/2016/12/fake-news-history-long-violent -214535.

77. See Samanth Subramanian, "Inside the Macedonian Fake-News Complex," *Wired*, February 15, 2017, https://www.wired.com/2017/02/veles-macedonia-fake-news/; Silverman and Alexander, "How Teens in the Balkans."

78. A. J. Liebling, "The Wayward Press: Do You Belong in Journalism?" *New Yorker*, May 14, 1960, 105.

79. Abby Ohlheiser, "This Is How the Internet's Fake News Writers Make Money," *Washington Post*, November 18, 2016, https://www.washingtonpost.com/news/the -intersect/wp/2016/11/18/this-is-how-the-internets-fake-news-writers-make-money /?utm_term=.7c4ee4d7e8d6.

80. Robert Thomson, "News Corp. CEO on Fake News, 'Digital Duopoly' and What Role Advertising Plays in All of It," *MediaShift*, April 3, 2017, http://mediashift.org/2017/04 /news-corp-ceo-fake-news-digital-duopoly-role-advertising-plays/.

81. Thomson, "News Corp. CEO."

82. Facebook, "Blocking Ads from Pages That Repeatedly Share False News," August 28, 2017, https://newsroom.fb.com/news/2017/08/blocking-ads-from-pages-that-repeatedly -share-false-news/.

83. Craig Silverman, Jeremy Singer-Vine, and Lam Thuy Vo, "In Spite Of the Crackdown, Fake News Publishers Are Still Earning Money from Major Ad Networks," *BuzzFeed*, April 4, 2017, https://www.buzzfeed.com/craigsilverman/fake-news-real-ads. For a more detailed discussion of how ad tech platforms are addressing their role supporting providers of fake news and disinformation, see Joshua A. Braun and Jessica L. Eklund, "Fake News, Real Money: Ad Tech Platforms, Profit-Drive Hoaxes, and the Business of Journalism," *Digital Journalism* 7, no. 1 (2019): 1–21.

84. "The evidence . . . demonstrates that independent news coverage grew as scale economies became more important." James T. Hamilton, *All the News That's Fit to Sell: How the Market Transforms Information Into News* (Princeton, NJ: Princeton University Press, 2004), 28. See also Gerald J. Baldasty, *The Commercialization of News in the Nineteenth Century* (Madison: University of Wisconsin Press, 1992).

   Some researchers have questioned whether the development of the norm of objectivity is tied to the commercialization of the press. "The notion that the move from partisanship to objectivity was economically motivated is widely believed but nowhere justified." Michael Schudson, "The Objectivity Norm in American Journalism," *Journalism* 2, no. 2 (2001): 149–170, 160.

85. "These Macedonians on Facebook didn't care if Trump won or lost the White House. They only wanted pocket money to pay for things—a car, watches, better cell phones, more drinks at the bar." Subramanian, "Inside the Macedonian Fake-News Complex."

   "We've found that a lot of fake news is financially motivated." Adam Mosseri, "News Feed FYI: Addressing Hoaxes and Fake News," *Facebook*, December 15, 2016, https://newsroom.fb.com/news/2016/12/news-feed-fyi-addressing-hoaxes-and-fake-news/.

   "Their reasons for launching these sites are purely financial, according to the Macedonians with whom BuzzFeed News spoke." Silverman and Alexander, "How Teens in the Balkans."

86. Alexios Mantzarlis, "Facebook Referrals Are Crucial for Traffic to Hyperpartisan and Fake News Sites," *Poynter*, November 28, 2016, https://www.poynter.org/2016/facebook-referrals-are-crucial-for-traffic-to-hyperpartisan-and-fake-news-sites/440132/.

87. Jacob L. Nelson, "Is 'Fake News' a Fake Problem?" *Columbia Journalism Review*, January 31, 2017, https://www.cjr.org/analysis/fake-news-facebook-audience-drudge-breitbart-study.php.

88. See, for example, Chris J. Vargo, Lei Guo, and Michelle A. Amazeen, "The Agenda-Setting Power of Fake News: A Big Data Analysis of the Online Media Landscape from 2014 to 2016," *New Media & Society* 20, no. 5 (2018): 2028–2049.

89. "Not surprisingly, we found the conversation around alternative narratives of mass shooting events to be largely fueled by content on alternative (as opposed to mainstream) media." Kate Starbird, "Examining the Alternative Media Ecosystem Through the Production of Alternative Narratives of Mass Shooting Events on Twitter," *Proceedings of the Eleventh International Conference on Web and Social Media* (Palo Alto, CA: AAAI Press, 2017), 230–239. See also Yochai Benkler, Robert Faris, and Hal Roberts, *Network Propaganda: Manipulation, Disinformation, and Radicalization in American Politics* (New York: Oxford University Press, 2018).

90. "By classifying all the content posted according to its political orientation we are able to identify the general political orientation of the users and measure levels of political homophily in their network." Elanor Colleoni, Alessandro Rozza, and Adam Arvidsson, "Echo Chamber or Public Sphere? Predicting Political Orientation and Measuring Political Homophily in Twitter Using Big Data," *Journal of Communication* 64, no. 2 (2014), 317–332, 319.

91. For details, see Joshua Green and Sasha Issenberg, "Inside the Trump Bunker, with Days to Go," *Bloomberg Businessweek*, October 27, 2016, https://www.bloomberg.com /news/articles/2016-10-27/inside-the-trump-bunker-with-12-days-to-go.

92. Christopher Wylie, *Written Statement to the United States Senate Committee on the Judiciary, In the Matter of Cambridge Analytica and Other Related Issues*, May 16, 2018, https://www.judiciary.senate.gov/imo/media/doc/05-16-18%20Wylie%20Testimony .pdf.

93. "While computational politics in its current form includes novel applications, the historical trends discussed in this paper predate the spread of the Internet. In fact, there was already a significant effort underway to use big data for purposes of marketing, and the progression of using marketing techniques for politics—and 'selling of the President'—clearly reflects longer-term trends. However, computational politics introduces significant qualitative differences to that long march of historical trends. Unlike previous data collection efforts (for example, collating magazine subscriptions or car type purchases) which required complicated, roundabout inferences about their meaning (does a magazine subscription truly signal a voter preference?) and allowed only broad profiling in the aggregate, this data provides significantly more individualized profiling and modeling, much greater data depth, and can be collected in an invisible, latent manner and delivered individually." Zeynep Tufekci, "Engineering the Public: Big Data, Surveillance, and Computational Politics," *First Monday* 19, no. 7 (2014), http:// firstmonday.org/article/view/4901/4097. See also Anthony Nadler, Matthew Crain, and Joan Donovan, *The Digital Influence Machine: The Political Perils of Online Ad Tech* (New York: Data & Society, 2018).

94. The data can be accessed at https://democrats-intelligence.house.gov/facebook-ads /social-media-advertisements.htm.

95. According to Senator Mark Warner, "It's been reported to me, and we've got to find this out, whether they were able to affect specific areas in Wisconsin, Michigan, Pennsylvania." Rachel Roberts, "Russia Hired 1,000 People to Create Anti-Clinton 'Fake News' in Key US States During Election, Trump-Russia Hearings Leader Reveals," *Independent*, March 30, 2017, http://www.independent.co.uk/news/world/americas /us-politics/russian-trolls-hilary-clinton-fake-news-election-democrat-mark-warner -intelligence-committee-a7657641.html.

96. Philip N. Howard, Bence Kollanyi, Samantha Bradshaw, and Lisa-Maria Neudert, "Social Media, News and Political Information During the US Election: Was Polarizing Content Concentrated in Swing States?" September 28, 2017, http://comprop.oii.ox.ac .uk/wp-content/uploads/sites/89/2017/09/Polarizing-Content-and-Swing-States.pdf. For a more detailed account of the range of election interference activities engaged in

by the Russian government, see United States of America v. Internet Research Agency LLC, Indictment in the United States District Court for the District of Columbia, filed February 16, 2018.

97. "WOLF BLITZER (HOST): Do these fake news trolls sometimes actually target President Trump himself? BRIAN TODD: According to the cybersecurity expert Clint Watts who you had on earlier, Wolf, they do, in fact, do that. Watts testified today that some outlets pushing fake or misleading stories will tweet right at President Trump during high volume periods when they know he's online. They're pushing conspiracy theories hoping that he clicks on one and cites one publicly." Media Matters Staff, "CNN: Fake News Trolls Pushing Conspiracy Theories 'Tweet Right at President Trump' Hoping That 'He Cites It Publicly,'" Media Matters for America, March 30, 2017, https://www.mediamatters.org/video/2017/03/30/cnn-fake-news-trolls-pushing-conspiracy-theories-tweet-right-president-trump-hoping-he-cites-it/215878.

98. Andrew Guess, Brendan Nyhan and Jason Reifler, "Selective Exposure to Misinformation: Evidence from the Consumption of Fake News During the 2016 U.S. Presidential Campaign," unpublished working paper, January 9, 2018, https://www.dartmouth.edu/~nyhan/fake-news-2016.pdf; Jacob L. Nelson and Harsh Taneja, "The Small, Disloyal Fake News Audience: The Role of Audience Availability in Fake News Consumption," *New Media & Society* 20, no. 10 (2018): 3720–3737.

99. Blasi, "Reading Holmes," 1357.

100. "The media that individuals consume on Facebook depends not only on what their friends share but also on how the News Feed ranking algorithm sorts these articles and what individuals choose to read." Eytan Bakshy, Solomon Messing, and Lada A. Adamic, "Exposure to Ideologically Diverse News and Opinion on Facebook," *Science* 348, no. 6239 (June 5, 2015), 1130–1132, 1130. See also Philip M. Napoli, "Social Media and the Public Interest: Governance of News Platforms in the Realm of Individual and Algorithmic Gatekeepers," *Telecommunications Policy* 39, no. 9 (2015): 751–760.

101. See, for example, Ivan Dylko, "The Dark Side of Technology: An Experimental Investigation of the Influence of Customizability Technology on Online Political Selective Exposure," *Computers in Human Behavior* 73 (2017): 181–190; Seth R. Flaxman, Sharad Goael, and Justin M. Rao, "Ideological Segregation and the Effects of Social Media on News Consumption," unpublished manuscript, May 2014, https://bfi.uchicago.edu/sites/default/files/research/flaxman_goel_rao_onlinenews.pdf, which found that "recent technological changes do increase ideological segregation." Cass Sunstein, *#Republic: Divided Democracy in the Age of Social Media* (Princeton, NJ: Princeton University Press, 2017).

102. See Starbird, "Examining the Alternative Media Ecosystem."

103. "Users with strong preferences for alternative information sources . . . are more susceptible to false information." Delia Mocanu, Luca Rossi, Qian Zhang, Marton Kasai, and Walter Quattrociocchi, "Collective Attention in the Age of (Mis)information," *Computers in Human Behavior* 51 (2015), 1198–1204, 1202.

"Polarized communities emerge around distinct types of contents and usual consumers of conspiracy news result to be more focused and self-contained on their specific contents." Alessandro Bessi, Mauro Coletto, George Alexandru Davidescu, Antonio Scala, Guido Caldarelli, and Walter Quattrociocchi, "Science vs. Conspiracy: Collective Narratives in the Age of Misinformation," *PLoS ONE* 10, no. 10 (2015), http://journals.plos.org/plosone/article?id=10.1371/journal.pone.0118093.

104. Walter Quattrociocchi, Antonio Scala, and Cass Sunstein, "Echo Chambers on Facebook," unpublished manuscript, June 2016, https://papers.ssrn.com/sol3/papers.cfm?abstract_id=2795110.

105. Vidya Narayanan, Vlad Barash, John Kelly, Bence Kollanyi, Lisa-Maria Neudert, and Philip N. Howard, "Polarization, Partisanship and Junk News Consumption Over Social Media in the US," Computational Propaganda Data Memo, February 6, 2018, http://comprop.oii.ox.ac.uk/research/polarization-partisanship-and-junk-news/.

106. This term is used in reference to the well-known spiral of silence, which posits that individuals who perceive their opinion to be in the minority will choose not to express that opinion, thus feeding into a downward spiral that systematically silences more and more of those holding that minority opinion, thereby creating a false impression of a widely shared majority opinion. See Elizabeth Noelle Neuman, *The Spiral of Silence: Public Opinion—Our Social Skin* (Chicago: University of Chicago Press,1994).

107. See Jonathan M. Ladd, *Why Americans Hate the Media and How It Matters* (Princeton, NJ: Princeton University Press, 2011), which illustrates how increased media fragmentation has interacted with demand for more partisan news to amplify partisanship and distrust of institutional news media.

108. "Starting in the 1980s, Americans began to report increasingly negative opinions of their opposing party." Amanda Taub, "The Real Story About Fake News Is Partisanship," *New York Times*, January 11, 2017, https://www.nytimes.com/2017/01/11/upshot/the-real-story-about-fake-news-is-partisanship.html. For a more detailed discussion of the relationship between fragmentation and political polarization, see Ricardo Gandour, "A New Information Environment: How Digital Fragmentation Is Changing the Way We Produce and Consume News," Knight Center for Journalism in America, 2016, https://knightcenter.utexas.edu/books/NewInfoEnvironmentEnglishLink.pdf. For a landmark study on the rise of media and audience fragmentation, see W. Russell Neuman, *The Future of the Mass Audience* (New York: Cambridge University Press, 1991).

109. "In the month leading up to the election, a quarter of Americans said they used biased news sites several times or more. Reliance on these websites appears to produce a distorted understanding of evidence, potentially promoting inaccurate beliefs even when evidence is understood correctly. It is sobering to recognize that online news may contribute to misperceptions even when consumers encounter a range of outlets and have been exposed to more accurate political information." R. Kelly Garrett et al. "Driving a Wedge Between Evidence and Beliefs: How Online Ideological News Exposure Promotes Political Misperceptions," *Journal of Computer Mediated Communication*, 21, no. 5 (2016): 331–348, 344.

110. Guess, Nyhan, and Reifler, "Selective Exposure to Misinformation," 1.

111. John H. McManus, "What Kind of Commodity Is News?" *Communication Research* 19, no. 6 (1992): 787–805, 794.

112. For an overview and advocacy of the concept of bounded rationality, see John Conlisk, "Why Bounded Rationality?" *Journal of Economic Literature* 34, no. 2 (1996): 669–700. For a discussion of the concept's relationship to the marketplace-of-ideas-metaphor, see Joseph Blocher, "Institutions in the Marketplace of Ideas," *Duke Law Journal* 57, no. 4 (2008): 821–889.

113. See McManus, "What Kind of Commodity Is News?" 793.

114. See, for example, Olivia Solon, "Only 20 percent of US Adults Have Information Overload, but Those Who Do Feel Burden," *Guardian*, December 7, 2016, https://www.theguardian.com/technology/2016/dec/07/information-overload-pew-study-digital-divide; Xiaoyan Qiu, Diego F. M. Oliveira, Alireza Sahami Shirazi, Alessandro Flammini, and Filippo Menczer, "Lack of Quality Discrimination in Online Information Markets," 2017, https://www.researchgate.net/publication/312194354_Lack_of_quality_discrimination_in_online_information_markets.

115. "One of the most prevalent heuristics used for evaluating credibility that was mentioned by focus group participants was relying on site or source reputation." Miriam J. Metzger, Andrew J. Flanagin, and Ryan B. Medders, " Social and Heuristic Approaches to Credibility Evaluation Online," *Journal of Communication* 60, no. 3 (2010): 413–439, 426.

116. "Whenever contracts for the exchange of a good are incomplete and sellers have leeway to shade its quality about which the consumer finds out only if it is too late . . . A key role in markets for such goods is assumed by trust." See Steffen Huck, Gabriele K. Lünser, and Jean-Robert Tyran, "Pricing and Trust," CEPR Discussion Paper No. DP6135, 2008, 1, https://papers.ssrn.com/sol3/papers.cfm?abstract_id=1133780, https://www.parisschoolofeconomics.eu/IMG/pdf/Huck2.pdf.

117. See Amy Mitchell, Elisa Shearer, Jeffrey Gottfried, and Kristine Lu, "How Americans Encounter, Recall and Act Upon Digital News," Pew Research Center, February 9, 2017, http://www.journalism.org/2017/02/09/how-americans-encounter-recall-and-act-upon-digital-news/.

118. See, generally, " 'Who Shared It?': How Americans Decide What News to Trust on Social Media," Media Insight Project, March 2017, http://mediainsight.org/PDFs/Trust%20Social%20Media%20Experiments%202017/MediaInsight_Social%20Media%20Final.pdf.

119. " 'Who Shared It?,' " 4–9.

120. "Those who trusted the sharer but saw the unknown outlet were more likely than those who did not trust the sharer and saw the reputable outlet to share the article, follow the sharer, sign up for news alerts from the source, and recommend the source to friends." " 'Who Shared It?,' " 10.

121. Maksym Gabielkov, Arthi Ramachandran, Augustin Chaintreau, and Arnaud Legout, "Social Clicks: What and Who Gets Read on Twitter?," paper presented at the ACM Sigmetrics / IFIP Performance Conference, Antibes Juan-les-Pins, France, June 2016, https://hal.inria.fr/hal-01281190/document.

122. "Twitter users are unlikely to be exposed to cross-ideological content from the cluster of users they followed as these were usually politically homogeneous." Itai Himelboim, Stephen McCreery, and Marc Smith, "Birds of a Feather Tweet Together: Integrating

Network and Content Analyses to Examine Cross-Ideology Exposure on Twitter," *Journal of Computer-Mediated Communication* 18, no. 2 (2013): 40–60, 40.

More ideologically extreme individuals have more homophilous social networks, which should "result in networks that embed their members in denser webs of like-minded associations, which could then insulate individuals from the demotivating effects of dissenting views, and may enable political behaviors to spread faster than they would through sparser networks." Andrei Boutyline and Robb Willer, "The Social Structure of Political Echo Chambers: Variation in Ideological Homophily in Online Networks," *Political Psychology* 38, no. 3 (2017): 551–569, 566–567.

123. "There is little overlap in the news sources [liberals and conservatives] turn to and trust." Amy Mitchell, Katerina Eva Matsa, Jeffrey Gottfried and Jocelyn Kiley, "Political Polarization and Media Habits," Pew Research Center, October 2014, 1, http://www .journalism.org/2014/10/21/political-polarization-media-habits.

"On many fronts, Americans are skeptical of 'the news media' in the abstract but generally trust the news they themselves rely on." "'My' Media Versus 'The' Media: Trust in News Media Depends on Which News Media You Mean," Media Insight Project, April 2017, 1, http://www.mediainsight.org/PDFs/Meaning%20of%20Media /APNORC_Trust_The_Media_2017.pdf.

124. See Goldman and Cox, "Speech, Truth, and the Free Market for Ideas," 23.

125. "The emergence of websites such as Weltner's Katrina Families and American Civil Rights Review illustrates a central feature of propaganda and cyber-racism in the digital era: the use of difficult-to-detect authorship and hidden agendas intended to accomplish political goals." Jessie Daniels, "Cloaked Websites: Propaganda, Cyber-Racism and Epistemology in the Digital Era," *New Media & Society* 11, no. 5 (2009): 658–683, 660.

126. "Organizations and individuals who deploy the strategies of 'black' and 'grey' propaganda online via cloaked websites can be more effective precisely because they conceal their intention and authorship." Daniels, "Cloaked Websites," 662.

127. Research indicates that social media users find it particularly difficult to accurately distinguish news posts from other types of social media posts. "Users and researchers often agree on defining social and political content, but are more likely to disagree on categorizing news content." Emily K. Vraga, Leticia Bode, Anne-Bennett Smithson, and Sonya Troller-Renfree, "Blurred Lines: Defining Social, News, and Political Posts on Facebook," *Journal of Information & Technology Politics* 13, no. 3 (2016): 272–294, 272.

128. Technological changes are likely to further enhance the ability to disguise fake news as legitimate news. "At corporations and universities across the country, incipient technologies appear likely to soon obliterate the line between real and fake. Or, in the simplest of terms, advancements in audio and video technology are becoming so sophisticated that they will be able to replicate real news—real TV broadcasts, for instance, or radio interviews—in unprecedented, and truly indecipherable, ways." Nick Bilton, "Fake News Is About to Get Even Scarier Than You Ever Dreamed," *Vanity Fair*, January 26, 2017, http://www.vanityfair.com/news/2017/01/fake-news-technology.

129. Roberts, "Russia Hired 1,000 People". For more details on the disinformation activities of Russia's Internet Research Agency, see Renee DiResta, Kris Shaffer, Becky Ruppel,

David Sullivan, Robert Matney, Ryan Fox, Jonathan Albright, Ben Johnson, *The Tactics & Tropes of the Internet Research Agency: Report Prepared for the United States Senate Select Committee on Intelligence* (November, 2018), https://disinformationreport.blob .core.windows.net/disinformation-report/NewKnowledge-Disinformation-Report -Whitepaper.pdf; Philip N. Howard, Bharath Ganesh, Dimitra Liotsiou, John Kelly, Camille Francois, *The IRA, Social Media, and Political Polarization in the United States, 2012–2018,* Computational Propaganda Project, University of Oxford, https://comprop.oii .ox.ac.uk/wp-content/uploads/sites/93/2018/12/The-IRA-Social-Media-and-Political -Polarization.pdf.

130. "There are dozens of proxy news sites presenting Russian propaganda, but with their affiliation with Russia disguised or downplayed." Christopher Paul and Miriam Matthews, "The Russian 'Firehouse of Falsehood' Propaganda Model," *RAND Corporation Perspective,* 2016, 2, http://www.rand.org/content/dam/rand/pubs/perspectives /PE100/PE198/RAND_PE198.pdf.

131. For more details, see Tim Mak, "Russian Influence Campaign Sought to Exploit Americans' Trust in Local News," *NPR,* July 12, 2018, https://www.npr.org/2018/07/12 /628085238/russian-influence-campaign-sought-to-exploit-americans-trust-in-local -news.

132. Jason Schartz, "Baby Breitbarts to Pop Up Across the Country?" *Politico,* April 30, 2018, https://www.politico.com/story/2018/04/30/breitbart-tennessee-fake-news-560670.

133. Schartz, "Baby Breitbarts."

134. *Piers Morgan Tonight* (air date July 18, 2012), CNN Transcripts, http://www.cnn.com /TRANSCRIPTS/1602/13/cnr.12.html. For a prescient discussion of the importance of transparency regarding the nature and motives of sources to the effective functioning of the First Amendment, see Amit Schejter, "Jacob's Voice, Esau's Hands: Transparency as a First Amendment Right in an Age of Deceit and Impersonation," *Hofstra Law Review* 35 (2007): 1489–1518.

135. *Piers Morgan Tonight.*

136. For a discussion of the challenges to the journalistic process of verifying news and information disseminated online, see Alfred Hermida, "Tweets and Truth: Journalism as a Discipline of Collaborative Verification," *Journalism Practice* 6, no. 5/6 (2012): 659–668.

137. "Our own study of over 1.25 million stories published online between April 1, 2015 and Election Day shows that a right-wing media network anchored around Breitbart developed as a distinct and insulated media system, using social media as a backbone to transmit a hyper-partisan perspective to the world. This pro-Trump media sphere appears to have not only successfully set the agenda for the conservative media sphere, but also strongly influenced the broader media agenda, in particular coverage of Hillary Clinton." Yochai Benkler, Robert Faris, Hal Roberts, and Ethan Zuckerman, "Study: Breitbart-Led Right-Wing Media Ecosystem Altered Broader Media Agenda," *Columbia Journalism Review,* March 3, 2017, https://www.cjr.org/analysis/breitbart -media-trump-harvard-study.php.

138. Josephine Lukito, Chris Wells, Yini Zhang, and Larisa Doroshenko, "The Twitter Exploit: How Russian Propaganda Infiltrated U.S. News," Report of the Social Media

and Democracy Research Group, University of Wisconsin, February 2018, https://www.researchgate.net/publication/323703483_The_Twitter_exploit_How_Russian_propaganda_infiltrated_US_news.

139. Josh Constine, "Facebook Shows Related Articles and Fact-Checkers Before You Open Links," *TechCrunch*, April 25, 2017, https://techcrunch.com/2017/04/25/facebook-shows-related-articles-and-fact-checkers-before-you-open-links/; Fergus Bell, "Here's a List of Initiatives That Hope to Fix Trust in Journalism and Tackle Fake News," *Medium*, April 25, 2017, https://medium.com/@ferg/heres-a-list-of-initiatives-that-hope-to-fix-trust-in-journalism-and-tackle-fake-news-30689feb402. For questions regarding the effectiveness of these initiatives, see Sam Levin, "Facebook Promised to Tackle Fake News. But the Evidence Shows It's Not Working," *Guardian*, May 16, 2017, https://www.theguardian.com/technology/2017/may/16/facebook-fake-news-tools-not-working.

140. Alfred Ng, "Facebook Deleted 583 Million Fake Accounts in the First Three Months of 2018," *CNET*, May 15, 2018, https://www.cnet.com/news/facebook-deleted-583-million-fake-accounts-in-the-first-three-months-of-2018/.

141. Bloomberg News, "Facebook Pulls 810 U.S. Accounts and Pages Spreading Fake News," *Ad Age*, October 11, 2018, https://adage.com/article/digital/facebook-pulls-810-u-s-accounts-pages-spreading-fake-news/315243/; Elizabeth Dwoskin and Tony Romm, "Facebook Says It Has Uncovered a Coordinated Disinformation Operation Ahead of the 2018 Midterm Elections," *Washington Post*, July 31, 2018, https://www.washingtonpost.com/technology/2018/07/31/facebook-says-it-has-uncovered-coordinated-disinformation-operation-ahead-midterm-elections/.

142. Del Harvey and Yoel Roth, "An Update on Our Elections Integrity Work," *Twitter*, October 1, 2018, https://blog.twitter.com/official/en_us/topics/company/2018/an-update-on-our-elections-integrity-work.html; Craig Timer and Elizabeth Dwoskin, "Twitter Is Sweeping Out Fake Accounts Like Never Before, Putting User Growth at Risk," *Washington Post*, July 6, 2018, https://www.washingtonpost.com/technology/2018/07/06/twitter-is-sweeping-out-fake-accounts-like-never-before-putting-user-growth-risk/; Nicholas Confessore and Gabriel J. X. Dance, "Battling Fake Accounts, Twitter to Slash Millions of Followers," *New York Times*, July 11, 2018, https://www.nytimes.com/2018/07/11/technology/twitter-fake-followers.html.

143. James Titcomb, "Twitter Removes Fifty Accounts Posing as Republican Party Members in Pre-Election Crackdown, *Telegraph*, October 2, 2018, https://www.telegraph.co.uk/technology/2018/10/02/twitter-removes-50-accounts-posing-us-republican-party-members/.

144. See, for example, Jonathan Albright, "Facebook and the 2018 Midterms: A Look at the Data," *Medium*, November 4, 2018, https://medium.com/s/the-micro-propaganda-machine/the-2018-facebook-midterms-part-i-recursive-ad-ccountability-ac090d276097?sk=b07db173bcb021f58089f498786a6024; Ben Collins, "Russian Propaganda Evades YouTube's Flagging System with BuzzFeed-Style Knockoffs," *NBC News*, April 19, 2018, https://www.nbcnews.com/tech/tech-news/russian-propaganda-evades-youtube-s-flagging-system-buzzfeed-style-knockoffs-n867431; Sheera Frenkel, "Facebook Tried to Reign in Fake Ads. It Fell Short in a California Race," *New York Times*,

June 3, 2018, https://www.nytimes.com/2018/06/03/technology/california-congressional-race-facebook-election-interference.html; Matthew Hindman and Vlad Barash, "Disinformation, Fake News, and Influence Campaigns on Twitter," Report prepared for the Knight Foundation, October 2018, https://knightfoundation.org/reports/disinformation-fake-news-and-influence-campaigns-on-twitter; Levin, "Facebook Promised to Tackle Fake News"; Laura Hazard Owen, "Has Facebook's Algorithm Change Hurt Hyperpartisan Sites? According to This Data, Nope," *Nieman Lab*, March 30, 2018, http://www.niemanlab.org/2018/03/has-facebooks-algorithm-change-hurt-hyperpartisan-sites-according-to-this-data-nope/.

145 Indeed, one could convincingly argue that the goal of these platforms is to host as many speakers, and as much speech, as possible, with relatively little consideration given to the nature of the speakers/speech—particularly in comparison to previous generations of content distributors.

146. 274 U.S. 357, 377.

147. For a useful case study of viral news, see Sapna Maheshwari, "How Fake News Goes Viral: A Case Study," *New York Times*, November 20, 2016, https://www.nytimes.com/2016/11/20/business/media/how-fake-news-spreads.html?_r=1.

148. See, generally, Howard Rosenberg and Charles S. Feldman, *No Time to Think: The Menace of Media Speed and the Twenty-Four-Hour News Cycle* (New York: Continuum, 2008).

149. This process dates back to the development of radio and progresses through the rise of twenty-four-hour news networks and the dissemination of news online.

150. For a review, see Helena Webb, Pete Burnap, Rob N. Procter, Omer F. Rana, Bernd Carsten Stahl, Matthew Williams, William Housley, Adam Edwards, and Marina Jirotka, "Digital Wildfires: Propagation, Verification, Regulation, and Responsible Innovation," *ACM Transactions on Information Systems* 34, no. 3 (2016), article 15.

151. "Our findings suggest that the presence of social media bots can indeed negatively affect democratic political discussion rather than improving it, which in turn can potentially alter public opinion and endanger the integrity of the Presidential election." Alessandro Bessi and Emilio Ferrara, "Social Bots Distort the 2016 U.S. Presidential Election Online Discussion," *First Monday*, November 7, 2016, http://journals.uic.edu/ojs/index.php/fm/article/view/7090.

Bots are used to create "the illusion of significant online popularity in order to build real political support" and "democratiz[e] propaganda through enabling nearly anyone to amplify online interactions for partisan ends." Samuel C. Woolley and Douglas R. Guilbeault, "Computational Propaganda in the United States of America: Manufacturing Consensus Online," Computational Propaganda Research Project Working Paper No. 2017.5, Oxford Internet Institute, 2017, 3, http://comprop.oii.ox.ac.uk/wp-content/uploads/sites/89/2017/06/Comprop-USA.pdf.

152. "When he testified before the Senate Intelligence Committee last week, former FBI agent Clint Watts described how Russians used armies of Twitter bots to spread fake news using accounts that seem to be Midwestern swing-voter Republicans." Gabe O'Connor and Avie Schneider, "How Russian Twitter Bots Pumped

Out Fake News During the 2016 Election," *NPR*, April 3, 2017, http://www.npr
.org/sections/alltechconsidered/2017/04/03/522503844/how-russian-twitter-bots
-pumped-out-fake-news-during-the-2016-election.

153. "During these critical months of the campaign, 20 top-performing false election stories from hoax sites and hyperpartisan blogs generated 8,711,000 shares, reactions, and
comments on Facebook. Within the same time period, the 20 best-performing election
stories from 19 major news websites generated a total of 7,367,000 shares, reactions, and
comments on Facebook." Craig Silverman, "This Analysis Shows How Viral Fake Election News Stories Outperformed Real News on Facebook," *BuzzFeed*, November 16, 2016,
https://www.buzzfeed.com/craigsilverman/viral-fake-election-news-outperformed
-real-news-on-facebook?utm_term=.cq7vVRjoK#.tgekXRJoE.

"Misinformation is often more viral and spreads with greater frequency than cor-
rective information." Craig Silverman, "Lies, Damn Lies, and Viral Content," Tow
Center for Digital Journalism, 45, https://academiccommons.columbia.edu/doi/10.7916
/D8Q8iRHH. For more recent research focusing on Twitter that reached similar con-
clusions, see Soroush Vosoughi, Deb Roy, Sinan Aral, "The Spread of True and False
News Online," *Science* 359 (2018): 1146-1151.

154. "Partisan skew" in the sharing of news stories on social media "holds not only
for high-activity users but also for low-activity ones." Jisun An, Daniele Quercia,
and Jon Crowcroft, "Partisan Sharing: Facebook Evidence and Societal Consequences," *Proceedings of the Second ACM Conference on Online Social Networks*,
October 2014, 17.

4. The Structure of the Algorithmic Marketplace of Ideas

1. For an exception, focusing on market failures in the marketplace of ideas within
the specific context of commercial speech, see Tamara Piety, "Market Failure in the
Marketplace of Ideas: Commercial Speech and the Problem That Won't Go Away,"
Loyola of Los Angeles Law Review 41 (2007): 181–225. For a more general overview of
forms of market failure that may affect the marketplace of ideas, see Darren Bush,
"'The Marketplace of Ideas': Is Judge Posner Chasing Don Quixote's Windmills?"
Arizona State Law Journal 32 (2000): 1107–1147. See also C. Edwin Baker, "Scope
of the First Amendment Freedom of Speech," *UCLA Law Review* 25, no. 5 (1978):
964–1040.

2. See Ronald H. Coase, "The Market for Goods and the Market for Ideas," *American
Economic Review* 64, no. 2 (1974): 384–391, 385.

3. See Philip M. Napoli, *Audience Economics: Media Institutions and the Audience
Marketplace* (New York: Columbia University Press, 2003).

4. This dynamic is reflected in the common adage, "If you're getting something for free,
then you're the product." See, for example, Hamish McNicol, "Facebook Will Always
Be Free but It Has a Massive Asset: Us," *Stuff*, March 28, 2017, http://www.stuff.co.nz
/business/89995576/facebook-will-always-be-free-but-it-has-a-massive-asset-us; Scott

Goodson, "If You're Not Paying for It, You Become the Product," *Forbes*, March 5, 2012, https://www.forbes.com/sites/marketshare/2012/03/05/if-youre-not-paying-for-it -you-become-the-product/#2140fabb5d6e. For a critique of this perspective, see Derek Powazek, "I'm Not the Product, but I Play One on the Internet," *Powazek*, December 18, 2012, http://powazek.com/posts/3229.

5. https://www.facebook.com/.

6. For details on the Cambridge Analytica scandal, and the nature of the user data that Facebook gathers and monetizes, see Philip Bump, "Everything You Need to Know About the Cambridge Analytica–Facebook Debacle," *Washington Post*, March 19, 2018, https://www.washingtonpost.com/news/politics/wp/2018/03/19/everything-you -need-to-know-about-the-cambridge-analytica-facebook-debacle/; Christopher Wyle, "Written Statement to the United States Senate Committee on the Judiciary, In the Matter of Cambridge Analytica and Other Related Issues," May 16, 2018, https://www .judiciary.senate.gov/imo/media/doc/05-16-18%20Wylie%20Testimony.pdf.

7. Russell Brandom, "Mark Zuckerberg Isn't Ruling Out a Paid Version of Facebook," *Verge*, April 10, 2018, https://www.theverge.com/2018/4/10/17220534/paid-facebook -ad-free-version-mark-zuckerberg-testimony.

8. Edmond Lee and Roni Molla, "The *New York Times* Digital Paywall Business Is Grow-ing as Fast as Facebook and Faster than Google," *Recode*, February 8, 2018, https:// www.recode.net/2018/2/8/16991090/new-york-times-digital-paywall-business -growing-fast-facebook-google-newspaper-subscription.

9. Stuart Cunningham, Terry Flew, and Adam Swift, *Media Economics* (New York: Palgrave Macmillan, 2015).

10. There is a substantial literature exploring the economic and strategic dimensions of public goods. This literature illustrates how the revenue potential of public goods can be realized through repurposing strategies such as windowing and versioning. A clas-sic example of windowing can be seen in how a motion picture migrates from theaters to on-demand platforms to premium cable to basic cable over an extended period of time, earning additional revenue at each step, but becoming available to consumers at progressively lower prices over time. In this way, windowing is a form of price discrim-ination that allows movie studios to make their films available at different price points over time. A related strategy is versioning, which involves making different versions of a media product available at the same time, again in an effort to price-discriminate. Once again we can look to the motion picture industry, where standard and 3-D ver-sions of a film are released simultaneously, with a 3-D ticket costing a fair bit more. Repurposing is not always about price discrimination. In some cases, it is about finding additional ways to monetize content over time (e.g., syndicating broadcast network television programs to local stations or small cable networks, or making segments of late-night talk shows available on YouTube the next morning).

11. See James T. Hamilton, *All the News That's Fit to Sell: How the Market Transforms Infor-mation Into News* (Princeton, NJ: Princeton University Press, 2004). "Because public goods are non-rivalrous (one person's consumption does not detract from another's) and non-excludable (difficult to monetize and to exclude from free riders), they differ

from other commodities, like cars or clothes, within a capitalistic economy." Victor Pickard, "The Great Evasion: Confronting Market Failure in American Media Policy," *Critical Studies in Media Communication 31*, no. 2 (2014), 153–159, 154.

12. "A person can consume a public good without paying for it, since it may be difficult or impossible to exclude any person from consumption." Hamilton, *All the News That's Fit to Sell*,8.

13. Since individuals do not calculate the full benefit to society of their learning about politics, they will express less than optimal levels of interest in public affairs coverage and generate less than desirable demands for news about government." Hamilton, *All the News That's Fit to Sell*,13.

14. "The inadequacy of commercial support for democracy-sustaining infrastructures suggests what should be obvious by now: the systematic underproduction of vital communications like journalistic media." Pickard, "The Great Evasion," 159.

15. James G. Webster, *The Marketplace of Attention: How Audiences Take Shape in the Digital Age* (New Haven, CT: Yale University Press, 2014).

16. See, for example, Thomas H. Davenport and John C. Beck, *The Attention Economy: Understanding the New Currency of Business* (Cambridge, MA: Harvard Business School Press, 2011); Tim Wu, *The Attention Merchants: The Epic Struggle to Get Inside Our Heads* (New York: Atlantic Books, 2017); Zeynep Tufekci, "Not This One," *American Behavioral Scientist 57*, no. 7 (2013): 848–870.

17. Philip M. Napoli, *Audience Evolution: New Technologies and the Transformation of Media Audiences* (New York: Columbia University Press, 2011).

18. Julia Angwin, Madeline Varner and Ariana Tobin, "Facebook Enabled Advertisers to Reach 'Jew Haters,'" *ProPublica*, September 14, 2017, https://www.propublica .org/article/facebook-enabled-advertisers-to-reach-jew-haters; Julia Angwin, Ariana Tobin and Madeleine Varner, "Facebooks (Still) Letting Housing Advertisers Exclude Users by Race," *ProPublica*, November 21, 2017, https://www.propublica.org/article /facebook-advertising-discrimination-housing-race-sex-national-origin.

19. Rhett Jones, "Facebook Offered Advertisers 'White Genocide' Option," November 2, 2018, *Gizmodo*, https://gizmodo.com/facebook-offered-advertisers-white-genocide-option -1830190052?fbclid=IwAR23MvocBxWz1OWi6m3wrRo8Qo138EPDRmKE3J5kx9F5qpwS -DaHtzLPEyE.

20. Maurice E. Stucke and Allen P. Grunes, "Antitrust and the Marketplace of Ideas," *Antitrust Law Journal 69*, no. 1 (2001): 249–302, 286.

21. Piety, "Market Failure in the Marketplace of Ideas," 189–190.

22. Richard A. Tybout, "Pricing Pollution and Other Negative Externalities," *Bell Journal of Economics and Management Science 3*, no. 1 (1972): 252–266. "We are left with the conclusion that the seemingly increased pervasiveness of falsity in public discussion is a phenomenon that may possibly be a consequence of a strong free speech culture, but is certainly not a phenomenon that a free speech regime is likely to be able to remedy." Frederick Schauer, "Facts and the First Amendment," *UCLA Law Review 57* (2009–2010): 897–919, 911–912.

23. James T. Hamilton, *Channeling Violence: The Economic Market for Violent Television Programming* (Princeton, NJ: Princeton University Press, 1998).

24. Hamilton, *Channeling Violence.*

25. Napoli, *Audience Economics.*

26. See, for example, Francis M. Bator, "The Anatomy of Market Failure," *Quarterly Journal of Economics* 72, no. 3 (1958): 351–379.

27. "The whole idea of economic efficiency is that the system should be responsive to consumers' tastes or preferences (subject to the limits of technology), not that it should produce certain goods in comparatively large quantities no matter what people want. Thus, if consumers have no very strong preference for truth as compared with other goods or dimensions of goods, then there is no reason to expect that the bundle of intellectual goods provided and "traded" in a competitive market will have maximum truth content. If people valued falsehood, then perfect competition would provide falsehood in a Pareto-optimal way." Alvin I. Goldman and James C. Cox, "Speech, Truth, and the Free Market for Ideas," *Legal Theory* 2 (1996): 1–32, 18.

28. Lyrissa Barnett Lidsky, "Nobody's Fools: The Rational Audience as First Amendment Ideal," *University of Illinois Law Review* 2010 (2010): 799–850, 839.

29. For a review, see Deborah Haas-Wilson, "Arrow and the Information Market Failure in Health Care: The Changing Content and Sources of Health Care Information," *Journal of Health Politics, Policy and Law* 26, no. 5 (2001): 1031–1044.

30. In this situation, news is not unlike a "lemon" purchased from an automobile seller. The poor quality of the information (or car) is not revealed until well after the purchase is finalized. For a discussion of asymmetrical information, see George A. Akerlof, "The Market for 'Lemons': Quality Uncertainty and the Market Mechanism," *Quarterly Journal of Economics* 84, no. 3 (1970): 483–500.

31. Alan Randall, "The Problem of Market Failure," *Natural Resources Journal* 23 (1983): 131–148.

32. Bator, "The Anatomy of Market Failure."

33. See chapter 3.

34. C. Edwin Baker, *Media Concentration and Democracy* (New York: Cambridge University Press, 2012).

35. Robert M. Entman and Steven S. Wildman, "Reconciling Economic and Non-Economic Perspectives on Media Policy: Transcending the 'Marketplace of Ideas,'" *Journal of Communication* 42, no. 1 (1992): 5–19; Philip M. Napoli, *Foundations of Communications Policy: Principles and Process in the Regulation of Electronic Media* (Cresskill, NJ: Hampton Press, 2001).

36. See, for example, Baker, *Media Concentration and Democracy*; Natalie Just, "Measuring Media Concentration and Diversity: New Approaches and Instruments in Europe and the U.S.," *Media, Culture & Society* 31, no. 1 (2009): 97–117.

37. See, for example, Philip M. Napoli (Ed.), *Media Diversity and Localism: Meaning and Metrics* (Mahwah, NJ: Erlbaum, 2007); Justin Schlosberg, *Media Ownership and Agenda Control: The Hidden Limits of the Information Age* (New York: Routledge, 2017).

38. Francine McKenna, "The Uncomfortable Question Zuckerberg Kept Facing: Is Facebook a Monopoly?" *MarketWatch*, April 11, 2018, https://www.marketwatch.com /story/the-uncomfortable-question-zuckerberg-kept-facing-is-facebook-a-monopoly -2018-04-11; Siva Vaidhyanathan, *Antisocial Media: How Facebook Disconnects Us and Undermines Democracy* (New York: Oxford University Press, 2018).

39. "Platform monopolies aren't the result of market forces breaking down. They're the results of markets working correctly, a phenomenon that economists call a 'natural monopoly.'" Alex Moazed and Nicholas L. Johnson, *Modern Monopolies: What It Takes to Dominate the Twenty-First-Century Economy* (New York: St. Martin's Press, 2016), 103.

40. "Google and Facebook Tighten Grip on US Digital Ad Market," *eMarketer*, September 21, 2017, https://www.emarketer.com/Article/Google-Facebook-Tighten-Grip-on-US-Digital -Ad-Market/1016494.

41. Eli Rosenberg, "'Twitter Is Part of the Problem': FCC Chairman Lambastes Company as Net-Neutrality Debate Draws Heat," *Washington Post*, November 28, 2017, https://www .washingtonpost.com/news/the-switch/wp/2017/11/28/twitter-is-part-of-the-problem -fcc-chairman-lambastes-company-as-net-neutrality-debate-draws-heat/?utm _term=.cf09accbe2b6.

42. Arguments that platforms such as Facebook and Google represent monopolistic situations requiring government intervention appear to have picked up steam of late. See, for example, Jonathan Taplin, *Move Fast and Break Things: How Facebook, Google, and Amazon Cornered Culture and Undermined Democracy* (New York: Hachette, 2017); Jon Swartz, "Soros: Beware IT Monopolies Facebook, Google," *Barron's*, January 25, 2018, https://www.barrons.com/articles/soros-beware-it-monopolies -facebook-google-1516923914. For an overview of the arguments for and against antitrust intervention, see Greg Ip, "The Antitrust Case Against Facebook, Google and Amazon," *Wall Street Journal*, January 16, 2018, https://www.wsj.com/articles /the-antitrust-case-against-facebook-google-amazon-and-apple-1516121561.

43. Jason Abbruzzese, "Facebook and Google Dominate in Online News—But for Very Different Topics," *Mashable*, May 23, 2017, http://mashable.com/2017/05/23/google -facebook-dominate-referrals-different-content/#3Px.3N762iqo.

44. Ariel Ezrachi and Maurice Stucke warn that the "invisible hand" of the market is being replaced by the "digitalized hand" of algorithmically controlled platforms. Ariel Ezrachi and Maurice E. Stucke, *Virtual Competition: The Promise and Perils of the Algorithm-Driven Economy* (Cambridge, MA: Harvard University Press, 2016), 209.

45. See Tarleton Gillespie, *Custodians of the Internet: Platforms, Content Moderation, and the Hidden Decisions That Shape Social Media* (New Haven, CT: Yale University Press, 2018).

46. Adam D. I. Kramer, Jamie E. Guillory, and Jeffrey T. Hancock, "Experimental Evidence of Massive-Scale Emotional Contagion Through Social Networks," *Proceedings of the National Academy of Sciences* 111, no. 24 (2014): 8788–8790.

47. Michael Nunez, "Former Facebook Workers: We Routinely Suppressed Conservative News," *Gizmodo*, May 9, 2016, https://gizmodo.com/former-facebook-workers-we -routinely-suppressed-conser-1775461006; Jonathan Albright, "Did Twitter Censor Occupy Wall Street?" *The Conversation*, October 11, 2011, https://theconversation.com

/did-twitter-censor-occupy-wall-street-3822; Allison Graves, "Did Google Adjust Its Autocomplete Algorithm to Hide Hillary Clinton's Problems?" *PunditFact*, June 23, 2016, http://www.politifact.com/punditfact/statements/2016/jun/23/andrew-napolitano/did -google-adjust-its-autocomplete-algorithm-hide-/.

48. Richard Epstein, "The Search Engine Manipulation Effect and Its Possible Impact on the Outcome of Election," *Proceedings of the National Academy of Sciences* 112, no. 33 (2015): E4512–E4521; Robert M. Bond, Christopher J. Fariss, Jason J. Jones, Adam D. I. Kramer, Cameron Marlow, Jaime E. Settle, and James H. Fowler, "A 61-Million Person Experiment in Social Influence and Political Mobilization," *Nature* 489 (2012): 295–298.

49. *Extremist Content and Russian Disinformation Online: Working with Tech to Find Solutions*, Hearing Before the United States Senate Committee on the Judiciary Subcommittee on Crime and Terrorism, October 31, 2017, https://www.judiciary.senate.gov /meetings/extremist-content-and-russian-disinformation-online-working-with-tech -to-find-solutions; Russia Investigative Task Force Open Hearing with Social Media Companies, Hearing Before the United States House of Representatives Permanent Select Committee on Intelligence, November 1, 2017, https://docs.house.gov/meetings /IG/IG00/20171101/106558/HHRG-115-IG00-Transcript-20171101.pdf.

50. Colin Stretch, General Counsel, Facebook, *Testimony Before the United States Senate Committee on the Judiciary Subcommittee on Crime and Terrorism*, October 31, 2017, https://www.judiciary.senate.gov/download/10-31-17-stretch-testimony.

51. "When viewed through an antitrust lens, news publishers are Facebook's competitors. They compete for users' time spent online, user data and advertising dollars. . . . Indeed, competitive biases baked into Facebook's design deserve a healthy portion of the responsibility for the rise of fake news. By pulling technological levers that keep users on its platform, thereby lessening clicks to news publishers' sites, Facebook has sped the decline of legitimate news and provided a breeding ground for the fake variety." Sally Hubbard, "Why Fake News Is an Antitrust Problem," *Forbes*, January 10, 2017, https://www.forbes.com/sites/washingtonbytes/2017/01/10/why-fake -news-is-an-antitrust-problem/#4c557dc730f1.

52. Ezrachi and Stucke, *Virtual Competition*, chapter 12.

53. Ezrachi and Stucke, *Virtual Competition*, 125.

54. Paul Armstrong, "Facebook Too Big to Fail? Three Warnings from Myspace," *Guardian*, July 29, 2014, https://www.theguardian.com/media/2014/jul/29/facebook-myspace -lessons-social-media-zuckerberg.

55. Armstrong, "Facebook Too Big to Fail?"

56. For more on network effects and social media, see Zsolt Katona, Peter Pal Zubszek, Miklos Sarvary, "Network Effects and Personal Influences: The Diffusion of an Online Social Network," *Journal of Marketing Research* 48, no. 3 (2011): 425–443.

57. See Eliot Jones, "Is Competition in Industry Ruinous?" *Quarterly Journal of Economics* 34, no. 3 (1920), 473–519; Maurice E. Stucke, "Is Competition Always Good?" *Journal of Antitrust Enforcement* 1, no. 1 (2013): 162–197.

58. Jones, "Is Competition in Industry Ruinous?"; Stucke, "Is Competition Always Good?"

59. Richard van der Wurff and Jan van Cuilenberg, "Impact of Moderate and Ruinous Competition on Diversity: The Dutch Television Market," *Journal of Media Economics* 14, no. 4 (2001): 213–229.

60. Stucke, "Is Competition Always Good?"

61. Consider, for instance, how much "user-generated content" is generated online with little or no expectation of financial reward.

62. See, for example, Michael Schudson, *Discovering the News: A Social History of American Newspapers* (New York: Basic Books, 1981).

63. See, for example, "Sinclair TV Chairman to Trump: 'We Are Here to Deliver Your Message,'" *Guardian*, April 10, 2018, https://www.theguardian.com/media/2018/apr/10/donald-trump-sinclair-david-smith-white-house-meeting.

64. Sydney Ember, "Sinclair Requires TV Stations to Air Segments That Tilt to the Right," *New York Times*, May 12, 2017, https://www.nytimes.com/2017/05/12/business/media/sinclair-broadcast-komo-conservative-media.html.

65. Sydney Ember and Andrew Ross Sorkin, "Meredith Bid for Time Inc. Said to Be Backed by Koch Brothers," *New York Times*, November 15, 2017, https://www.nytimes.com/2017/11/15/business/media/koch-brothers-time-meredith.html.

66. See, for example, Tom Evens and Laurence Hauttekeete, "From Hero to Zero: How Commercialism Ruined Community Radio in Flanders," *Radio Journal* 6, nos. 2/3 (2008): 95–112; Lars W. Nord, "Newspaper Competition and Content Diversity: A Comparison of Regional Media Markets in Sweden," *Papeles de Europa* 26, no. 1 (2013): 1–13; van der Wurff and van Cuilenberg, "Impact of Moderate and Ruinous Competition."

67. See, for example, *Europe Economics, Market Definition in the Media Sector: Economic Issues*, Report for the European Commission, 2002, http://ec.europa.eu/competition/sectors/media/documents/european_economics.pdf.

68. For an overview of this perspective, see Gordon Tullock, *On Voting: A Public Choice Approach* (Northampton, MA: Edward Elgar, 1998).

69. "Most economists . . . compare voters to consumers who shrewdly 'vote their pocketbooks.'" Bryan Caplan, *The Myth of the Rational Voter: Why Democracies Choose Bad Policies* (Princeton, NJ: Princeton University Press, 2007), 18.

70. "It's probably best to jettison the term 'self-interest' altogether . . . [and] refer to 'inclusive interests.' Something is in a person's 'inclusive interests' when it advances their or their family members' everyday, typical goals," as well as those of "their friends, allies, and social networks." Jason Weeden and Robert Kurzban, *The Hidden Agenda of the Political Mind: How Self-Interest Shapes Our Opinions and Why We Won't Admit It* (Princeton, NJ: Princeton University Press, 2014), 39–40.

71. Because "electoral outcome is detached from electoral 'choice' for each voter," voting becomes a form of "expressive behavior [that reflects] various kinds of ethical and ideological principles that are suppressed in the market setting. Politics, therefore, gives much freer range to ethical considerations than do markets." Geoffrey Brennan and Loren Lomasky, *Democracy and Decision: The Pure Theory of Electoral Preference* (New York: Cambridge University Press, 1993), 15–16.

72. "Voter irrationality is precisely what economic theory implies once we adopt introspectively plausible assumptions about human motivation." Caplan, *The Myth of the Rational Voter*, 3.

73. "The key debate in these discussions . . . is how much interests matter in driving political opinions. In chapter 2 we responded to claims that self-interest hardly matters: When we run simple tests of these simple claims, quite often the simple claims are simply untrue." Weeden and Kurzban, *The Hidden Agenda*, 203.

74. White, blue-collar voters voted for Trump not "because they're irrational, but because they are self-interested—something generally true of voters on both sides." Robert Kurzban and Jason Weeden, "No, Trump Voters Were Not Irrational," *Washington Post*, November 9, 2016, https://www.washingtonpost.com/news/in-theory /wp/2016/11/09/no-trump-voters-were-not-irrational/?utm_term=.45ad6fae23c6. See also David Goodhart, "White Self-Interest Is Not the Same Thing as Racism," *American Renaissance*, March 2, 2017, https://www.amren.com/news/2017/03/white-self-interest -not-thing-racism/; Ned Barnett, "Duke Professor Dispels Myth About Trump and Working-Class Voters," *News-Observer*, June 10, 2017, http://www.newsobserver.com /opinion/opn-columns-blogs/ned-barnett/article155509549.html.

75. "It is said that the Trump electorate wanted to blow up the status quo." Daniel Henninger, "The Trump Question," *Wall Street Journal*, January 18, 2017, https://www.wsj .com/articles/the-trump-question-1484784436.

76. "Our analysis shows Trump accelerated a realignment in the electorate around racism, across several different measures of racial animus—and that it helped him win. By contrast, we found little evidence to suggest individual economic distress benefited Trump." Sean McElwee and Jason McDaniel, "Economic Anxiety Didn't Make People Vote Trump, Racism Did," *Nation*, May 8, 2017, https://www.thenation.com/article /economic-anxiety-didnt-make-people-vote-trump-racism-did/

77. "An important obstacle to the first woman president remains: the hidden, internalized bias many people hold against career advancement by women. And perhaps surprisingly, there is evidence that women hold more of this bias, on average, than men do." Carl Bialik, "How Unconscious Sexism Could Help Explain Trump's Win," *Five ThirtyEight*, January 21, 2017, https://fivethirtyeight.com/features/how-unconscious -sexism-could-help-explain-trumps-win/.

78. See, for example, Martha C. White, "Trump Voters Stand to Suffer Most from Obamacare Repeal and Trade War," *NBC News*, February 6, 2017, http://www.nbcnews .com/business/business-news/trump-voters-stand-suffer-most-obamacare-repeal -trade-war-n717491; Paul Krugman, "Coal Country Is a State of Mind," *New York Times*, March 31, 2017, https://www.nytimes.com/2017/03/31/opinion/coal-country-is-a-state -of-mind.html; Andrew Restuccia, Matthew Nussbaum, and Sarah Ferris, "Trump Releases Budget Hitting His Own Voters Hardest," *Politico*, May 22, 2017, http:// www.politico.com/story/2017/05/22/trump-budget-cut-social-programs-238696; Amanda Taub, "Why Americans Vote 'Against Their Interest': Partisanship," *New York Times*, April 12, 2017, https://www.nytimes.com/2017/04/12/upshot/why-americans -vote-against-their-interest-partisanship.html?_r=0; Catherine Rampell, "Why the

White Working Class Votes Against Itself," *Washington Post*, December 22, 2016, https://www.washingtonpost.com/opinions/why-the-white-working-class-votes-against-itself/2016/12/22/3aa65c04-c88b-11e6-8bee-54e800ef2a63_story.html?utm_term=.99d233ea82fb; Neil H. Buchanan, "Why Did So Many Americans Vote to Be Poorer?" *Newsweek*, January 15, 2017, http://www.newsweek.com/neil-buchanan-why-did-so-many-americans-vote-be-poorer-542453; Neil Macdonald, "Trump's Poor and Rural Supporters Line Up to Take Their Economic Beating," *CBC News*, April 5, 2017, http://www.cbc.ca/news/opinion/americans-voting-for-cuts-1.4055389.

79. "Donald Trump's most ardent supporters are likely to be hit the hardest if he makes good on his promise to dismantle the Affordable Care Act and embark on trade wars with China and Mexico." White, "Trump Voters Stand to Suffer Most."

    "Donald Trump, whose populist message and promises to help American workers propelled him to the White House, issued a budget proposal on Tuesday that instead takes aim at the social safety net on which many of his supporters rely." Restuccia et al., "Trump Releases Budget."

80. Paul Waldman, "The GOP Tax Plan Is Moving Forward. It's a Big Scam on Trump's Base," *Washington Post*, November 16, 2017, https://www.washingtonpost.com/blogs/plum-line/wp/2017/11/16/the-gop-tax-plan-is-moving-forward-its-a-big-scam-on-trumps-base/?utm_term=.07cd832ee214; Sam Berger, "The GOP Tax Bill Would Hit Trump Supporters Hardest," *Real Clear Policy*, November 28, 2017, http://www.realclearpolicy.com/articles/2017/11/28/the_gop_tax_bill_would_hit_trump_supporters_hardest.html; John Harwood, "Trump's Core Supporters Are About to Be Handed the Bill for Tax Reform," *CNBC*, November 16, 2017, https://www.cnbc.com/2017/11/16/trumps-core-supporters-are-about-to-be-handed-the-bill-for-tax-reform.html.

81. Berger, "The GOP Tax Bill."

82. "Why do people vote against their economic interests? The answer, experts say, is partisanship. Party affiliation has become an all-encompassing identity that outweighs the details of specific policies." Taub "Why Americans Vote."

83. Kathleen Hall Jamieson, *Cyber-War: How Russian Hackers and Trolls Helped Elect a President* (New York: Oxford University Press, 2018).

84. "Even if all of the needed data mysteriously appeared, after the fact we have no good way to isolate the effects of troll-generated and hacked content from the impact of multiple other sources and forms of electoral communication." Jamieson, *Cyber*-War, 208.

85. See Social Science Research Council, Social Data Initiative, Request for Proposals, July 2018, https://s3.amazonaws.com/ssrc-cdn2/5bbcff044d422.pdf.

86. See Social Science One, Dataverse, 2018, https://socialscience.one/facebook-dataverse.

5. The Public-Interest Principle in Media Governance: Past and Present

1. For more extensive discussions of the public interest concept, see Denis McQuail, *Media Performance: Mass Communication and the Public Interest* (Thousand Oaks, CA: Sage, 1992); Philip M. Napoli, *Foundations of Communications Policy: Principles and Process in the Regulation of Electronic Media* (Cresskill, NJ: Hampton Press, 2001).

2. Uwe Hasebrink, "The Role of the Audience Within Media Governance: The Neglected Dimension of Media Literacy, *Media Studies* 3, no. 6 (2012): 58–73; Natali Helberger, "From Eyeball to Creator—Toying with Audience Empowerment in the Audiovisual Media Services Directive, *Entertainment Law Review* 6 (2008): 128–137; Ganaele Langlois, "Participatory Culture and the New Governance of Communication: The Paradox of Participatory Media," *Television & New Media* 14 (2012): 91–105.

3. Avshalom Ginosar, "Media Governance: A Conceptual Framework or Merely a Buzzword?" *Communication Theory* 23 (2013): 356–374, 357; see also David Nolan and Tim Marjoribanks, "'Public Editors' and Media Governance at the *Guardian* and the *New York Times*," *Journalism Practice* 5, no. 1 (2011): 3–17.

4. See, for example, Council of Europe, *Public Service Media Governance: Looking to the Future*,2009,https://teledetodos.es/index.php/documentacion/publicaciones-e-informes/139-public-service-media-governance-looking-to-the-future-psm-gobernance-2009/file; Kari Karppinen and Hallvard Moe, "A Critique of 'Media Governance,'" in *Communication and Media Policy in the Era of the Internet*, ed. Maria Loblich and Senta Pfaff-Rudiger, (Nomos: Baden-Baden, 2013), 69–80; Manuel Puppis, "Media Governance: A New Concept for the Analysis of Media Policy and Regulation," *Communication, Culture & Critique* 3, no. 2 (2010): 134–149.

5. Eva Lievens, Peggy, Valcke and Pieter Jan Valgaeren, State of the Art on Regulatory Trends in Media: Identifying Whether, What, How and Who to Regulate on Social Media. Report from User Empowerment in Social Media Culture (EMSOC) (December, 2011).

6. Tarleton Gillespie, "The Politics of 'Platforms,'" *New Media & Society* 12, no. 3 (2010): 347–364, 348.

7. Napoli, *Foundations of Communications Policy*.

8. See, for example, Steven M. Barkin, *American Television News: The Media Marketplace and the Public Interest* (Armonk, NY: M. E. Sharpe, 2003); Jeremy Iggers, *Good News, Bad News: Journalism Ethics and the Public Interest* (Boulder, CO: Westview Press, 1999).

9. For detailed discussions of media industry self-regulatory codes, see Angela J. Campbell, "Self-Regulation and the Media," *Federal Communications Law Journal* 51 (1999): 711–771; Bruce A. Linton, "Self-Regulation in Broadcasting Revisited," *Journalism Quarterly* 64 (1987): 483–490; and Mark MacCarthy, "Broadcast Self-Regulation: The NAB Codes, Family Viewing Hour, and Television Violence," *Cardozo Arts & Entertainment Law Journal* 13 (1995): 667–696. These authors devote particular attention to the rather unusual history of the National Association of Broadcasters' (NAB) Radio and Television Codes, which were in place for roughly fifty and thirty years, respectively, before being eliminated in the early 1980s. Their elimination came about as a result of a Department of Justice (DOJ) suit that charged that the provisions in the Television Code that limited commercial minutes and the total number of commercials per broadcast hour manipulated the supply of commercial time and thus violated the Sherman Antitrust Act. Although the DOJ suit addressed only the advertising guidelines contained in the code—not the programming guidelines—the NAB abandoned the entire code in the wake of the DOJ action.

10. "ASNE Statement of Principles," *ASNE*, 2018, http://asne.org/asne-principles.

11. "SPJ Code of Ethics," *Society of Professional Journalists*, 2014, https://www.spj.org /ethicscode.asp.

12. "ASNE Statement,"

13. "SPJ Code,"

14. "RTDNA Code of Ethics," *RTDNA*, 2015, https://www.rtdna.org/content/rtdna_code _of_ethics.

15. Alfred Hermida, Fred Fletcher, Darryl Korell, and Donna Logan, "Share, Like, Recommend: Decoding the Social Media News Consumer," *Journalism Studies* 13, no. 5–6 (2012): 815–824.

16. Luke Goode, "Social News, Citizen Journalism and Democracy," *New Media & Society* 11, no. 8 (2010): 1287–1305.

17. Mark Zuckerberg, "Bringing the World Closer Together," *Facebook*, June 22, 2017, https://www.facebook.com/zuck/posts/10154944663901634.

18. "Our Company," *Twitter*, 2018, https://about.twitter.com/en_us/test-pages1/c20 -masthead-text-version.html.

19. Evgeny Morozov, *The Net Delusion: The Dark Side of Internet Freedom* (New York: Public Affairs, 2011); Astrid Taylor, *The People's Platform: Taking Back Power and Culture in the Digital Age* (New York: Metropolitan Books, 2014).

20. See, for example, Jessi Hempel, "Social Media Made the Arab Spring, but Couldn't Save It," *Wired*, January 26, 2016, https://www.wired.com/2016/01/social-media-made -the-arab-spring-but-couldnt-save-it/.

21. See, for example, Yochai Benkler, *The Wealth of Networks: How Social Production Transforms Markets and Freedom* (New Haven, CT: Yale University Press, 2006); Clay Shirky, *Here Comes Everybody: The Power of Organizing Without Organizations* (New York: Penguin, 2008).

22. As Robert Gehl describes this mind-set, "the sovereign interactive consumer is the master of digital flows" and is thus "equipped to deal with massive, ubiquitous advertising networks, the complex interaction between first- and third-party Web analytics; myriad flows of personal data; and, of course, the sophisticated noopower of advertisements that play on fears, memories, and desires." Robert W. Gehl, *Reverse Engineering Social Media: Software, Culture, and Political Economy in New Media Capitalism* (Philadelphia: Temple University Press, 2014), 110, 112. Of course, we could add to this list the various forms of misinformation and fake news that populate the social media sphere.

23. Quoted in Ravi Somaiya, "How Facebook Is Changing the Way Its Users Consume Journalism," *New York Times*, October 26, 2014, https://www.nytimes.com/2014/10/27 /business/media/how-facebook-is-changing-the-way-its-users-consume-journalism. html (emphasis added).

24. Geert Lovink, *Networks Without a Cause: A Critique of Social Media* (Malden, MA: Polity Press, 2011), 34.

25. Jay Rosen, "Why Do They Give Us Tenure?" *PressThink*, October 25, 2014, http:// pressthink.org/2014/10/why-do-they-give-us-tenure/.

26. Motahhare Eslami et al., "'I Always Assumed That I Wasn't Really That Close to [Her]': Reasoning About Invisible Algorithms in the News Feed," *Proceedings of the*

Thirty-Third Annual ACM Conference on Human Factors in Computing Systems, April 2015, 153–162.

27. Elia Powers, "My News Feed Is Filtered? *Digital Journalism* 5, no. 10 (2017): 1315–1335.

28. Tarleton Gillespie, "Facebook's Algorithm—Why Our Assumptions Are Wrong, and Our Concerns Are Right," *Culture Digitally*, July 4, 2014, http://culturedigitally.org/2014/07/facebooks-algorithm-why-our-assumptions-are-wrong-and-our-concerns-are-right/.

29. Mark Zuckerberg, "Continuing Our Focus for 2018," *Facebook*, January 19, 2018, https://www.facebook.com/zuck/posts/10104445245963251?pnref=story.

30. Zuckerberg, "Continuing Our Focus for 2018."

31. Zuckerberg, "Continuing Our Focus for 2018."

32. Zuckerberg, "Continuing Our Focus for 2018."

33. For a discussion of the political dynamics and controversies surrounding audience measurement, see Philip M. Napoli, *Audience Evolution: New Technologies and the Transformation of Media Audiences* (New York: Columbia University Press, 2011).

34. Will Oremus, "Who Controls Your Facebook Feed," *Slate*, January 3, 2016, http://www.slate.com/articles/technology/cover_story/2016/01/how_facebook_s_news_feed_algorithm_works.html.

35. Oremus, "Who Controls Your Facebook Feed."

36. Adam Mosseri, "Helping Ensure News on Facebook Is from Trusted Sources," *Facebook*, January 19, 2018, https://newsroom.fb.com/news/2018/01/trusted-sources/.

37. For similar critiques, see Will Oremus, "What Could Go Wrong With Facebook's Plan to Rank News Sources by 'Trustworthiness,'" *Slate*, January 18, 2018, https://slate.com/technology/2018/01/facebook-will-rank-new-sources-by-trustworthiness-what-could-go-wrong.html.

38. Virginia Held, *The Public Interest and Individual Interests* (New York: Basic Books, 1970).

39. Tom McKay, "Facebook Is Now Trying to Hire 'News Credibility Specialists' to Deal with Its Fake News Problem," *Gizmodo*, June 7, 2018, https://gizmodo.com/facebook-is-now-trying-to-hire-news-credibility-special-1826654472.

40. Fairness, Accountability, and Transparency in Machine Learning, "Principles for Accountable Algorithms and a Social Impact Statement for Algorithms," n.d., https://www.fatml.org/resources/principles-for-accountable-algorithms.

41. Association of Computing Machinery, "Statement on Algorithmic Transparency and Accountability," January 12, 2017, https://www.acm.org/binaries/content/assets/public-policy/2017_usacm_statement_algorithms.pdf.

42. Partnership on AI, "About Us," n.d., https://www.partnershiponai.org/about/.

43. For more details on recent efforts to bring greater social responsibility to algorithmic decision-making, see Aaron Rieke, Miranda Bogen, and David G. Robinson, *Public Scrutiny of Automated Decisions: Early Lessons and Emerging Methods: An Upturn and Omidyar Network Report*, February 2018, http://omidyar.com/sites/default/files/file_archive/Public%20Scrutiny%20of%20Automated%20Decisions.pdf.

44. Communications Act of 1934, Pub. L. No. 416, 48 Stat. 1064 (1934).

45. Dean M. Krugman and Leonard N. Reid, "The Public Interest as Defined by FCC Policymakers," *Journal of Broadcasting* 24, no. 3 (1980): 311–325.

46. For a detailed discussion, see Napoli, *Foundations of Communications Policy*.

47. Mark S. Fowler and Daniel L. Brenner, "A Marketplace Approach to Broadcast Regulation," *Texas Law Review* 60 (1982): 1–51, 3–4.

48. See, for example, Reed Hundt, "The Public's Airwaves: What Does the Public Interest Require of Television Broadcasters?" *Duke Law Journal* 45 (1996): 1089–1129; Cass R. Sunstein, "Television and the Public Interest," *University of California Law Review* 88 (2000): 499–564.

49. See, for example, Napoli, *Foundations of Communications Policy*.

50. Napoli, *Foundations of Communications Policy*.

51. Federal Communications Commission, *Protecting and Promoting the Open Internet, Report and Order*, March 12, 2015, https://transition.fcc.gov/Daily_Releases/Daily _Business/2015/db0312/FCC-15-24A1.pdf.

52. Ajit Pai, "Restoring Internet Freedom," Federal Communications Commission, December 14, 2015, https://www.fcc.gov/restoring-internet-freedom.

53. Napoli, *Foundations of Communications Policy*.

54. NBC v. United States, 319 U.S. 190 (1943), 213.

55. NBC v. United States, 216.

56. See, for example, Lawrence Gasman, *Telecompetition: The Free Market Road to the Information Highway* (Washington, DC: CATO Institute, 1994).

57. See, for example, Robert W. McChesney, *Telecommunications, Mass Media, and Democracy: The Battle for the Control of U.S. Broadcasting, 1928–1935* (New York: Oxford University Press, 1993).

58. Eli M. Noam, "Why TV Regulation Will Become Telecom Regulation," in *Communications: The Next Decade*, ed. Ed Richards, Robin Foster, and Tom Kiedrowski (London: Ofcom, 2016), 67–72, 67.

59. Noam, "Why TV Regulation Will Become Telecom Regulation."

60. Noam, "Why TV Regulation Will Become Telecom Regulation," 68.

61. See, for example, Charles W. Logan, Jr., "Getting Beyond Scarcity: A New Paradigm for Assessing the Constitutionality of Broadcast Regulation," *California Law Review* 85, no. 6 (1997): 1687–1747.

62. See, for example, CBS v. Federal Communications Commission, 453 U.S. 367 (198); Hundt, "The Public's Airwaves."

63. See, for example, R. Clark Wadlow and Linda M. Wellstein, "The Changing Regulatory Terrain of Cable Television," *Catholic University Law Review* 35, no. 3 (1986): 705–736.

64. A common misperception is that the pervasiveness rationale has been successfully applied only within the context of broadcasting. However, the Supreme Court has drawn on this rationale to uphold the constitutionality of laws requiring cable systems to block indecent programming on leased access channels. See, for example, Denver Area Educational Telecommunications Consortium v. FCC, 116 S. Ct. 2374 (1996); Robert Kline, "Freedom of Speech on the Electronic Village Green: Applying the First Amendment Lessons of Cable Television to the Internet," *Cornell Journal of Law & Public Policy* 6, no. 1 (1996): 23–60.

65. Federal Communications Commission v. Pacifica Foundation, 438 U.S. 726 (1978), 748.

66. Communications Decency Act of 1996, Pub. L. No. 104–104 (Tit. V), 110 Stat. 133 (February 8, 1996).

67. Reno v. ACLU, 521 U.S. 844 (1997), 869.

68. United States v. Southwestern Cable Co., 392 U.S. 157 (1968).

69. United States v. Southwestern Cable Co.

70. Henry Geller and Donna Lampert, "Cable, Content Regulation, and the First Amendment," *Catholic University Law Review* 32 (1983): 603–631.

71. United States v. Southwestern Cable Co.

72. Napoli, *Foundations of Communications Policy*.

73. United States v. Southwestern Cable Co., 178.

74. David Lazarus, "Facebook Says You 'Own' All the Data You Post. Not Even Close, Say Privacy Experts," *Los Angeles Times*, March 19, 2018, http://www.latimes.com/business /lazarus/la-fi-lazarus-facebook-cambridge-analytica-privacy-20180320-story.html. A former Cambridge Analytica employee launched a change.org petition, with the accompanying hashtag #OwnYourData, focused on compelling Facebook to treat user data as the property of the users; see Brittany Kaiser, "Tell Facebook: Our Data Is Our Property," https://www.change.org/p/tell-facebook-our-data-is-our-property-ownyourdata.

75. Jack M. Balkin, "Information Fiduciaries and the First Amendment," *UC Davis Law Review* 49 (2016): 1185–1234.

76. U.S. v. AT&T, Memorandum Opinion, June 12, 2018, http://www.dcd.uscourts.gov /sites/dcd/files/17-2511opinion.pdf.

77. Philip M. Napoli and Deborah L. Dwyer, "Media Policy in a Time of Political Polarization and Technological Evolution," *Publizistik* 63, no. 4 (2018): 583–601.

78. Jon Sallet, "FCC Transaction Review: Competition and the Public Interest," Federal Communications Commission, August 12, 2014, https://www.fcc.gov/news-events/blog /2014/08/12/fcc-transaction-review-competition-and-public-interest.

79. Jon Sallet, "FCC Transaction Review."

80. The reality in this situation is that Time Warner did not hold only one broadcast license; there were a number of broadcast licenses associated with the satellite distribution of Time Warner's many cable networks. See Jeff John Roberts, "AT&T's Bid for Time Warner Could Get Tripped Up by CNN Satellites," *Fortune*, October 26, 2016, http://fortune.com/2016/10/26/att-time-warner-fcc-2/.

81. Jon Brodkin, "AT&T/Time Warner Seems Headed for FCC Review, Whether AT&T Likes It or Not," *Ars Technica*, October 26, 2016, https://arstechnica.com/tech-policy /2016/10/atttime-warner-seems-headed-for-fcc-review-whether-att-likes-it-not/.

82. David Leiberman, "FCC Approves Time Warner TV Station Sale, Likely Helping AT&T Deal," *Deadline Hollywood*, April 17, 2017, http://deadline.com/2017/04 /fcc-approves-time-warner-tv-station-sale-likely-helping-att-deal-1202070989/.

83. John Eggerton, "Ajit Pai Agrees to Confirm FCC's Non-Role in AT&T–Time Warner Review. *Broadcasting & Cable*, March 8, 2017, http://www.broadcastingcable.com/news /washington/ajit-pai-agrees-confirm-fccs-non-role-att-time-warner-review/163899. As for the relevance of the licenses associated with the distributions of Time Warner's cable networks, according to one report, because "they involve technical, mostly

backhaul, functions [they] either might not have to be sold to AT&T or can be replaced by distribution technologies that don't use the public airwaves." David Lieberman, "FCC Approves Time Warner TV Station Sale, Likely Helping AT&T Deal," *Deadline*, April 17, 2017, https://deadline.com/2017/04/fcc-approves-time-warner-tv -station-sale-likely-helping-att-deal-1202070989/. It is worth noting, that under questioning from members of Congress, Chairman Pai promised an independent legal review of whether the FCC has authority to review the merger, but no such review has yet been produced.

84. Mike Ananny and Tarleton Gillespie, "Public Platforms: Beyond the Cycle of Shock and Exceptions," paper presented at the annual meeting of the International Communication Association, San Diego, CA, May 2017, 2–3.

85. Philip M. Napoli and Robyn Caplan, "When Media Companies Insist They're Not Media Companies, Why They're Wrong, and Why It Matters, *First Monday* 22, no. 5 (2017), http://firstmonday.org/ojs/index.php/fm/article/view/7051/6124.

86. Tarleton Gillespie, *Custodians of the Internet: Platforms, Content Moderation, and the Hidden Decisions That Shape Social Media* (New Haven, CT: Yale University Press, 2018).

87. Julia Angwin and Hannes Grassegger, "Facebook's Secret Censorship Rules Protect White Men from Hate Speech but Not Black Children," *ProPublica*, June 28, 2017, https:// www.propublica.org/article/facebook-hate-speech-censorship-internal-documents -algorithms.

88. Angwin and Grassegger, "Facebook's Secret Censorship Rules." For a more recent analysis and critique of Facebook's guidelines for moderating global political speech (based on leaked documents), see Max Fisher, "Inside Facebook's Secret Rulebook for Global Political Speech," *New York Times*, December 27, 2018, https://www.nytimes .com/2018/12/27/world/facebook-moderators.html.

89. Melissa Eddy and Mark Scott, "Delete Hate Speech or Pay Up, Germany Tells Social Media Companies," *New York Times*, June 30, 2017, https://www.nytimes.com /2017/06/30/business/germany-facebook-google-twitter.html.

90. Federal Communications Commission, "Broadcasting False Information," n.d., http:// transition.fcc.gov/cgb/consumerfacts/falsebroadcast.pdf.

91. Federal Communications Commission, "Broadcasting False Information."

92. Federal Communications Commission, "The Public and Broadcasting," July 2008, https://www.fcc.gov/media/radio/public-and-broadcasting#DISTORT.

93. Federal Communications Commission, "The Public and Broadcasting."

94. Chad Raphael argues that the FCC's news distortion regulations are more "symbolic" than genuine. Chad Raphael, "The FCC's Broadcast News Distortion Rules: Regulation by Drooping Eyelid," *Communication Law and Policy* 6 (2001): 485–539. For a similar critique, see William B. Ray, *FCC: The Ups and Downs of Radio-TV Regulation* (Ames: Iowa State University Press, 1989).

95. Dave Saldana, "A Law Against Lying on the News: Why Canada Has One and the U.S. Doesn't," *Yes!*, March 17, 2011, http://www.yesmagazine.org/people-power/a-law -against-lying-on-the-news.

96. Lane Wallace, "Should Lying Be Illegal? Canada's Broadcasters Debate." *Atlantic*, March 23, 2011, https://www.theatlantic.com/international/archive/2011/03/should-lying-be-illegal-canadas-broadcasters-debate/72866/.

97. Arthur Chu, "Mr. Obama, Tear Down This Liability Shield," *TechCrunch*, September 29, 2015, https://techcrunch.com/2015/09/29/mr-obama-tear-down-this-liability-shield/.

98. Steve Waldman and the Working Group on Information Needs of Communities, *The Information Needs of Communities: The Changing Media Landscape in a Broadband Age* (Washington, DC: Federal Communications Commission, 2011), https://books.google.com/books/about/Information_Needs_of_Communities.html?id=bLulzihSxPEC&printsec=frontcover&source=kp_read_button#v=onepage&q&f=false.

99. Waldman et al., *The Information Needs of Communities*. For a more detailed discussion of the FCC's report, see Philip M. Napoli and Lewis Friedland, "U.S. Communications Policy Research and the Integration of the Administrative and Critical Communication Research Traditions, *Journal of Information Policy* 6 (2016): 41–65.

100. See, for example, Robert W. McChesney and John Nichols, *The Death and Life of American Journalism: The Media Revolution That Will Begin the World Again* (New York: Nation Books, 2010); Robert W. McChesney and Victor Pickard, eds., *Will the Last Reporter Please Turn Out the Lights: The Collapse of Journalism and What Can Be Done to Fix It* (New York: New Press, 2011).

101. Advisory Committee on Public Interest Obligations of Digital Television Broadcasters, *Charting the Digital Broadcasting Future* (Washington, DC: The Benton Foundation, 1998).

102. Advisory Committee on Public Interest Obligations of Digital Television Broadcasters, *Charting the Digital Broadcasting Future.*

103. Advisory Committee on Public Interest Obligations of Digital Television Broadcasters, *Charting the Digital Broadcasting Future.*

104. Advisory Committee on Public Interest Obligations of Digital Television Broadcasters, *Charting the Digital Broadcasting Future.*

105. For a detailed account of this process, see Anthony E. Varona, "Changing Channels and Bridging Divides: The Failure and Redemption of American Broadcast Television Regulation," *Minnesota Journal of Law, Science & Technology* 6, no. 1 (2004): 1–116.

106. See, for example, Pablo J. Boczkowski and C.W. Anderson, *Remaking the News: Essays on the Future of Journalism Scholarship in the Digital Age* (Cambridge, MA: MIT Press, 2017).

107. For an examination of this phenomenon, see Jacob Nelson, *Partnering with the Public: The Pursuit of Audience Engagement in Journalism*, unpublished doctoral dissertation, Northwestern University, June 2018.

108. Nelson, *Partnering with the Public.*

109. Robert W. McChesney, *Communication Revolution: Critical Junctures and the Future of Media* (New York: New Press, 2007).

110. McChesney, *Communication Revolution.*

6. Reviving the Public Interest

1. Alexis Madrigal, "Why Donald Trump Was the 'Perfect Candidate' for Facebook," *Atlantic*, February 26, 2018.

2. Jack M. Balkin, "Free Speech in the Algorithmic Society: Big Data, Private Governance, and New School Speech Regulation," *U.C. Davis Law Review* 51 (2018): 1149–1210.

3. Tess Townsend, "Google Has Banned 200 Publishers Since It Passed a New Policy Against Fake News," *Recode*, January 25, 2017, https://www.recode.net/2017/1/25/14375750 /google-adsense-advertisers-publishers-fake-news.

4. Craig Silverman, Jeremy Singer-Vine, and Lam Thuy, "In Spite of the Crackdown, Fake News Publishers Are Still Earning Money from Major Ad Networks," *BuzzFeed News*, April 4, 2017, https://www.buzzfeed.com/craigsilverman/fake-news-real-ads?utm_term =.gmv1JDdEmx#.hkkNeAB81G.

5. Joshua Gillin, "The More Outrageous the Better: How Clickbait Ads Make Money for Fake News Sites," *PunditFact*, October 4, 2017, http://www.politifact.com/punditfact /article/2017/oct/04/more-outrageous-better-how-clickbait-ads-make-mone/.

6. Seth Fiegerman, "Facebook, Google, Twitter to Fight Fake News with 'Trust Indicators'", *CNN*, November 16, 2017, http://money.cnn.com/2017/11/16/technology/tech-trust -indicators/index.html.

7. Jon Fingas, "YouTube Will Fight Fake News by Offering Workshops to Teens," *Engadget*, April 23, 2017, https://www.engadget.com/2017/04/23/youtube-fake-news -teen-workshops/.

8. Louise Matsakis, "YouTube Will Link Directly to Wikipedia to Fight Conspiracy Theories," *Wired*, March 13, 2018, https://www.wired.com/story/youtube-will-link -directly-to-wikipedia-to-fight-conspiracies/.

9. Nick Statt, "Twitter Says It Exposed Nearly 700,000 People to Russian Propaganda During US Election," *Verge*, January 19, 2018, https://www.theverge.com/2018/1/19/16911086 /twitter-russia-propaganda-us-presidential-election-bot-accounts-findings.

10. lvin I. Goldman and James C. Cox, "Speech, Truth, and the Free Market for Ideas," *Legal Theory* 2 (1996): 1–32, 23.

11. Tessa Lyons, "Replacing Disputed Flags with Related Articles," *Facebook Newsroom*, December 20, 2017, https://newsroom.fb.com/news/2017/12/news-feed-fyi-updates -in-our-fight-against-misinformation/.

12. Jeff Smith, Grace Jackson, and Seetha Raj, "Designing Against Misinformation," *Medium*, December 20, 2017, https://medium.com/facebook-design/designing-against -misinformation-e5846b3aa1e2.

13. Sam Levin, "Facebook Promised to Tackle Fake News. But the Evidence Shows It's Not Working," *Guardian*, May 16, 2017, https://www.theguardian.com/technology/2017 /may/16/facebook-fake-news-tools-not-working.

14. James E. Sneegas and Tamyra A. Plank, "Gender Differences in Pre-Adolescent Reactance to Age-Categorized Television Advisory Labels," *Journal of Broadcasting & Electronic Media* 42, no. 4 (1998): 423–434.

15. Brad Bushman and Joanne Cantor, "Media Ratings for Violence and Sex: Implications for Policymakers and Parents," *APA PsycNET* 58, no. 2 (2003): 130–141.

16. Smith, Jackson, and Raj, "Designing Against Misinformation."

17. Sara Su, "New Test with Related Articles," *Facebook Newsroom*, April 25, 2017, https://newsroom.fb.com/news/2017/04/news-feed-fyi-new-test-with-related-articles/.

18. Twitter Public Policy, "Update: Russian Interference in 2016 US Election," *Twitter Blog*, September 28, 2017, https://blog.twitter.com/official/en_us/topics/company/2017/Update-Russian-Interference-in-2016--Election-Bots-and-Misinformation.html.

19. Jack Nicas, "YouTube Cracks Down on Conspiracies, Fake News," *MarketWatch*, October 5, 2017, https://www.marketwatch.com/story/youtube-cracks-down-on-conspiracies-fake-news-2017-10-05.

20. Smith, Jackson and Raj, "Designing Against Misinformation."

21. Thuy Ong, "Facebook Is Shrinking Fake News Posts in the News Feed," *Verge*, April 30, 2018, https://www.theverge.com/2018/4/30/17301390/facebook-fake-news-newsfeed.

22. Laura Hazard Owen, "Facebook Might Downrank the Most Vile Conspiracy Theories. But It Won't Take Them Down," *Nieman Lab*, July 13, 2018, http://www.niemanlab.org/2018/07/facebook-might-downrank-the-most-vile-conspiracy-theories-but-it-wont-take-them-down/.

23. Hanna Kozlowska, "Facebook Is Actually Going to Start Removing Fake News—or at Least Some of It," *Quartz*, July 18, 2018, https://qz.com/1331476/facebook-will-start-removing-fake-news-that-could-cause-harm/; Joseph Menn, "Facebook to Ban Misinformation on Voting in Upcoming U.S. Elections," *Reuters*, October 15, 2018, https://www.reuters.com/article/us-facebook-election-exclusive/exclusive-facebook-to-ban-misinformation-on-voting-in-upcoming-u-s-elections-idUSKCN1MP2G9.

24. Jack Nicas, "YouTube Tweaks Search Results as Las Vegas Conspiracy Theories Rise to Top," *Wall Street Journal*, October 5, 2017, https://www.wsj.com/articles/youtube-tweaks-its-search-results-after-rise-of-las-vegas-conspiracy-theories-1507219180.

25. Alfred Ng, "Facebook Deleted 583 Million Fake Accounts in the First Three Months of 2018," *CNET*, May 15, 2018, https://www.cnet.com/news/facebook-deleted-583-million-fake-accounts-in-the-first-three-months-of-2018/.

26. Bloomberg News, "Facebook Pulls 810 U.S. Accounts and Pages Spreading Fake News," *Ad Age*, October 11, 2018, https://adage.com/article/digital/facebook-pulls-810-u-s-accounts-pages-spreading-fake-news/315243/; Elizabeth Dwoskin and Tony Romm, "Facebook Says It Has Uncovered a Coordinated Disinformation Operation Ahead of the 2018 Midterm Elections," *Washington Post*, July 31, 2018, https://www.washingtonpost.com/technology/2018/07/31/facebook-says-it-has-uncovered-coordinated-disinformation-operation-ahead-midterm-elections/.

27. Del Harvey and Yoel Roth, "An Update on Our Elections Integrity Work," *Twitter*, October 1, 2018, https://blog.twitter.com/official/en_us/topics/company/2018/an-update-on-our-elections-integrity-work.html; Craig Timer and Elizabeth Dwoskin, "Twitter Is Sweeping Out Fake Accounts like Never Before, Putting User Growth at Risk," *Washington Post*, July 6, 2018, https://www.washingtonpost.com/technology/2018/07/06/twitter-is-sweeping-out-fake-accounts-like-never-before-putting-user-growth

-risk/; Nicholas Confessore and Gabriel J. X. Dance, "Battling Fake Accounts, Twitter to Slash Millions of Followers," *New York Times*, July 11, 2018, https://www.nytimes.com/2018/07/11/technology/twitter-fake-followers.html.

28. James Titcomb, "Twitter Removes 50 Accounts Posing as Republican Party Members in Pre-Election Crackdown, *Telegraph*, October 2, 2018, https://www.telegraph.co.uk/technology/2018/10/02/twitter-removes-50-accounts-posing-us-republican-party-members/.

29. Jessica Davies, "Facebook's European Media Chief: Fake News Is a Game of 'Whack-a-Mole,'" *Digiday*, January 12, 2017, https://digiday.com/uk/facebooks-european-media-chief-addresses-fake-news-game-whack-mole/.

30. Ricardo Bilton, "A New App Aims to Burst Filter Bubbles by Nudging Readers Toward a More 'Balanced' Media Diet," *Nieman Lab*, March 9, 2017, http://www.niemanlab.org/2017/03/a-news-app-aims-to-burst-filter-bubbles-by-nudging-readers-toward-a-more-balanced-media-diet/; Michael A. Chandler, "Feeling Stuck in Your Social Media Bubble? Here's the Latest in a Growing Class of Apps Designed to Help," *Washington Post*, April 18, 2017, https://www.washingtonpost.com/news/inspired-life/wp/2017/04/18/feeling-stuck-in-your-social-media-bubble-heres-the-newest-of-in-a-growing-class-of-apps-designed-to-help/?utm_term=.19ad0d7a72f6.

31. Tom Wheeler, "How Social Media Algorithms Are Altering Our Democracy," *Medium*, November 1, 2017, https://medium.com/Brookings/how-social-media-algorithms-are-altering-our-democracy-97aca587ec85.

32. Jeremy Kahn, "AI is 'Part of the Answer' to Fake News, Facebook Scientist Says," *Bloomberg*, May 23, 2018, https://www.bloomberg.com/news/articles/2018-05-23/ai-part-of-the-answer-to-fake-news-facebook-scientist-says. For details on how Facebook is using artificial intelligence in its efforts to combat fake news, see Nicholas Thompson, "Exclusive: Facebook Opens Up About False News," *Wired*, May 23, 2018, https://www.wired.com/story/exclusive-facebook-opens-up-about-false-news/.

33. Noah Kulwin, "Facebook Is Hiring 1000 More People to Block Fake News Ads," *Vice*, October 2, 2017, https://news.vice.com/en_us/article/pazmgy/facebook-is-hiring-1000-more-people-to-block-fake-news-ads.

34. Richi Iyengar, "Google Is Hiring 10,000 People to Clean Up YouTube," *CNN*, December 6, 2017, https://money.cnn.com/2017/12/05/technology/google-youtube-hiring-reviewers-offensive-videos/index.html.

35. Issie Lapowsky, "NewsGuard Wants to Fight Fake News with Humans, not Algorithms," *Wired*, August 23, 2018, https://www.wired.com/story/newsguard-extension-fake-news-trust-score/.

36. See Joshua Benton, "Facebook's Message to Media: We Are Not Interested in Talking to You About Your Traffic. . . . That Is the Old World and There Is No Going Back," *Nieman Lab*, August 13, 2018, http://www.niemanlab.org/2018/08/facebooks-message-to-media-we-are-not-interested-in-talking-to-you-about-your-traffic-that-is-the-old-world-and-there-is-no-going-back/.

37. Alex Hardiman, "Removing Trending from Facebook," June 1, 2018, Facebook Newsroom, https://newsroom.fb.com/news/2018/06/removing-trending/.

38. "After this change, we expect news to make up roughly 4 percent of News Feed, down from 5 percent today." Mark Zuckerberg, Facebook, January 19, 2018, https://www.facebook.com/zuck/posts/10104445245963251.

39. Hardiman, "Removing Trending from Facebook."

40. Nic Newman with Richard Fletcher, Antonis Kalogeropoulos, David A. L. Levy, and Rasmus Kleis Nielsen, *Reuters Institute Digital News Report 2018*, http://media.digitalnewsreport.org/wp-content/uploads/2018/06/digital-news-report-2018.pdf?x89475.

41. Newman et al., *Reuters Institute Digital News Report*.

42. Josh Schwartz, "What Happens When Facebook Goes Down? People Read the News," *Nieman Lab*, October 22, 2018, http://www.niemanlab.org/2018/10/what-happens-when-facebook-goes-down-people-read-the-news/.

43. Karissa Bell, "WhatsApp Will Pay Researchers up to $50,000 to Study Its Fake News Epidemic," *Mashable*, July 5, 2018, https://mashable.com/2018/07/05/whatsapp-research-fake-news-grants/#kBcSkqZm2qqL; see also Jim Waterson, "Fears Mount Over WhatsApp's Role in Spreading Fake News," *Guardian*, June 17, 2018, https://www.theguardian.com/technology/2018/jun/17/fears-mount-over-whatsapp-role-in-spreading-fake-news.

44. Many of the news stories that users share on WhatsApp are stories that these users initially encountered on social media platforms; Newman et al., *Reuters Institute Digital News Report*.

45. Philip M. Napoli, *Foundations of Communications Policy: Principles and Process in the Regulation of Electronic Media* (Cresskill, NJ: Hampton Press, 2001).

46. Philip M. Napoli, "Diminished, Enduring, and Emergent Diversity Policy Concerns in an Evolving Media Environment," *International Journal of Communication* 5 (2011): 1182–1196.

47. Napoli, "Diminished, Enduring, and Emergent Diversity Policy Concerns."

48. See, for example, Natali Helberger, Kari Karppinen, and Lucia D'Acunto, "Exposure Diversity as a Design Principle for Recommender Systems," *Information, Communication & Society* 21, no. 2 (2018): 191–207; Natali Helberger, "Exposure Diversity as a Policy Goal," *Journal of Media Law* 4, no. 1 (2012): 65–92.

49. Philip M. Napoli, "Exposure Diversity Reconsidered," *Journal of Information Policy* 1 (2011): 246–259.

50. Media diversity researchers often refer to "horizontal" diversity (the diversity of content/sources consumed *across* audience members) and "vertical" diversity (the diversity of content/sources consumed *within* each audience member). See, for example, Philip M. Napoli, "Rethinking Program Diversity Assessment: An Audience-Centered Approach," *Journal of Media Economics* 10, no. 4 (1997): 59–74; Elain J. Yuan, "Measuring Diversity of Exposure in Guangzhou's Television Market," *Asian Journal of Communication* 18 (2008): 155–171. The point of such a distinction is to recognize the possibility that while media consumption in the aggregate might appear quite diverse, the media consumption activities of the individual media users contributing to this aggregate may not be very diverse at all.

51. Richard H. Thaler and Cass R. Sunstein, *Nudge: Improving Decisions About Health, Wealth, and Happiness* (New York: Penguin Books, 2008).

52. Helberger at al., "Exposure Diversity as a Design Principle."

53. This point takes us back to the idea, presented in chapter 2, that social media platforms have traditionally emphasized personal significance to the neglect of social significance in the design of their news curation algorithms. See Michael A. DeVito, "A Values-Based Approach to Understanding Story Selection in the Facebook News Feed," *Digital Journalism* 5, no. 6 (2017): 753–773.

54. For a discussion of "diversity by design" and its potential role in facilitating exposure diversity, see Natali Helberger, "Diversity by Design," *Journal of Information Policy* 1 (2011): 441–469.

55. Sandra Braman, "The Limits of Diversity," in *Media Diversity and Localism: Meaning and Metrics*, ed. P. M. Napoli (Mahwah, NJ: Erlbaum, 2007), 139–150.

56. See, for example, Eric Alterman, "How False Equivalence Is Distorting 2016 Election Coverage," *Nation*, June 2, 2016, https://www.thenation.com/article/how-false-equivalence-is-distorting-the-2016-election-coverage/; Thomas E. Mann, "False Equivalence in Covering the 2016 Campaign," *Brookings*, June 2, 2016, https://www.brookings.edu/blog/fixgov/2016/06/02/false-equivalence-in-covering-the-2016-campaign/.

57. "Informing citizens in a way that enables them to act as citizens has traditionally been the responsibility of the press." Irene Costera Meijer, "The Public Quality of Popular Journalism: Developing a Normative Framework," *Journalism Studies* 2, no. 2 (2001): 189–205, 189.

58. Mark Cooper, "The Future of Journalism: Addressing Pervasive Market Failure with Public Policy," in *Will the Last Reporter Please Turn Out the Lights*, ed. Robert W. McChesney and Victor Pickard, (New York: Free Press, 2011), 320–339, 322.

59. See, for example, Lee Drutman, "Learning to Trust Again," *New Republic*, February 23, 2018, https://newrepublic.com/article/146895/learning-trust; Telly Davidson, "Giving Up the Ghost of Objective Journalism," *American Conservative*, March 29, 2018, http://www.theamericanconservative.com/articles/giving-up-the-ghost-of-objective-journalism-fakenews-yellow-journalism/.

60. For a discussion of this issue, see Lee McIntyre, *Post-Truth* (Cambridge, MA: MIT Press, 2018).

61. In 1947, Winston Churchill stated, "Many forms of government have been tried, and will be tried in this world of sin and woe. No one pretends that democracy is perfect or all-wise. Indeed it has been said that democracy is the worst form of government except for all those other forms that have been tried from time to time"; see International Churchill Society, https://winstonchurchill.org/resources/quotes/the-worst-form-of-government/.

62. Matthew Ingram, "Facebook Touches the Third Rail by Discussing Accreditation of Journalists," *Columbia Journalism Review*, March 26, 2018, https://www.cjr.org/the_new_gatekeepers/facebook-accreditation-journalists.php.

63. Quoted in Ingram, "Facebook Touches the Third Rail."

64. A high-profile example is the removal of Alex Jones's Infowars from platforms such as Twitter, Facebook, and YouTube. See Jack Nicas, "Alex Jones and Infowars Content

Is Removed from Apple, Facebook, and YouTube," *New York Times*, August 6, 2018, https://www.nytimes.com/2018/08/06/technology/infowars-alex-jones-apple -facebook-spotify.html; Sara Salinas, "Twitter Permanently Bans Alex Jones and Infowars Accounts," *CNBC*, September 6, 2018, https://www.cnbc.com/2018/09/06 /twitter-permanently-bans-alex-jones-and-infowars-accounts.html.

65. Anna Gonzalez and David Schulz, "Helping Truth with Its Boots: Accreditation as an Antidote to Fake News," *Yale Law Journal Forum* 127 (2017): 315–336.

66. See, for example, Dan Gilmor, *We the Media: Grassroots Journalism by the People, for the People* (Sebastapol, CA: O'Reilly, 2004); Lucas Graves, "Everyone's a Reporter," *Wired*, September 1, 2005, https://www.wired.com/2005/09/everyones-a-reporter/.

67. For details on the accreditation process, see Sunanda Creagh, "The Conversation's FactCheck Granted Accreditation by International Fact-Checking Network at Poynter," *Conversation*, https://theconversation.com/the-conversations-factcheck-granted -accreditation-by-international-fact-checking-network-at-poynter-74363.

68. International Fact-Checking Network, "Code of Principles," Poynter Institute, 2018, https:// www.poynter.org/international-fact-checking-network-fact-checkers-code-principles.

69. International Fact-Checking Network, "Code of Principles."

70. Tessa Lyons, "Increasing Our Efforts to Fight False News," *Facebook*, June 21, 2018, https://newsroom.fb.com/news/2018/06/increasing-our-efforts-to-fight-false-news/.

71. See, for example, Edward S. Herman and Noam Chomsky, *Manufacturing Consent: The Political Economy of the Mass Media* (New York: Pantheon, 1988).

72. See, for example, Michael Parenti, *Inventing Reality: The Politics of News Media*, 2nd ed. (Belmont, CA: Wadsworth, 1992).

73. For a "propaganda model" of the mass media, see Herman and Chomsky, *Manufacturing Consent*, 1–36.

74. In support of this argument, Tim Wu offers an historical description of evolutionary patterns in the media and telecommunications sectors. Each communications technology became "a highly centralized and integrated new industry. . . . Without exception, the brave new technologies of the twentieth century . . . eventually evolved into privately controlled industrial behemoths, the 'old media' giants of the twenty-first, through which the flow and nature of content would be strictly controlled. . . . History also shows that whatever has been closed too long is ripe for ingenuity's assault: in time a closed industry can be opened anew, giving way to all sorts of technical possibilities and expressive uses for the medium before he effort to close the system likewise begins again."). Tim Wu, *The Master Switch: The Rise and Fall of Information Empires* (New York: Vintage, 2010), 6. For additional work in this area, see Matthew Hindman, *The Internet Trap: How the Digital Economy Builds Monopoly and Undermines Democracy* (Princeton, NJ: Princeton University Press, 2018).

75. For an account of the increased emphasis on audience and revenue maximization that took hold in journalism in the 1980s and 1990s, see John H. McManus, *Market-Driven Journalism: Let the Citizen Beware?* (Thousand Oaks, CA: Sage, 1994).

76. Ken Auletta, *Three Blind Mice: How the TV Networks Lost Their Way* (New York: Random House, 1991).

77. See, for example, Natali Helberger, Jo Pierson, and Thomas Poell, "Governing Online Platforms: From Contested to Collaborative Responsibility," The *Information Society* 34, no. 1 (2018): 1–14.

78. Mark Zuckerberg, "A Blueprint for Content Governance and Enforcement," Facebook, November 15, 2018, https://www.facebook.com/notes/mark-zuckerberg/a-blueprint -for-content-governance-and-enforcement/10156443129621634/. More details about the structure or authority of this independent council had not been released at the time this book was going to press.

79. See Angela J. Campbell, "Self-Regulation of the Media," *Federal Communications Law Journal* 51, no. 3 (1999): 711–772.

80. See, for example, Robert Corn-Revere, "Regulation by Raised Eyebrow," *Student Lawyer*, February 1988, 26–29.

81. Unlike other media sectors, which have collectively developed mechanisms for dealing with adult or offensive content, social media platforms have operated unilaterally. Facebook's approach is different from Twitter's, which is different from YouTube's, which is different from Snapchat's, etc.

82. Howard Homonoff, "Nielsen, ComScore, and Rentrak: Keeping Score of Media Measurement," *Forbes*, October 5, 2015, https://www.forbes.com/sites/howardhomonoff/2015 /10/05/nielsen-comscore-and-rentrak-keeping-score-in-media-measurement /#325db6eb21d9; Nat Worden, "Nielsen's Post-IPO Challenge: Preserving Ratings Monopoly," *Wall Street Journal*, January 25, 2011, https://www.wsj.com/articles/SB10 0014240527487046980045761041033979700050; see also Daniel Biltereyst and Lennart Soberon, "Nielsen Holdings," in *Global Media Giants*, ed. Benjamin Birkinbine, Rodrigo Gomez, and Janet Wasko (New York: Routledge, 2017), 447–463.

83. For a discussion and analysis of this position, see Harsh Taneja, "Audience Measurement and Media Fragmentation: Revisiting the Monopoly Question," *Journal of Media Economics* 26, no. 3 (2013): 203–219.

84. Alex Moazed and Nicholas L. Johnson, *Modern Monopolies: What It Takes to Dominate the Twent-First Century Economy* (New York: St. Martin's Press, 2016).

85. See Philip M. Napoli, "Audience Measurement and Media Policy: Audience Economics, the Diversity Principle, and the Local People Meter," *Communication Law & Policy* 10, no. 4 (2005): 349–283.

86. For a more detailed discussion, see James G. Webster, Patricia F. Phalen, and Lawrence W. Lichty, *Ratings Analysis: Audience Measurement and Analytics*, 4th ed. (New York: Routledge, 2013).

87. Asaf Greiner, "Invasion of the Ad Fraud Super Bots," *Forbes*, November 30, 2017, https:// www.forbes.com/sites/forbestechcouncil/2017/11/30/invasion-of-the-ad-fraud-super -bots/#24d7d4a07996; Max Read, "How Much of the Internet is Fake? Turns out a lot of it, Actually," *New Yorker*, December 26, 2018, http://nymag.com/intelligencer/2018/12 /how-much-of-the-internet-is-fake.html.

88. See, for example, Samantha Bradshaw and Philip N. Howard, "Challenging Truth and Trust: A Global Inventory of Organized Social Media Manipulation," Computational Propaganda Project, Oxford University, July 2018, http://comprop.oii.ox.ac.uk

/wp-content/uploads/sites/93/2018/07/ct2018.pdf; Dan Jerker B. Svantesson and William van Caenegem, "Is It Time for an Offense of 'Dishonest Algorithmic Manipulation for Electoral Gain?" *Alternative Law Journal* 42, no. 3 (2017): 18–189.

89. See chapter 2 in this volume.

90. See, for example, Jane Bambauer, "Is Data Speech?" *Stanford Law Review* 66 (2014): 57–120; Josh Blackman, "What Happens If Data Is Speech?" *Journal of Constitutional Law* 16 (2014): 25–36.

91. For more detailed discussions of the First Amendment ambiguities surrounding algorithms and audience measurement systems, see Stuart M. Benjamin, "Algorithms and Speech," *University of Pennsylvania Law Review* 161, no. 6 (2013): 1445–1494; Oren Bracha, "The Folklore of Informationalism: The Case of Search Engine Speech," *Fordham Law Review* 82, no. 4 (2014): 1629–1687; Philip M. Napoli, "Audience Measurement, the Diversity Principle, and the First Amendment Right to Construct the Audience," *St. John's Journal of Legal Commentary* 24, no. 2 (2009): 359–385; Tim Wu, "Machine Speech," *University of Pennsylvania Law Review* 161, no. 6 (2013): 1495–1533.

92. Jon Lafayette, "Taking the Measure of Audience Measurement," *Broadcasting & Cable*, November 6, 2017, http://www.broadcastingcable.com/news/currency/taking-measure -audience-measurement/169879.

93. "History and Mission of the MRC," Media Rating Council, http://mediaratingcouncil .org/History.htm. For more historical detail, see Napoli, "Audience Measurement and Media Policy."

94. See "2019 Membership," Media Rating Council, http://mediaratingcouncil.org/Member %20Companies.htm.

95. "Minimum Standards for Media Rating Research," Media Rating Council, Inc., 2011, http://mediaratingcouncil.org/MRC%20Minimum%20Standards%20-%20December %202011.pdf, 5.

96. Mike Ananny and Kate Crawford, "Seeing Without Knowing: Limitations of the Transparency Ideal and Its Application to Algorithmic Accountability," *New Media & Society* 20, no. 3 (2018): 973–989.

97. European Commission, "Code of Practice on Disinformation," September 26, 2018, https://ec.europa.eu/digital-single-market/en/news/code-practice-disinformation.

98. Samuel Stolton, "Disinformation Crackdown: Tech Giants Commit to EU Code of Practice," *EURACTIV*, September 26, 2018, https://www.euractiv.com/section/digital /news/disinformation-crackdown-tech-giants-commit-to-eu-code-of-practice/.Seealso European Commission, *Code of Practice on Disinformation*, September 26, 2018, https:// ec.europa.eu/digital-single-market/en/news/code-practice-disinformation.

99. Fairness, Accuracy, Inclusiveness, and Responsiveness in Ratings Act of 2005, S. 1372, 109th Congress, 1st Session, https://www.congress.gov/109/bills/s1372/BILLS-109s1372is .pdf.

100. Wolfgang Schulz and Thorsten Held, *Regulated Self-Regulation as a Form of Modern Government* (Eastleigh, UK: John Libbey, 2004).

101. See, for example, Statements of Patrick J. Mullen, President, Tribune Broadcasting Company and Gale Metzger, Former President, Statistical Research Inc., S. 1372, The Fair

Ratings Act, Hearing Before the Committee on Commerce Science, and Transportation, U.S. Senate, 109th Congress, 1st Session, July 27, 2005.

102. See, for example, Statement of Kathy Crawford, President, Local Broadcast, Mindshare, S. 1372, The Fair Ratings Act, Hearing Before the Committee on Commerce Science, and Transportation, U.S. Senate, 109th Congress, 1st Session, July 27, 2005.

103. See Statement of George Ivie, Executive President/CEO, Media Rating Council, S. 1372, The Fair Ratings Act, Hearing Before the Committee on Commerce Science, and Transportation, U.S. Senate, 109th Congress, 1st Session, July 27, 2005.

104. For a discussion of the European regulatory context, see Mira Burri, "Cultural Diversity in the Internet Age: In Search of New Tools That Work," *Communications & Strategies* 1, no. 101 (2016): 63–85; Robin Mansell, "The Public's Interest in Intermediaries," *Info* 17, no. 6 (2015): 8–18. In the United Kingdom, where concerns about the influence of fake news accelerated in the wake of that country's Brexit vote, a 2019 report produced by the House of Commons recommended actions such as the creation of an independent regulatory body to craft and oversee a compulsory code of ethics for social media platforms. See House of Commons, Digital Culture, Media and Sport Committee, *Disinformation and "Fake News": Final Report* (February, 2019), https://publications.parliament.uk/pa/cm201719/cmselect/cmcumeds/1791/1791.pdf. For an overview of regulatory actions taking place in Europe, see Petros Iosifidis and Leighton Andrews, "Regulating the Internet Intermediaries in a Post-Truth World: Beyond Media Policy?" *International Communication Gazette* (in press).

105. For a detailed proposal in this regard, see Danielle Keats Citron and Benjamin Wittes, "The Problem Isn't Just Backpage: Revising Section 230 Immunity," *Georgetown Law and Technology Review* 2 (2018): 435–473.

106. Senator Mark Warner, "Potential Policy Proposals for Regulation of Social Media and Technology Firms," July 2018, https://regmedia.co.uk/2018/07/30/warner_social_media_proposal.pdf.

107. Steven T. Walther, Federal Election Commission, December 15, 2017, http://saos.fec.gov/aodocs/2017-12.pdf.

108. Margaret Sessa-Hawkins, "FEC's New Facebook Ruling Requires Ad Sharing Info Yet Gives Reformers Little to Like," *MapLight*, January 8, 2018, https://maplight.org/story/fecs-new-facebook-ruling-requires-ad-sharing-info-yet-gives-reformers-little-to-like/.

109. Tom Udall and David Price, " 'We the People' Democracy Reform Act of 2017 Sponsored by Senator Udall and Representative Price," https://www.tomudall.senate.gov/imo/media/doc/WE%20THE%20PEOPLE%20DEMOCRACY%20REFORM%20ACT%20SUMMARY.pdf; "Honest Ads Act," Congress.gov, 2017, https://www.congress.gov/bill/115th-congress/senate-bill/1989/text.

110. Samantha Masunaga and David Pierson, "Facebook Under Scrutiny as FTC Confirms It Is Investigating Privacy Practices," *Los Angeles Times*, March 26, 2018, http://www.latimes.com/business/technology/la-fi-tn-facebook-ftc-20180326-story.html.

111. National Association of Attorneys General, Letter to Mark Zuckerberg, March 26, 2018, https://www.attorneygeneral.gov/wp-content/uploads/2018/03/2018-03-26-Letter-to-Facebook.pdf.

112. Social Media Privacy Protection and Consumer Rights Act of 2018, 115th Congress, 2nd Session, https://www.scribd.com/document/377302061/S-Social-Media-Privacy -Protection-and-Consumer-Rights-Act-of-2018.

113. Customer Online Notification for Stopping Edge-provider Network Transgressions Act, 115th Congress, 2nd Session, https://www.markey.senate.gov/imo/media/doc /CONSENT%20Act%20text.pdf.

114. General Data Protection Regulation, European Parliament, April 2016, https://eur-lex .europa.eu/legal-content/EN/TXT/PDF/?uri=CELEX:32016R0679.

115. Social Media Privacy Protection and Consumer Rights Act of 2018, 115th Congress, 2nd Session, https://www.scribd.com/document/377302061/S-Social-Media-Privacy -Protection-and-Consumer-Rights-Act-of-2018.

116. Customer Online Notification for Stopping Edge-provider Network Transgressions Act.

117. See, for example, Jeffrey L. Blevins and Duncan H. Brown, "Political Issue or Policy Matter? The Federal Communication Commission's Third Biennial Review of Broad-cast Ownership Rules," *Journal of Communication Inquiry* 30, no. 1 (2006): 21–41; Robert M. Entman and Steven S. Wildman, "Reconciling Economic and Non-Economic Per-spectives on Media Policy: Transcending the 'Marketplace of Ideas,'" *Journal of Com-munication* 42, no. 1 (1992): 5–19; Napoli, *Foundations of Communications Policy.*

118. See, for example, Ellen Goodman, "Media Policy Out of the Box: Content Abundance, Attention Scarcity, and the Failure of Digital Markets," *Berkeley Technology Law Journal* 19, no. 4 (2004): 1389–1472.

119. European Commission, "Call for Applications for the Selection of Members of the High Level Group on Fake News," November 12, 2017, https://ec.europa.eu/digital -single-market/en/news/call-applications-selection-members-high-level-group-fake -news.

120. European Commission, *A Multi-Dimensional Approach to Disinformation: Report of the Independent High Level Group on Fake News and Online Disinformation*, 2018, https:// ec.europa.eu/digital-single-market/en/news/final-report-high-level-expert-group -fake-news-and-online-disinformation.

121. Reuters Staff, "Britain to Set Up Unit to Tackle 'Fake News': May's Spokesman," *Reuters*, January 23, 2018, https://www.reuters.com/article/us-britain-politics-fakenews /britain-to-set-up-unit-to-tackle-fake-news-mays-spokesman-idUSKBN1FC2AL.

122. House of Commons, Digital, Culture, Media and Sport Committee, "Disinforma-tion and 'Fake News': Interim Report," July 24, 2018, https://publications.parliament. uk/pa/cm201719/cmselect/cmcumeds/363/363.pdf. House of Commons, "Disin-formation and 'Fake News': Final Report" For a similar governmental algorithmic audits proposal in the Canadian context, see Edward Greenspon and Taylor Owen, "Democracy Divided: Countering Disinformation and Hate in the Digital Public Sphere," Public Policy Forum, August 2018, https://www.ppforum.ca/publications /social-marketing-hate-speech-disinformation-democracy/.

123. Yasmeen Serhan, "Macron's War on 'Fake News,'" *Atlantic*, January 6, 2018, https://www .theatlantic.com/international/archive/2018/01/macrons-war-on-fake-news/549788/.

124. "French Lawmakers Adopt 'Fake News' Bill," *Guardian*, October 10, 2018, https://guardian.ng/news/french-lawmakers-adopt-fake-news-bill/.

125. Mathieu Rosemain, Michael Rose, and Gwenaelle Barzic, "France to 'Embed' Regulators at Facebook in Fight Against Hate Speech," *Reuters*, November 12, 2018, https://www.reuters.com/article/france-facebook-macron/france-to-embed-regulators-at-facebook-in-fight-against-hate-speech-idUSL8N1XM1HY.

126. "Germany Starts Enforcing Hate Speech Law," *BBC News*, January 1, 2018, http://www.bbc.com/news/technology-42510868.

127. Kristen Chick and Sarah Miller Llana, "Is Germany's Bold New Law a Way to Clean Up the Internet or Is It Stifling Free Expression?" *Christian Science Monitor*, April 8, 2018, https://www.csmonitor.com/World/Europe/2018/0408/Is-Germany-s-bold-new-law-a-way-to-clean-up-the-internet-or-is-it-stifling-free-expression.

128. Andrea Shalal, "German States Want Social Media Law Tightened," *Business Insider*, November 12, 2018, https://www.businessinsider.com/r-german-states-want-social-media-law-tightened-media-2018-11.

129. Tim Wu, "Is the First Amendment Obsolete?" Knight First Amendment Institute Emerging Threats Series, 2017, https://knightcolumbia.org/sites/default/files/content/Emerging%20Threats%20Tim%20Wu%20Is%20the%20First%20Amendment%20Obsolete.pdf.

130. Wu, "Is the First Amendment Obsolete?"

131. Zeynep Tufekci, "It's the (Democracy-Poisoning) Golden Age of Free Speech," *Wired*, January 16, 2018, https://www.wired.com/story/free-speech-issue-tech-turmoil-new-censorship/.

132. Wu, "Is the First Amendment Obsolete?"

133. Hustler Magazine, Inc. v. Falwell, 485 U.S. 46 52 (1988).

134. For a transcript of the *Meet the Press* broadcast in which the term was famously introduced, see Rebecca Sinderbrand, "How Kellyanne Conway Ushered in the Era of 'Alternative Facts,'" *Washington Post*, January 22, 2017, https://www.washingtonpost.com/news/the-fix/wp/2017/01/22/how-kellyanne-conway-ushered-in-the-era-of-alternative-facts/?utm_term=.b633a394a39f.

135. Frederick Schauer, "Facts and the First Amendment," *UCLA Law Review* 57 (2009–2010): 897–919, 907.

136. Schauer, "Facts and the First Amendment," 902.

137. See T. M. Scanlon, Jr., "Freedom of Expression and Categories of Expression," *University of Pittsburgh Law Review* 40 (1978–1979): 519–550.

138. See, for example, Alex Kozinski and Stuart Banner, "Who's Afraid of Commercial Speech?" *Virginia Law Review* 76, no. 4 (1990): 627–653.

139. For overviews, see Robert B. Horwitz, "The First Amendment Meets Some New Technologies: Broadcasting, Common Carriers, and Free Speech in the 1990s," *Theory and Society* 20, no. 1 (1991): 21–72; Napoli, *Foundations of Communications Policy*.

140. "Although the umbrella and scope of general First Amendment protections have broadened over the past several decades, this expansion has proceeded by way of the displacement of a collectivist or communication version of the First Amendment

tradition in favor of the individualistic or individual liberty model of free speech." Horwitz, "The First Amendment Meets Some New Technologies," 25.

141. Stanley Ingber, "Rediscovering the Communal Worth of Individual Rights: The First Amendment in Institutional Contexts," *Texas Law Review* 69, no. 1 (1990): 1–108.

142. Richard H. Fallon, Jr., "Two Senses of Autonomy," *Stanford Law Review* 46, no. 4 (1994): 875–905.

143. See, for example, Jack M. Balkin, "Digital Speech and Democratic Culture: A Theory of Freedom of Expression for the Information Society," *New York University Law Review* 79 (2004): 1–55.

144. Alexander Meiklejohn, *Free Speech and Its Relation to Self-Government* (Port Washington, NY: Kennikat Press, 1948/1972), 25.

145. See, for example, Owen Fiss, *The Irony of Free Speech* (Cambridge, MA: Harvard University Press, 1996); Cass Sunstein, *Democracy and the Problem of Free Speech* (New York: Free Press, 1993).

146. Balkin, "Free Speech in the Algorithmic Society," 1152.

147. See, for example, Balkin, "Digital Speech and Democratic Culture"; Fiss, *The Irony of Free Speech*; Meiklejohn, *Free Speech and Its Relation to Self-Government*; Sunstein, *Democracy and the Problem of Free Speech*.

148. Napoli, *Foundations of Communications Policy*.

149. See, for example, Tim Worstall, "Google and Facebook Are Dominant but Not Monopolies," *Forbes*, May 10, 2017, https://www.forbes.com/sites/timworstall/2017/05/10/google -and-facebook-are-dominant-but-not-monopolies/#7e2bec7136d4.

150. See W. Russell Neuman, ed., *Media, Technology, and Society: Theories of Media Evolution* (Ann Arbor: University of Michigan Press, 2010).

151. For a critique of regulatory approaches dictated by the characteristics of individual communications conduits, see Jim Chen, "Conduit-Based Regulation of Speech," *Duke Law Journal* 54, no. 6 (2005): 1359–1456.

152. Napoli, *Foundations of Communications Policy*.

153. See, for example, Breck P. McAllister, "Lord Hale and Business Affected with a Public Interest," *Harvard Law Review* 43, no. 5 (1930): 759–791, http://www.jstor.org /stable/1330729; Walton H. Hamilton, "Affectation with Public Interest," *Yale Law Review* 39, no. 8 (1930): 1089–1112, http://www.jstor.org/stable/790369.

154. Mark Cooper, "The Long History and Increasing Importance of Public-Service Principles for 21st Century Public Digital Communications Networks," *Journal on Telecommunications and High Technology Law* 12 (2014): 1–54.

155. It is worth noting that some have argued that social media platforms should be treated as utilities; see, for example, Mark Andrejevic, "Search and Social as Public Utilities: Rethinking Search Engines and Social Networking as Public Goods," *Media International Australia* 146 (2013): 143–132; Iosifidis and Andrews, "Regulating the Internet Intermediaries."

156. Frank Pasquale, "Internet Nondiscrimination Principles: Commercial Ethics for Carriers and Search Engines," *University of Chicago Legal Forum* 2008, no. 6 (2008): 263–299.

157. Wolff Packing Co. v. Court of Industrial Relations, 262 U.S. 522 (1923), 535.

158. For a similar contention that social media platforms should be perceived as being affected with the public interest, see Jack M. Balkin, "The Three Laws of Robotics in the Age of Big Data," *Ohio State Law Journal* 78, no. 5 (2017): 1217–1241.

159. For a more detailed discussion of the media ecosystem concept, see C. W. Anderson, "Media Ecosystems: Some Notes Toward a Genealogy of the Term and an Application of It to Journalism Research," paper presented at the ESF Exploratory Workshop on Mapping Digital News Ecosystems, May 2013.

160. See, for example, Reed Hundt, "The Public's Airwaves: What Does the Public Interest Require of Television Broadcasters?" *Duke Law Journal* 45, no. 6 (1996): 1089–1130; Fiss, *The Irony of Free Speech*; Sunstein, *Democracy and the Problem of Free Speech*; Cass Sunstein, *Republic.com 2.0* (Princeton, NJ: Princeton University Press, 2008).

161. Natasha Lomas, "Germany's Social Media Hate Speech Law Is Now in Effect," *Tech-Crunch*, October 2, 2017, https://techcrunch.com/2017/10/02/germanys-social-media-hate-speech-law-is-now-in-effect/.

162. For a discussion of this methodological approach, see Philip M. Napoli, "Assessing Media Diversity: A Comparative Analysis of the FCC's Diversity Index and the EC's Media Pluralism Monitor," in *Media Pluralism: Concepts, Risks and Global Trends*, ed. Peggy Valcke, Miklós Sükösd and Roberet G. Picard (Hampshire, UK: Palgrave, 2015), 141–151.

163. Lee C. Bollinger, "Freedom of the Press and Public Access: Toward a Theory of Partial Regulation of the Mass Media," *Michigan Law Review* 75, no. 1 (1976): 1–42.

164. "Regulation both responds to constitutional traditions and cuts against them." Bollinger, "Freedom of the Press and Public Access," 27.

165. Bollinger, "Freedom of the Press and Public Access," 32.

166. Too often, discussions of the practices or regulation of social media platforms tend to conflate social media with the Internet as a whole.

Conclusion

1. Joshua A. Tucker, Andrew Guess, Pablo Barbera, Cristian Vaccari, Alexandra Siegel, Sergey Sanovich, Denis Stukal, and Brendan Nyhan, "Social Media, Political Polarization, and Political Disinformation," report prepared for the Hewlett Foundation, March 2018, https://hewlett.org/wp-content/uploads/2018/03/Social-Media-Political-Polarization-and-Political-Disinformation-Literature-Review.pdf.

2. Matthew Hindman and Vlad Barash, "Disinformation, 'Fake News' and Influence Campaigns on Twitter," report prepared for the Knight Foundation, October 2018, https://knightfoundation.org/reports/disinformation-fake-news-and-influence-campaigns-on-twitter; Jaime E. Settle, *Frenemies: How Social Media Polarizes America* (New York: Cambridge University Press, 2018).

3. Hunt Allcott, Matthew Gentzkow, and Chuan Yu, "Trends in the Diffusion of Misinformation on Twitter," unpublished working paper, October 2018, http://web.stanford.

edu/~gentzkow/research/fake-news-trends.pdf. See also Paul Resnick, Aviv Ovadya, and Garlin Gilchrist, "Iffy Quotient: A Platform Health Metric for Misinformation," report from the Center for Social Media Responsibility, University of Michigan, October 2018, https://csmr.umich.edu/wp-content/uploads/2018/10/UMSI-CSMR-Iffy-Quotient-Whitepaper-810084.pdf.

4. Kathleen Hall Jamieson, *Cyberwar: How Russian Hackers and Trolls Helped Elect a President—What We Don't, Can't and Do Know* (New York: Oxford University Press, 2018).

5. See, for example, Hunt Allcott and Matthew Gentzkow, "Social Media and Fake News in the 2016 Election," *Journal of Economic Perspectives* 31, no. 2 (2017): 211–236; Andrew Guess, Brendan Nyhan, and Jason Reifler, "Selective Exposure to Misinformation: Evidence from the Consumption of Fake News During the 2016 U.S. Presidential Campaign," unpublished working paper, 2018, https://www.dartmouth.edu/~nyhan/fake-news-2016.pdf; Jacob Nelson, "Fake News, Fake Problem? An Analysis of the Fake News Audience in the Lead-Up to the 2016 Election," paper presented at the Telecommunications Policy Research Conference, Arlington, VA, September 2017; Frederik J. Zuiderveen Borgesius, Damian Trilling, Judith Möller, Balázs Bodó, Claes H. de Vreese, and Natali Helberger, "Should We Worry About Filter Bubbles?" *Internet Policy Review* 5, no. 1 (2016): 1–16. It is worth noting that little of the work in this vein engages in any kind of robust media-effects research, instead drawing inferences from estimates of audience exposure and engagement.

6. Josh Schwartz, "What Happens When Facebook Goes Down? People Read the News," *Nieman Lab*, October 22, 2018, http://www.niemanlab.org/2018/10/what-happens-when-facebook-goes-down-people-read-the-news/.

Index